SUSTAINABLE FOOD FUTURES

Securing sustainable food for everyone is one of the world's most pressing challenges, but research, policy, and programmes remain fragmented, and effective solutions have been slow to emerge. This book takes on these challenges by proposing a range of solutions that can advance pathways towards sustainable food futures.

Complete with recipes, this book is structured so that readers are taken in a logical progression through discussions of solutions, highlighting the need to recognise the importance of place and the importance of participation, and to challenge dominant descriptions of markets, through to re-designing food systems.

The solutions presented in this book are based on real-world cases, but discussions remain deliberately broad to encourage thinking in new ways. Cases are drawn from Africa, Asia, Europe, and North and South America. The book is of relevance to those interested in sustainable food futures, and can serve as a supplementary textbook for a wide range of courses in food studies and related disciplines.

Jessica Duncan is an Assistant Professor in the Rural Sociology Group, Wageningen University, the Netherlands. She is the author of *Global Food Security Governance: Civil Society Engagement in the Reformed Committee on World Food Security* (Routledge, 2015).

Megan Bailey is an Assistant Professor in the Marine Affairs Program and Canada Research Chair, Integrated Ocean and Coastal Governance, Dalhousie University, Canada.

Routledge Studies in Food, Society and the Environment

Feeding Cities
Improving local food access, security and sovereignty
Edited by Christopher Bosso

The Right to Food Guidelines, Democracy and Citizen Participation
Country case studies
Katharine S.E. Cresswell Riol

Peasants Negotiating a Global Policy Space
La Vía Campesina in the Committee on World Food Security
Ingeborg Gaarde

Public Policies for Food Sovereignty
Social movements and the state
Edited by Annette Desmarais, Priscilla Claeys and Amy Trauger

Sustainable Food Futures
Multidisciplinary solutions
Edited by Jessica Duncan and Megan Bailey

Food and Cooking Skills Education
Why teach people how to cook?
Anita Tull

For further details please visit the series page on the Routledge website:
www.routledge.com/books/series/RSFSE/

SUSTAINABLE FOOD FUTURES

Multidisciplinary Solutions

Edited by
Jessica Duncan and Megan Bailey

Routledge
Taylor & Francis Group

LONDON AND NEW YORK

earthscan
from Routledge

First published 2017
by Routledge
2 Park Square, Milton Park, Abingdon, Oxon OX14 4RN

and by Routledge
711 Third Avenue, New York, NY 10017

Routledge is an imprint of the Taylor & Francis Group, an informa business

British Library Cataloguing-in-Publication Data
A catalogue record for this book is available from the British Library

Library of Congress Cataloging-in-Publication Data
A catalog record for this book has been requested

ISBN: 978-1-138-20616-8 (hbk)
ISBN: 978-1-138-20700-4 (pbk)
ISBN: 978-1-315-46313-1 (ebk)

Typeset in Bembo
by Apex CoVantage, LLC

Dedicated to Christopher Henry, without whom this book likely would have been published on time. We hope we have begun, and can continue, to inspire you to be part of the next generation of solution citizens.

CONTENTS

List of figures   *x*
List of tables   *xi*
List of recipes   *xii*
Notes on contributors   *xiii*
Acknowledgements   *xx*

1   Sustainable food futures: multidisciplinary solutions   1
    Jessica Duncan and Megan Bailey

PART I
Recognizing place   **15**

2   Cultural relevance in Arctic food security initiatives   17
    Carie Hoover, Colleen Parker, Claire Hornby, Sonja Ostertag,
    Kayla Hansen-Craik, Tristan Pearce, and Lisa Loseto

3   Rebuilding consumers' trust in food: community-
    supported agriculture in China   34
    Zhenzhong Si

4   Place-based food systems: "re-valuing local" and fostering
    socio-ecological sustainability   46
    Susanna E. Klassen and Hannah Wittman

5 Recovering farmland commons   61
   Jamie Baxter

PART II
Enhancing participation   **75**

6 The political economy of customary land rights in
   Mozambique: lessons from a food sovereignty movement   77
   Helena Shilomboleni

7 Small-scale aquaculture in the Bolivian Amazon: a
   contextually-based solution for positive social and
   economic outcomes   89
   *Tiffanie Rainville, Sean Irwin, Verónica R. Hinojosa Sardán,
   Cintya Castellón Antezana, and Widen Abastoflor Sauma*

8 Building 'a world where many worlds fit': indigenous
   autonomy, mutual aid, and an (anti-capitalist) moral
   economy of the (rebel) peasant   103
   Levi Gahman

PART III
Challenging markets   **117**

9 Knowing how to bring food to the market: appreciating
   the contribution of intermediary traders to the future of
   food availability in Sub-Saharan Africa   119
   Mirjam Schoonhoven-Speijer, Ellen Mangnus, and Sietze Vellema

10 Certify sustainable retailers?   133
    Simon R. Bush

11 The solution cannot be conventionalized: protecting the
    alterity of fairer and more sustainable food networks   145
    Raquel Ajates Gonzalez

PART IV
Designing sustainable food futures   **161**

12 Cultured meat, better than beans?   163
    Cor van der Weele

13 Soil currency: exploring a more equitable, sustainable, and
participatory economic system 175
Randall Coleman

14 From pirate islands to communities of hope: reflections on
the circular economy of food systems 186
Stefano Pascucci and Jessica Duncan

PART V
Conclusions **201**

15 Caution: road work ahead 203
Jessica Duncan and Megan Bailey

Index *215*

FIGURES

2.1 Main Inuit and Aboriginal geographic settlement regions of the
Canadian Arctic 18

2.2 Identifying how the proposed solutions fit with the three
components of food security: food access, food availability, and
food quality 22

4.1 The Lower Fraser Valley region of southwestern BC, Canada 50

6.1 Members of an UNAC farmers association water their land in
the early morning hours 80

7.1 Gender gaps in APNI organization (2016) 96

7.2 Serving suggestion 99

9.1 Produce and cash flows in the oilseed sector in Uganda 123

9.2 Produce and cash flows in the cereal sector in Mali 124

11.1 Double hourglass: strategies to tackle power imbalances in the
food system 147

11.2 Transparency: Esnetik's double labeling 154

13.1 Soil-erg exhibit at dOCUMENTA(13), Kassel, Germany 176

TABLES

2.1 Comparison of select grocery prices from March 2015 in
Nunavut compared to the Canadian average   21

8.1 Abbreviated timeline of events that led to the Zapatista Uprising   105

9.1 An overview of assets and skills used in intermediary trade   126

11.1 Cooperative initiatives exploring new practices to protect
their alterity   148

13.1 Waste to soil currency exchange rate   179

14.1 Typology of cases using circular economy principles to design
food systems   193

15.1 Matching key questions to solutions found in this book   204

RECIPES

Chapter 1	Whole roasted cauliflower with tahini sauce	10
Chapter 2	Caribou stew	28
Chapter 3	Scrambled eggs with tomatoes	43
Chapter 4	Hearty seasonal salad	55
Chapter 5	Fresh collard wraps with quick pickled onion and green tomato salsa	69
Chapter 6	Mozambican coconut chicken	86
Chapter 7	Bolivian pacú from Yapacaní	99
Chapter 8	How 'To Rebel and Struggle'	114
Chapter 9	Ugandan g-nut and sim-sim sauce	130
Chapter 10	Canh chua cá tra (sweet and sour pangasius fish soup)	140
Chapter 11	Political maftoul (giant couscous) warm salad with roasted vegetables	155
Chapter 12	Chili con carne cultivada	172
Chapter 13	Mel's soil mix	183
Chapter 14	Frittata di maccheroni (leftover pasta frittata)	198
Chapter 15	Ugly fruit fondue	211

CONTRIBUTORS

Cintya Castellón Antezana, born in Cochabamba, Bolivia, is a biologist with a specialty in limnology and aquaculture. She completed a Masters of Environmental Science in 2008 and an international Diploma in Rural Business Development (2012) with a gender focus. She has worked for 18 years in aquaculture, and moved to Yapacaní in 2009 to work on aquaculture development in the region as Technical Aquaculture Development staff for the Peasant Farming Promotion Centre (CEPAC). Her focus is small-scale, family-based aquaculture, with female leadership. She is now leading a small laboratory and business undertaking reproduction of Amazon fish species.

Megan Bailey is an Assistant Professor and Canada Research Chair (Tier II) at Dalhousie University's Marine Affairs Program. Megan holds degrees in zoology and resource management, and focuses on understanding how public and private approaches to fisheries and seafood governance can combine to contribute to sustainable fish futures. Her research interests are in seafood value chain governance, traceability, and Fair Trade fish. Megan serves on the Scientific and Technical Advisory Committee of the International Pole and Line Foundation, on the Board of Directors for the Ecology Action Centre, and on the Communications Committee of the Fishermen and Scientists Research Society. When not working, Megan enjoys reading, cooking, and spending time on the lake with her family.

Jamie Baxter is an Assistant Professor at the Schulich School of Law, Dalhousie University. He writes and teaches in the areas of property, land regulation, food, and agriculture. Jamie holds degrees in economics and law from McMaster University, the University of Toronto, and Yale, and was a Canada-US Fulbright Scholar at the University of Kentucky.

Simon R. Bush is Professor and Chair of Environmental Policy at Wageningen University. He is currently the principal investigator of three research programs. Two of these focus on the relationship between government and business in the sustainable management of tuna fisheries in the Western and Central Pacific and Indonesia. The other focuses on supermarket-supported, area-based management and certification of aquaculture in Southeast Asia.

Randall Coleman is a social entrepreneur, educator, and sustainable development practitioner. He has co-founded an international development nongovernmental organization (Can YA Love) and created an experiential learning tool called The Food Trade Game. Randall currently works for the Non-GMO Project and has consulted for various non-profit, for-profit, and intergovernmental organizations, providing expertise on research, sustainability, and database management. He is a member partner of the Sustainable Food Systems Programme, a project of the 10YFP United Nations Environment Programme (UNEP). You can see his work on sustainable development in various publications and speaking engagements around the world. Randall has a Master of Public Policy from American University and a BA in Government and Politics from the University of Maryland.

Jessica Duncan is Assistant Professor in Rural Sociology at Wageningen University (the Netherlands). She holds a PhD in Food Policy from City University London. Her research areas include food policy, food security, global governance, environmental policy, and participation. More specifically, she researches the science-policy-participation interface by studying the relationships between governance organizations, systems of food provisioning, the environment, and the actors engaged in and across these spaces. She is interested in better understanding ways in which actors participate in policy-making processes; and analysing how the resulting policies are shaped, implemented, challenged, and resisted, and what this means for societal transformation. She is an Associate Editor for the journal *Food Security* and an advisor to the Traditional Cultures Project.

Levi Gahman is a radical geographer from Kansas (ancestral Osage territories) whose background includes time spent as a sawmill laborer, farmhand, substance abuse/trauma counselor, disability resource center facilitator, and community organizer. His work draws upon feminist, Fanonian, and Foucauldian perspectives to critically interrogate the discursive, material, spatial, and socio-psychological products of global capitalism, ongoing colonialisms, and hetero-patriarchal social relations. Levi's current research investigates how resistance and mutual aid can create pathways out of structural violence towards social harmony. He received a PhD in Interdisciplinary Studies (Gender Studies and Human Geography) from the University of British Columbia and is now with the University of the West Indies (Trinidad and Tobago), where he remains a loyal but stumbling advocate of hope, collectivity, playfulness, and the Zapatista's Sixth Declaration of the Lacandon Jungle.

Raquel Ajates Gonzalez is a Postdoctoral Researcher at University of Dundee working on GROW, a Horizon 2020 project setting up a citizen observatory that aims to make a vital contribution to global environmental monitoring and empower growers across Europe with knowledge of sustainable soil management practices. Before that, Raquel was a Teaching Fellow at the Innovative Food System Teaching and Learning programme at the Centre for Food Policy at City University of London, where she also completed her MSc and PhD degree. Her research interests include cooperatives in food and farming, defining sustainable food systems, agroecology and the politics of evidence-based policy-making processes.

Kayla Hansen-Craik was born and raised in the community of Inuvik, Northwest Territories. Before attending the University of Manitoba, where she is pursuing her BA in Environmental Studies, she worked with communities across the Inuvialuit Settlement Region as a Fisheries Resource Specialist for the Fisheries Joint Management Committee (a co-management board responsible for managing fish and marine mammals in the region).

Carie Hoover is a Postdoctoral Researcher at the University of Manitoba. She works closely with Fisheries and Oceans Canada Central and Arctic Division, and the co-management boards of the Inuvialuit Settlement Region. Her research focuses on ecosystem impacts of climate change, improving the use of indicators in ecosystem management within the Beaufort Sea ecosystem, and the impacts these changes have on local communities.

Claire Hornby is a marine mammal researcher with Fisheries and Oceans Canada, Freshwater Institute. Originally from British Columbia, Claire completed a BSc in Conservation Biology from the University of British Columbia in 2010. In 2013, Claire moved to Winnipeg and completed a MSc degree in the Department of Environment and Geography. Her current fields of interest are biology, ecology, and management of Arctic ecosystems, specifically population health, habitat use, and spatial modeling of marine mammal distributions.

Sean Irwin is originally from the Canadian prairies and now lives in Victoria, British Columbia, where he is a doctoral candidate in the Department of Geography at the University of Victoria. He has a Masters of International Trade from the University of Saskatchewan and a Masters of Rural Development from Brandon University. His research seeks pathways towards socioeconomic development for rural people and communities in the global South. He is particularly interested in food systems, food security, value chains, small-scale farmers, and globalization. His master's research focused on Southern Belizean cacao farmers and their experiences engaging in international trade.

Susanna E. Klassen completed her Master's of Science in Integrated Studies in Land and Food Systems from the University of British Columbia, which explored the topic of food sovereignty in the British Columbia blueberry industry. She used this case study to explore how multi-scalar socio-ecological system dynamics contribute to sustainability of the local agricultural system, focusing on labor, livelihoods, and management practices. Through the study of complex socio-ecological relationships in agriculture, Susanna hopes to make valuable contributions to food system sustainability in a way that is both reflective of global challenges and synergistic with local context. In her spare time, Susanna enjoys cooking, baking, and fermenting. She received a BSc in Environmental Science from McGill University in 2013.

Lisa Loseto is a research scientist at Fisheries and Oceans Canada in Winnipeg. Lisa's research largely focuses on characterizing beluga health and habitat use in the Western Canadian Arctic. Her research attempts to better understand beluga diet, trends in contaminants, and impacts of climate change to beluga health that combines Western science and traditional knowledge. Lisa's research programs are carried out in partnership with communities and co-management boards of the Inuvialuit Settlement Region. She strives to serve all Canadians by providing knowledge and advice to decision makers and by helping to empower the people of the north through scientific knowledge combined with their own knowledge of the lands and waters of their home.

Ellen Mangnus is a Post-Doctoral Researcher at the Human Geography group, Utrecht University. Her research focusses on the impact of Dutch investors on local food security in Ghana, Ethiopia, and Kenya, and involves two PhD researchers and several master's students. Her PhD, at Wageningen University, was on cereal trading practices of farmers and traders in South Mali. Prior to working in academics, she worked as an advisor on sustainable economic development at the Royal Tropical Institute in Amsterdam. For eight years, she was involved in advisory services for policy makers and practitioners in development in both East and West Africa. She adores writing and regularly publishes in the Dutch magazines *VORK* and *Vice Versa*.

Sonja Ostertag is a Natural Sciences and Engineering Research Council (NSERC) Visiting Fellow at the Freshwater Institute, Fisheries and Oceans Canada. Sonja works closely with beluga harvesters in the Inuvialuit Settlement Region to support the inclusion of Indigenous Knowledge and local observations in beluga monitoring and management.

Colleen Parker has a background in Environmental Biology and Geography. Her master's work focused on food security in the context of changing socio-economic and climatic conditions in Ulukhaktok, Northwest Territories (NWT). She now works for an environmental nongovernmental organization in Inuvik, NWT, with a focus on marine conservation.

Stefano Pascucci is a Professor in Sustainability and Circular Economy at the University of Exeter Business School (UK) and visiting researcher at Wageningen

University (the Netherlands). He holds a PhD in Agricultural Economics and Policy. His research interests are related to the organization, innovation, and sustainability of international food value chains, and more recently to circular economy. Stefano has published, among others, in *Agriculture and Human Values, Journal of Cleaner Production, European Review of Agricultural Economics, Food Policy, Journal of Business Ethics,* and *Agricultural Systems.* Stefano serves as a member of the editorial board of the *British Food Journal.* He is a member of the Institutional and Organizational Economics Academy and alumnus of the Ronald Coase Institute. When not working, he likes to run, read, cook, and enjoy food and friends.

Tristan Pearce's research focuses on the human dimensions of global environmental change, in particular the vulnerability and adaptation of communities and socioecological systems to climate change. He is currently working on these issues in partnership with Indigenous communities in the Canadian Arctic, Pacific Islands, and Australia, and the mining sector in Canada. He has a particular interest in subsistence livelihoods, food security, and traditional knowledge (TK), including the generation and transmission of TK and its role in adaptation to environmental change.

Tiffanie Rainville is from Ottawa, Canada, and has lived in Bolivia since 2011, where she works as International Program Director and Field Officer for the Amazon Fish for Food project (www.pecesvida.org/en). She completed her BSc in Biology and Health at Queen's University. Her Master of Environmental Studies from Dalhousie University took her to two of Ecuador's coastal areas, where she studied the impacts and perceptions of climate change in mangrove ecosystems and fishing communities. Her current research interests include gender in fisheries and aquaculture, implementing and reflecting on scaling-up processes, participatory research, and the impact of fish on food security.

Verónica R. Hinojosa Sardán has a bachelor's degree in economics and a Masters in Environmental Socioeconomics (2002) from the Centre for Research and Education (CATIE) of Costa Rica. She has worked for the Peasant Farming Promotion Centre (CEPAC) since 2004, specializing in local economic and value chain development, and business development, and is responsible for gender mainstreaming throughout these areas. She also focuses on organizational strengthening for producer associations (2007–2010). Verónica is a professor at the Postgraduate Unit from the Faculty of Agricultural Sciences from the Autonomous University Gabriel René Moreno (UAGRM). Currently, she works for the Amazon Fish for Food project as a specialist in Economic Development and Organizational Strengthening and Gender (2015–2017).

Widen Abastoflor Sauma was born in Sucre and now lives in Santa Cruz de la Sierra, Bolivia. He is a chemical engineer, and has a diploma in Rural Business Development from the Centre for Research and Education (CATIE) of Costa Rica. He is the founder of the Peasant Farming Promotion Centre (CEPAC), and a specialist in Food Security and Value Chains. He is currently leading projects in local economic development, coordinating livelihood research, designing the value chain for farmed pacú fish in Yapacaní, and promoting a female-led model for aquaculture development which addresses poverty and food security issues in the region. Widen coordinates CEPAC's strong focus on both gender and communication and information technology.

Mirjam Schoonhoven-Speijer is a PhD candidate at the Knowledge, Technology and Innovation group of Wageningen University, the Netherlands. Her research focuses on three ways of getting oilseeds in Northern Uganda from the farmer to the market: traders, cooperatives, and contract farming. The study is interdisciplinary, using theories from development economics, sociology, and organizational studies. The aim of the research is to understand better how farmers and other market actors make markets work for them, as opposed to the often-heard phrase of 'making markets work for the poor'. This reflects well her interest in going beyond mainstream approaches, and instead finding new ways to study rural markets, hopefully contributing to new food solutions. She holds a Bachelor in Development Studies and a Research Master in Social and Cultural Science, both from Radboud University Nijmegen, the Netherlands.

Helena Shilomboleni is a Postdoctoral Fellow at Balsillie School of International Affairs in Canada this Fall. She received her PhD in 2017 in Social and Ecological Sustainablity from the University of Waterloo, Canada. Her primary area of research examines how the divergent agrarian models of the African Green Revolution and Africa's Food Sovereignty movements shape our understanding of food security and agricultural sustainability in southern Africa. She holds an MA in Global Governance from the University of Waterloo.

Zhenzhong Si is a Postdoctoral Fellow at Balsillie School of International Affairs in Canada. He holds a PhD in Geography from the University of Waterloo in Canada. His research interests include sustainable food systems, rural development, food security, food safety, and land management. His doctoral research examined government- and civil-society driven initiatives in the emerging ecological agriculture sector, Alternative Food Networks, and rural development in China. He has also been involved in "Hungry Cities Partnership", an international research project interrogating urban food security, food safety, and inclusive growth in the food economy in the Global South. Dr. Si has also conducted research on the socioeconomic implications of land management programs and policy changes in rural China.

Sietze Vellema is Associate Professor at the Knowledge, Technology and Innovation group, Wageningen University, and senior researcher at the Partnerships Resource Centre, Rotterdam School of Management, the Netherlands. His interest is to understand why and how different actors collaborate in solving organizational, managerial, and technical problems related to inclusive development and sustainable food provision. He studies partnerships, certification, and institutional arrangements in agri-food chains and supervises PhD candidates in different fields:

collective action in oil palm, shea, and sesame in West Africa; trading practices in East and West Africa; food safety and consumer practices in Southeast Asia; labels, governance, and service delivery in global commodity trade; and coordination and diversity in banana production in Asia. Sietze leads action research focusing on value chains, partnerships, poverty, and food security in Africa. He is an integrative thinker, and as editor-in-chief of *NJAS – Wageningen Journal of Life Sciences*, he enables a scientific platform for interdisciplinary and transdisciplinary research on complex and persistent problems in agricultural production, food and nutrition security, and natural resource management.

Cor van der Weele is Professor of humanistic philosophy at Wageningen University, the Netherlands. She was trained as a biologist and a philosopher; her PhD in philosophy of biology focused on metaphors as tools of selective attention in explanations of embryological development. About ten years ago, she learned about the idea of cultured meat through bio-artist Oron Catts. She has been studying the development of responses and ideas on cultured meat in interdisciplinary projects, working and publishing with lab pioneers, social scientists, and designers. In the field of meat alternatives, selective attention remains a core interest.

Hannah Wittman is Academic Director of the Centre for Sustainable Food Systems at the University of British Columbia and Associate Professor in the Institute for Resources, Environment and Sustainability (IRES). She is a rural sociologist who conducts community-based research related to food sovereignty, agrarian reform, agroecology, agrarian citizenship, and health equity in Canada and Latin America. Her recent edited books include *Environment and Citizenship in Latin America: Natures, Subjects and Struggles*; *Food Sovereignty: Reconnecting Food, Nature and Community*; and *Food Sovereignty in Canada: Creating Just and Sustainable Food Systems*.

ACKNOWLEDGEMENTS

We would firstly like to extend a huge thank-you to each of the contributors to this book. You have inspired us, kept us honest to our collective vision, and provided much food for thought. We would also like to acknowledge Angela Straathof: thanks for getting dirty with us and sharing your knowledge of soil. A giant thank-you is owed to Kathleen Short, who spent countless hours reading over every word in this book, checking references and formatting. The idea for this book transpired while we were guest editing a special issue – "Towards Sustainable Food Futures" – of the journal *Solutions*. Thanks to the editors of the journal for believing in our original idea, and giving us the space and time to work with an exciting group of emerging scholars who share our passion for thinking about solutions. Finally, we would like to thank Tom and Alex. To say this book could not have happened without your support is an understatement.

1

SUSTAINABLE FOOD FUTURES

Multidisciplinary solutions

Jessica Duncan and Megan Bailey

Introduction

Voltaire once said that "no problem can withstand the assault of sustained think-ing"*. In this book, we put that statement to the test. The problems plaguing food systems are well researched and well known. A growing global population, growing inequity, urbanization, and exceeded planetary boundaries are all expected to con-tribute to a food insecure future. This presents a complex and troubling challenge: how can we support transformation towards sustainable and just food systems? One thing that is clear, is that the objective of future food systems can no longer be to simply maximize productivity. We are now faced with having to grapple with "a far more complex landscape of production, rural development, environmental and social justice outcomes" (Pretty et al., 2010, p. 221).

As academics, we write about these outcomes and teach about the problems fac-ing the food system. Our discussions are focused on understanding and identifying problems, and much less focused on solutions. It is for this reason that we set out to explore solutions in this book. The solutions we have collected address problems across different scales and contexts. They take different entry points and start from different perspectives. The solutions are creative, imaginative, and practical, all to varying degrees. Some seek to work with existing institutions, others aim to tear them down.

The problem with solutions

While the challenges of feeding nine billion people are well articulated (Grethe et al., 2013), and also critiqued (Tomlinson, 2011), innovative solutions remain elusive and time is of the essence. While we are promoting solutions in this book, we are keenly aware of the problems with solutions. What works in a particular place, at a particular time, under a particular set of circumstances, will not necessarily work again, or elsewhere. We also recognize that many of the current problems to which solutions are being proposed are the result of previous attempts at solving problems. In this regard, we must find a balance between caution, reflexivity, and action. We must find a way of engaging in deep reflection, in transparent collaboration, without becoming entrapped in an endless cycle of consultation and reflection. At a certain point, we need a little less conversation, a little more action.

As this book makes clear, solutions to the myriad problems related to food systems are not only to be found in new scientific discoveries. They are being developed and implemented by people responding to challenges in their communities, and in their countries. A key challenge remains in shifting patterns of thought and assumptions of where and how solutions can be found. We also recognize that proposing alternatives can prove challenging. For example, ask any advocate of organic farming how many times they have been asked about whether organic agriculture can feed the world. This question itself reflects a mode of thinking that limits us. It divides the conversation into two camps, but perhaps more importantly, the question rests on the faulty assumption that world food security can be achieved by a single set of agricultural practices. Such an approach works to restrict much-needed out-of-the-box thinking, and is why Pablo Tittonell (2013, p. 5) proposed to turn the question around and ask: can conventional agriculture feed the world, noting "[t]his is obviously a rhetorical question, because we know that the answer is no". The big question we are thus asking in this book is: what kind of practices can feed the world?

Overview

The difficulty of creating categories

In approaching this question, we identified four broad practices that have the potential to support pathways towards sustainable food futures. These four practices serve as four thematic clusters around which this book is organized: Recognizing place; Enhancing participation; Challenging markets; and Designing sustainable food futures. Organizing the book this way allows us to move outside of disciplinary silos and across disciplinary subjects, and beyond the limitations of country borders and sectors. The thematic categories allow for comparison around key practices and values, and can thus add new dimensions to ongoing theoretical discussions while also disrupting the status quo. By organizing the book this way, we can highlight novel interconnections, and identify emerging points of convergence, but also conflicts and contradictions.

At the same time, we recognize the limitations of creating such categories. Specifically, we recognize that categorization is an exercise in power, one we have not taken lightly as editors. We acknowledge that while categories can help to structure, they also serve to restrict diversity, present problems of representation, and are subject to simplifications that we anticipate many readers will find problematic. To complicate matters, we note that neither markets nor designs, nor place for that matter, determine how food provisioning is carried out. Instead, they "provide the context in which different positions are possible. Together, these constitute room for maneuver" (van der Ploeg, 1992, p. 9).

This room for maneuver represents cracks in the dominant logic. Some of the solutions proposed in this book aim to fill up cracks, while others are proposing solutions that create new cracks. There are also many people working to pave over the cracks – to maintain the current path we are on – despite the overwhelming evidence that this path is not sustainable (Leach, Raworth & Rockström, 2013; Steffen et al., 2015). Business as usual is not an option and as such, we have not sought out solutions that keep us on this path.

In what follows, we expand upon the structure of the book, including the chapter categorization that we eventually settled on.

Recognizing place

A call to recognize place may seem a bit strange at first. You are certainly in a place right now, reading this. This place is almost certainly recognizable to you. Perhaps it is your home, the library, your office, the bus, or a café. These are all places, but the point we are interested in is that the place matters. Depending on your own reading preferences, you may find the bus a rather distracting, or even nauseating, place to read. Some of you may find the soundscape of your local café, and the gaze of fellow coffee drinkers, helpful for staying focused. Yet, while place is fundamental to our experience and practices, it rarely makes an appearance in our investigations.

Massey (2009) highlights the political potential of place, and conceptualizes place as "political entities" within space, in which negotiation, conflict, competition, and agreement ensue. This perspective on place is important insofar as it can create spaces for political debate and discussion, and can facilitate the inclusion of new perspectives. In particular, Massey (2004) argues that a politics of place beyond place needs to consider and critically analyze the power relations sustaining a particular identity of place. The combination of a sense of place and place as a political entity are at the core of our call to recognize place in the development of solutions.

As the chapters in this section make clear, the role of place is fundamental in the development of community-led policies in the Arctic, in the advancement of community-supported agriculture in China, in the problematization of the "local", and in the development of a diversity of farmland commons to address the limitations of increased concentration and privatization of farmland.

More specifically, in Chapter 2, Carie Hoover and her colleagues introduce us to challenges facing Arctic communities where governmental policies and related programs have supported a transition away from local – country – foods. These policies have facilitated a loss of traditional knowledge and traditional diet, and a dependence on expensive and often unhealthy foods. This loss is happening concurrently with major environmental change that is also shifting the way Inuit interact with and relate to place. The result is a situation where the ability of people to shape their diets in a way consistent with their culture is restricted. To address this problem, they propose culturally relevant solutions that include the transmission of environmental knowledge and land skills, and redirecting policies and programs to support these activities, including hunting resources and community storage.

In Chapter 3, Zhenzhong Si's solution sets out to address a widespread lack of trust in the Chinese food system, brought about in part by promotion of an agricultural sector dependent on the usage of chemical pesticides and synthetic fertilizer. The resulting food supply chains are delocalized and elongated, distancing farmers from consumers and creating distrust between them. Si provides concrete examples of how community-supported agriculture (CSA) in China not only addresses the sustainability challenges confronting the conventional Chinese food system, but also works to address declining social trust and the marginalization of peasants. Here, the idea of, and connection to, place is reinvigorated for consumers through connection with food production and provision.

In Chapter 4, Susanna Klassen and Hannah Wittman also grapple with the problems associated with limited trust and increasing distance in food supply chains. Like Si, they turn to localized food production as a solution pathway, but instead of focusing on CSA, they explore the idea of place-based food systems as a way to reconsider the meaning and value of localized agricultural production. Their engagement with the concept of place-based food systems contributes to ongoing critical discussion about the meaning and implications of 'local food'. Indeed, in this chapter, they compare conceptualizations of localized and place-based food systems through a case study of the blueberry industry in British Columbia, Canada. By presenting place-based food systems as a solution, they illustrate the complex and intersecting drivers contributing to key dynamics, including social and ecological diversification, sustainable nutrient cycling, and connection to place.

Building on the idea of the local and the fundamental importance of place to sustainable food futures, in Chapter 5 Jamie Baxter illustrates the relationship between disaggregation and redistribution of property rights to food insecurity. He highlights how food insecurity is linked to a lack of clear, enforceable, and sufficiently long-term property rights. To address this problem, Baxter examines the idea of the "farmland commons" as a promising solution to the linked problems of food and farmland insecurity. He explores opportunities and tensions surrounding the idea of farmland commons, leading him to conclude that to sustain the diversity of farmland commons arrangements, it is important that principles for good institutional design are identified, and that legal and other reforms are implemented. The collection of chapters in this section call on us to recognize place in the development of food solutions, and show us, in different ways, how we can do this.

Enhancing participation

There is broad agreement around the importance of people being able to participate in processes that impact their lives. Indeed, participation of a diverse range of people is increasingly being seen as fundamental to the development of policies, programs, and practices that are built on the basis of uncertain knowledge and socio-cultural evolution (Voss & Kemp, 2006, p. 15) (e.g. food security, climate change, sustainability). As such, enhanced participation reflects, in part, a strategy for tackling complexity, uncertainty, and multiple values through the input of various communities of knowledge (Kasemir et al., 2000; Mielke et al., 2016). We actively recognize that participation "is a problematic and contested ground, but one with the potential to deliver real benefits to those who have hitherto been incorporated" (Parfitt, 2004, p. 538). Towards that end, a growing body of evidence from developing countries shows that participation and ownership in the design of rules can increase voluntary compliance (World Bank, 2017).

The chapters that make up this section propose various solutions for sustainable food futures that are grounded in principles of enhanced participation. In Chapter 6, Helena Shilomboleni reflects on the state of customary land rights in Mozambique and draws lessons from the food sovereignty movement to contribute to contemporary debates on land reform in Sub-Saharan Africa. She notes that while many African countries have fairly strong legal provisions that recognize customary-based land rights, the laws may be poorly implemented. Focusing on a case in the district of Marracune, she shows how improving land law training and participatory governance is key to a sustainable food future. She explains how, in response to increased pressure on land use, the National Union of Mozambican Peasants is teaching farmers about the land law. A key outcome of the solution is that when marginalized people are given a voice and the necessary tools to participate, they can shift relations of power.

In Chapter 7, Tiffanie Rainville and her colleagues reiterate the importance and value of developing programs that specifically target women but that also take context into account. Their review of a small-scale, family-based aquaculture farm in Bolivia's Southern Amazon region shows how supporting the uptake of aquaculture practices by marginalized groups is having important impacts on livelihoods. The project presented in the chapter started to work with women but also employed a place-based participatory approach, and has managed to reduce social, environmental, and economic vulnerability while also improving resilience, food security, and gender equality.

In Chapter 8, the final chapter of this section on participation, Levi Gahman shows how participation in resistance is a key solution. Importantly, he highlights how this form of participation can work towards multiplicity. Specifically, he describes how in Mexico, the Zapatistas are constructing *un mundo donde quepan muchos* (a world where many worlds fit) by claiming autonomy and actively rejecting neoliberalism. More specifically, he describes how the Zapatistas are building an economy of solidarity that incorporates gender equality, mutual aid, food sovereignty, and Indigenous culture. He highlights the work that has been done in these communities to adopt more inclusive language, and how this has supported a shift towards more fair and just social relations. The radical solution presented in this chapter illustrates how resistance, while difficult, can be a solution for decolonizing food systems.

Challenging markets

Since the end of the nineteenth century, an idealized vision of economic growth and the market has influenced the development not only of economics, but social policy more broadly. However, as Leyshon (2005, p. 859) notes, in "[p]rivileging the ideal over the actual, the dominant ways of thinking and seeing constitute an impoverished approach to economies and the range of possibilities they offer for diverse and alternative economic futures".

Markets, "the structures through which goods and services are exchanged" (van der Ploeg, 2015, p. 16), are one of the key institutions mediating how food production and trade are governed. These institutions reflect societal values, and thus, they need to be continually engaged with, reformed, reimagined, and reconstructed to reflect current values. At the same time, they need to be flexible enough to take on the fact that no single value set can represent the diversity of values we find in the world.

While markets are "heralded as the ideal system for coordinating complex transactions between producers and consumers" (Gibson-Graham, Cameron & Healy, 2013, p. 85), the globalization of food and commodity markets – understood by a combination of the international circulation of food products as commodities, the transnational expansion of food-based corporations, and an increasingly globalized governance system – have brought to bear growing economic and cultural inequities across the world (Phillips, 2006). The use of globalized markets in sustainable food movements has been proposed as potentially antithetical to the processes by which sustainability improvements should be made (Taylor, 2005; Konefal, 2013). The chapters in this section directly challenge the role of the market, or current market mechanisms through their solutions.

In Chapter 9, Mirjam Schoonhoven-Speijer, Ellen Mangnus, and Sietze Vellema propose a solution to the problem of productionism in food security; that is, the focus on increased production at the expense of addressing other key challenges such as access, affordability, and stability. In their chapter, they explore how food is made available through non-conventional channels, specifically the informal nature of commercial transactions; and they question whether these actually hinder the provision of food in rural and urban markets, as much of the existing literature suggests. Drawing on studies from Mali and Uganda, they outline the important roles played by intermediary traders, highlighting, for example, the stability and their long-term presence. From here, they propose an innovative solution for food security: the organization of skill-based education to transform food trade.

In Chapter 10, Simon Bush questions the dominant model of third-party eco-certification in sustainable aquaculture production. He points to limits of these certification schemes, especially when applied to producers in developing countries, and asks how certification can transform industries towards sustainability if the capabilities of small-holders to comply with related standards remains low. To answer this question, he focuses on aquaculture small-holders and proposes a new form of retail-targeted certification that reverses the burden of proof that currently rests with producers. In his proposed model, it is not small-holders who have to demonstrate sustainability, but rather the buyers and retailers. Such a model could give important recognition to retailers, and could foster inclusive and effective support for improving the production practices of small-holders.

In Chapter 11, the last of this section, Raquel Ajates Gonzalez presents a framework for overcoming the tendency of alternatives to the conventional food system being taken up by the very system they are seeking to subvert. The result is the continuation of current dynamics and the simultaneous weakening of alternatives. To address this, she outlines solution-based strategies being employed by actors operating in Alternative Food Networks. These actors are working to combat the marketization of social justice and ecological public health ideals, and practices by and for the benefit of industrial food regimes. A layered framework for analysis is proposed, made up of four interconnected categories: rediscovering new allies, fostering diversity, rethinking access to resources while redefining success, and democratizing knowledge production. Together, these strategies are promoting fairer and more sustainable food systems and simultaneously challenging the lack of diversity in conventional food relations while preventing the co-optation of alternative practices. What unites the chapters in this section is that they all start by challenging the logic of the dominant economic system and put forward solutions to address what they see to be current limitations to sustainable food futures.

Designing sustainable food futures

Up to this point, the chapters in this book have drawn on empirical and experiential evidence of diverse solutions. Of course, if we are thinking about sustainable food futures, we also require forward-thinking solutions. The chapters in this next section do this by engaging with questions and practices related to the design of sustainable food futures. They focus on shifting values and advancing technologies and principles to support these shifts, be it towards a non-monetary currency, animal-free meat, or circular designs. Perhaps not surprisingly, these solutions make use of technological innovations, but they are not blind calls for technological solutions. In this sense, the solutions that make up this chapter support Garrett Hardin's problematization of a reliance on technology and technical solutions. He argues that solutions to our problems are not to be found in technical solutions, but through a reformulation of human ideals and values (Hardin, 1968). But maybe more to the point today is that a match between technical solutions and human values is needed. A sustainable food future necessitates "changes in the way food is produced, stored, processed, distributed, and accessed" (Godfray et al., 2010, p. 812).

We acknowledge that technology has a large and ever-increasing role in facilitating these changes, but we recognize that technological advancements have also been a key contributor to an industrial food system with devastating social-ecological consequences. For example, technological advances are one of the primary drivers of overfishing (Jacquet, 2009). Technological gains have often meant making people and processes more efficient, and so have been important where labor costs are high. But it is also a deliberate and political decision to focus on technology, as one could also decide to make natural capital more efficient – for example, through practices like conservation agriculture (Hobbs, 2007) – or to do both. We can see that key questions emerge around how best to utilize technological gains for the benefit of food producers and consumers, where "benefit" has to be in line with society's values. The chapters in this section grapple with this tension and explore technical solutions as possible means to just and sustainable food futures.

In Chapter 12, Cor van der Weele addresses the problems related to raising rates of meat consumption. She interrogates the idea of cultured meat, a meat alternative developed from animal cells, which has been advanced as a solution. Her work on cultured meat shows that the mere idea of cultured meat opens up discussions about what constitutes "normal" meat and uncovers widespread ambivalence about what meat is. While she concludes that what cultured meat may mean for us in the future remains uncertain, it is clear that a space has opened in which "normal" meat comes to appear less normal.

In Chapter 13, Randall Coleman challenges us to reflect on how we ascribe value to what matters to us. He takes on the dominant economic system by creating a new one, based on compost. In this new economy, household waste is exchanged for fresh produce. Taking inspiration from alternative currencies, he proposes the idea of soil currency, complete with an exchange rate based on volume of inputs of household organic waste to volume of compost needed to grow crops.

In Chapter 14, Stefano Pascucci and Jessica Duncan explore the principles of the circular economy and apply them to food production. They examine multiple cases where these principles are being applied to varying degrees. Based on these cases, they propose a typology to begin to classify the growing number of circular food initiatives as being either an Island of Pirates, a Spider in the Web, a Town of Renaissance, or a Community of Hope. The typology is then used to uncover key tensions, ambiguities, and potentials emerging from the designs of circular food systems.

A revolution with cooking

Thinking about the future world we want to live in, we draw inspiration from a well-quoted statement attributed to Emma Goldman: "a revolution without dancing is not a revolution worth having"***. We agree, and would add that "a revolution without cooking and sharing food is not a revolution worth having". This led us to the idea of including recipes with each chapter. Cooking can be a revolutionary act. In this sense, recipes can also act as solution pathways to sustainable food futures.

Recipes are much more than instructions on how to cook a meal. They are culture, they are tradition, and they tell stories. Consider the cookbook *Handmade* (Palmera, 2016) that shares the stories of 34 women from Sri Lanka and their experiences of war through their recipes. In the book's summary, the authors note: "Food is their life and a language they are at ease with. So what better way to tell their story than through food?" (Palmera, 2016). Another cookbook, *With Our Own Hands* (van Oudenhoven & Haider, 2015), provides a rich ethnographic account of the people who live in Pamir mountains that stand between Afghanistan and Tajikistan. The book includes over 100 recipes and provides a rich understanding of the ecological, agricultural, and cultural heritage of a region that produces a diverse array of walnuts, apples, pears, apricots, mulberries, and over 150 varieties of wheat. In a more light-hearted example, *Recipes for a Beautiful Life: A Memoir in Stories*, Rebecca Barry (2016) integrates recipes into her memoir of motherhood (and of marriage, work, meditation, and other manners of life's components). The recipes give the reader insight into her thought process and states of mind throughout life's challenges, which provide an added, sometimes hilarious, depth to the memoirs. Taken together, these cookbooks show us how, through recipes, we can gain access to histories: insights into cultures, rituals, and traditions that in some instances are disappearing.

The recipes included in this book are admittedly far less ambitious, but the idea to include them was certainly inspired by these projects. In the context of this book, the recipes serve as examples of how authors try to put their solutions into practice. They highlight the culture, the taste, the creativity, and the fun of these solutions. In presenting these recipes, we acknowledge tradition, culture, and place, but we also recognize that recipes are adaptations. You will likely develop your own adaptations, depending on where you live, what foods you can access, and what you like to eat. These recipes are thus another reminder that context matters, and panaceas are a straw (wo)man. So, we encourage you to eat your way through this book, and as you do, to think through the questions that the authors have posed at the end of each of the chapters. These questions are meant to encourage deeper thinking on the solutions being proposed, but they are also meant to get us thinking critically about the limitations and challenges inherent to the solution.

Conclusions

This book should be read and understood as a complex, and at times contradictory, multidisciplinary contribution. Each author has drawn on their own disciplinary expertise and experience to develop relevant questions and corresponding research-and-solution formulation. Thus, while we run the risk of maintaining disciplinary silos, we seek to combat this by raising critical questions and supporting dialogue across the chapters.

The solutions proposed in this book can be read as an atlas of possibilities. There are multiple roads we can, and must, travel to bring us towards our destination: just and sustainable food futures. And yet, overwhelmingly it appears that instead of moving towards a brighter future, we continue with a status quo that is not good enough. To reach sustainable food futures, we require diligent and creative route planning. Not every route will work for everyone, or every context. Some routes will require us to go off road, while others take us along the toll roads. Others set about redefining what we know to be a road, and some may lead us directly to road blocks. It is our hope that the majority will lead us to new social-technical or social-economic arrangements that promote just, sustainable, and fair food futures.

RECIPE: WHOLE ROASTED CAULIFLOWER WITH TAHINI SAUCE

One evening we decided to co-host a dinner party. We hosted it on a weekday, and to share the cooking load, we told everyone it would be potluck. The idea of a potluck is that everyone contributes a dish to the meal. Ideally, some coordination is involved to ensure that appetizers, salads, main courses, and desserts are covered. We both grew up in Canada where potlucks are very common. However, we were hosting the dinner in the Netherlands. On the evening of the dinner, we rushed back from work, put together a salad, and made this cauliflower dish. As the guests started to arrive, it became clear that very few of them had realized it was a potluck (in fact, many thought that "potluck" was the name of the dish we would be making, like a casserole, or a Dutch stampot). The reality of having to share one cauliflower among 10 hungry people began to sink in. The recipe is delicious, but it is best served alongside a main dish. In the end, we managed to quickly prepare enough improvised dishes and the evening was a success, but it was a good lesson for us on just how important it is to be clear with instructions and to not make assumptions.

Ingredients

- 1 large cauliflower
- 2 cloves of garlic
- 1 teaspoon smoked paprika
- 2 tablespoons apple cider vinegar
- olive oil
- salt
- freshly ground black pepper
- 1 lemon, zest and juice
- 1 can of chopped plum tomatoes (400 g)

Tahini sauce

- 1 cup tahini sesame seed paste
- 3/4 cup lukewarm water, or more if needed for a smoother consistency

- 2 cloves raw garlic (or 5 cloves roasted garlic)
- 1/4 cup fresh lemon juice (or more to taste)
- 1/4 tsp salt (or more to taste)

Method

1 Preheat the oven to 180°C/350°F.
2 In a blender, mix 2 cloves garlic, 1 generous splash of olive oil, 2 teaspoons salt, some black pepper, the juice of 1 lemon, 1 teaspoon smoked paprika, and 2 tablespoons apple cider vinegar.
3 Trim the outer cauliflower leaves. Cut the stalk so the cauliflower can sit flat. Place the cauliflower in a medium casserole pan that has a lid.
4 Pour the blended spices (step 2) over the cauliflower and rub them in.
5 Cover the cauliflower and place the pan, with the lid on, into a preheated oven for 1 hour (or until the cauliflower is tender). Remove the lid and continue baking for another 15–20 minutes.
6 Take the pan out of the oven and pour in a can of chopped plum tomatoes. Sprinkle lemon zest and thyme leaves, and return the dish back to the oven for 10 more minutes, or until the cauliflower takes on a golden look.
7 Meanwhile, place the ingredients for the tahini sauce into a blender or food processor and blend until smooth.
8 When the cauliflower is done and out of the oven, drizzle it with the tahini sauce and extra virgin olive oil. You can also put toasted almonds, parsley, or pomegranate seeds on top.
9 Cut the dish like a pie and serve.
10 Hope you explained the concept of potluck better than we did so that you have other things to eat with this! We would suggest a pilaf or couscous dish (see Chapter 9 for a great recipe!).

Questions

1 From your perspective, what is the most pressing problem facing food systems?
2 We identified four themes: place, participation, markets, and future designs. Which of these themes do you think will have the biggest impact on advancing sustainable food futures, and why?
3 Why is there still a tendency to apply a "one size fits all" model of sustainability? What are the implications of such an approach?

Notes

* See https://en.wikiquote.org/wiki/Talk:Voltaire.
** See https://en.wikiquote.org/wiki/Emma_Goldman.

References

Barry, R. (2016) *Recipes for a Beautiful Life: A Memoir in Stories*. Toronto, Simon & Schuster.

Gibson-Graham, J. K., Cameron, J. & Healy, S. (2013) *Take Back the Economy: An Ethical Guide for Transforming Our Communities*. Minneapolis, University of Minnesota Press.

Godfray, H. C. J., Beddington, J. R., Crute, I. R., Haddad, L., Lawrence, D., Muir, J. F., Pretty, J., Robinson, S., Thomas, S. M. & Toulmin, C. (2010) Food security: The challenge of feeding 9 billion people. *Science*. 327 (5967), 812–818.

Grethe, H., Bahrs, E., Becker, T., Birner, R., Brockmeier, M., Dabbert, S., Doluschitz, R., Lippert, C. & Thiele, E. (2013) Challenges of global change for agricultural development and world food security. *Berichte Uberlandwirtschaft*. Stuttgart, W. Kohlhammer GMBH, I A Jochen Krauss. 91 (1).

Hardin, G. (1968) The tragedy of the commons. *Science*. 162 (3859), 1243–1248. Available from: doi: 10.1126/science.162.3859.1243 [Accessed: 10th March 2017].

Hobbs, P. R. (2007) Conservation agriculture: What is it and why is it important for future sustainable food production? *The Journal of Agricultural Science*. 145 (2), 127. Available from: doi: 10.1017/S0021859607006892 [Accessed: 10th March 2017].

Jacquet, J. (2009) Silent water: A brief examination of the marine fisheries crisis. *Environment, Development and Sustainability*. 11 (2), 255–263. Available from: doi: 10.1007/s10668-007-9108-1 [Accessed: 10th March 2017].

Kasemir, B., Dahinden, U., Swartling, Å. G., Schüle, R., Tabara, D. & Jaeger, C. C. (2000) Citizens' perspectives on climate change and energy use. *Global Environmental Change*. 10 (3), 169–184. Available from: doi: 10.1016/S0959-3780(00)00022-4 [Accessed: 10th March 2017].

Konefal, J. (2013) Environmental movements, market-based approaches, and neo-liberalization. *Organization & Environment*. 26 (3), 336–352. Available from: doi: 10.1177/1086026612467982 [Accessed: 10th March 2017].

Leach, M., Raworth, K. & Rockström, J. (2013) Between social and planetary boundaries: Navigating pathways in the safe and just space for humanity. In: Hackmann, H., Caillods, F., Moser, S., Berkhout, F., Daniel, L., Feliciano, D., Martin, O. & Marques, E. (eds.) *World Social Sciences Report*. Paris, UNESCO, pp. 84–89. Available from: doi: 10.1787/9789264203419-en [Accessed: 10th March 2017].

Leyshon, A. (2005) Introduction: Diverse economies. *Antipode*. 37 (5), 856–862. Available from: doi: 10.1111/j.0066-4812.2005.00535.x [Accessed: 10th March 2017].

Massey, D. (2004) Geographies of responsibility. *Geografiska Annaler, Series B: Human Geography*. 86 (1), 5–18. Available from: doi: 10.1111/j.0435-3684.2004.00150.x [Accessed: 10th March 2017].

Massey, D. (2009) Concepts of space and power in theory and in political practice. *Documents d'Ànalisi Geogràfica*. 55, 15–26.

Mielke, J., Vermaßen, H., Ellenbeck, S., Fernandez Milan, B. & Jaeger, C. (2016) Stakeholder involvement in sustainability science – a critical view. *Energy Research & Social Science*. 17, 71–81. Available from: doi: 10.1016/j.erss.2016.04.001 [Accessed: 10th March 2017].

Palmera. (2016) *Handmade*. Strathfield, Australia, Palmera.

Parfitt, T. (2004) The ambiguity of participation. *Third World Quarterly*. 25 (3), 537–556.

Phillips, L. (2006) Food and globalization. *Annual Review of Anthropology*. 35 (1), 37–57. Available from: doi: 10.1146/annurev.anthro.35.081705.123214 [Accessed: 10th March 2017].

Pretty, J., Sutherland, W. J., Ashby, J., Auburn, J., Baulcombe, D., Bell, M., Bentley, J., Bickersteth, S., Brown, K., Burke, J., Campbell, H., Chen, K., Crowley, E., Crute, I., Dobbelaere, D., Edwards-Jones, G., Funes-Monzote, F., Godfray, H. C. J., Griffon, M., Gypmantisiri, P., Haddad, L., Halavatau, S., Herren, H., Holderness, M., Izac, A.-M., Jones, M., Koohafkan, P.,

Lal, R., Lang, T., McNeely, J., Mueller, A., Nisbett, N., Noble, A., Pingali, P., Pinto, Y., Rabbinge, R., Ravindranath, N. H., Rola, A., Roling, N., Sage, C., Settle, W., Sha, J. M., Shiming, L., Simons, T., Smith, P., Strzepeck, K., Swaine, H., Terry, E., Tomich, T. P., Toulmin, C., Trigo, E., Twomlow, S., Vis, J. K., Wilson, J. & Pilgrim, S. (2010) The top 100 questions of importance to the future of global agriculture. *International Journal of Agricultural Sustainability*. 8 (4), 219–236. Available from: doi: 10.3763/ijas.2010.0534 [Accessed: 10th March 2017].

St. Martin, K., Roelvink, G. & Gibson-Graham, J. K. (2015) An economic politics for our times. In: St. Martin, K., Roelvink, G. & Gibson-Graham, J. K. (eds.) *Making Other Worlds Possible: Performing Diverse Economies*. Minneapolis, University of Michigan Press, pp. 12–25.

Steffen, W., Richardson, K., Rockstrom, J., Cornell, S. E., Fetzer, I., Bennett, E. M., Biggs, R., Carpenter, S. R., de Vries, W., de Wit, C. A., Folke, C., Gerten, D., Heinke, J., Mace, G. M., Persson, L. M., Ramanathan, V., Reyers, B. & Sorlin, S. (2015) Planetary boundaries: Guiding human development on a changing planet. *Science*. 347 (6223), 1259855–1259855. Available from: doi: 10.1126/science.1259855 [Accessed: 10th March 2017].

Taylor, P. L. (2005) In the market but not of it: Fair trade coffee and forest stewardship council certification as market-based social change. *World Development*. 33 (1), 129–147. Available from: doi: 10.1016/j.worlddev.2004.07.007 [Accessed: 10th March 2017].

Tittonell, P. A. (2013) *Farming systems ecology: Towards ecological intensification of world agriculture*. [Lecture] Wageningen, Wageningen University, 16th May 2013.

Tomlinson, I. (2011) Doubling food production to feed the 9 billion: A critical perspective on a key discourse of food security in the UK. *Journal of Rural Studies*. 29, 81–90. Available from: doi: 10.1016/j.jrurstud.2011.09.001 [Accessed: 10th March 2017].

van der Ploeg, J. D. (1992) Styles of farming: An introductory note on concepts and methodology. In: De Haan, H. & Douwe van der Ploeg, J. (eds.) *Endogenous Regional Development in Europe: Theory, Method and Practice*. Luxembourg, Office for Official Publications of the European Communities, pp. 7–30.

van der Ploeg, J. D. (2015) Newly emerging, nested markets: A theoretical introduction. In: Hebinck, P., Van der Ploeg, J. D. & Schneider, S. (eds.) *Rural Development and the Construction of New Markets*. Oxon, Routledge, pp. 16–40.

van Oudenhoven, F. & Haider, J. (2015) *With Our Own Hands*. Volendam, LM Publishers.

Voss, J.-P. & Kemp, R. (2006) Sustainability and reflexive governance: Introduction. In J. P., Bauknecht, D. & Kemp, R. (eds.) *Reflexive Governance for Sustainable Development*. Cheltenham, Edward Elgar, pp. 3–28.

World Bank (2017) *World development report 2017: Governance and the law*. World Bank Group. Available from: www.worldbank.org/en/publication/wdr2017 [Accessed 10th March 2017].

PART I

Recognizing place

2

CULTURAL RELEVANCE IN ARCTIC FOOD SECURITY INITIATIVES

*Carie Hoover, Colleen Parker, Claire Hornby,
Sonja Ostertag, Kayla Hansen-Craik,
Tristan Pearce, and Lisa Loseto*

Introduction to the Arctic: landscape, history, and food security

Inuit, the Indigenous People inhabiting the Arctic regions of Greenland, Canada, Alaska, and the Russian Far East, have adapted to living in harsh Arctic conditions for thousands of years. In Canada, there are more than 50 Inuit communities across the Canadian Arctic that fall under a variety of land claims across territories and provinces (Figure 2.1): Yukon, Northwest Territories (NT), Nunavut (NU), Quebec, and Nunatsiavut. Many of the communities in these territories or provinces are located above or near the Arctic Circle (66°30' N), and nearly all are located in remote locations accessible only by airplanes. While summer temperatures can reach upwards of 35°C, winter temperatures can drop below −60°C when factoring in windchill effects, with wind speeds ranging from 50–80 km/h and temperatures remaining below freezing for up to 8 months of the year (Government of Canada, 2015). In high-latitude Canadian communities, polar nights (24-hour period with no sunrise) last up to 4.5 months, and 24-hour daylight lasts up to 5.5 months (National Research Council Canada, 2015). The resulting short growing season combined with extensive permafrost (soil frozen throughout the year) limits agricultural approaches to food production. Historically, Inuit have relied heavily on wild populations of terrestrial and marine species for food, warm clothing, and tools, with the historic seasonal movement of Inuit centered on seasonal food availability (e.g., caribou, whales, seals, and fish) (Kelly, 1983; Friesen, 2002).

Food security exists when people at all times can acquire safe, nutritionally adequate, and culturally acceptable foods in a manner that maintains human dignity (FAO, 2002; Gregory, Ingram & Brklacich, 2005). This has been broken down into food access, food availability, and food quality. In an Inuit context, food *availability* denotes sufficient availability of the store food and country food (hunted or trapped

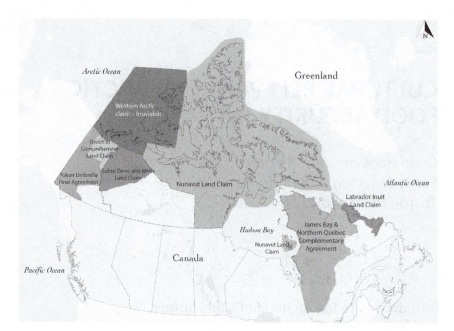

FIGURE 2.1 Main Inuit and Aboriginal geographic settlement regions of the Canadian Arctic, as represented by associated land claims: Yukon (Yukon Umbrella Final Agreement); Northwest Territories (Gwich'in Comprehensive Land Claim, Western Arctic Claim, Sahtu Dene Metis Land Claim); Nunavut (Nunavut Land Claim); Quebec (James Bay and Northern Quebec Agreement); and Nunatsiavut (an autonomous area of Newfoundland and Labrador claimed under the Labrador Inuit Land Claim)

Source: Authors, adapted from www.northernstrategy.gc.ca/cns/cns-eng.asp

animals, other foods gathered from the land) components of the food system to meet demand; food *access* refers to the "ability of households and individuals to access adequate resources to acquire store and traditional foods for a nutritious diet"; and food *quality* involves the "ability to obtain safe food of sufficient nutritional and cultural value" (Ford, 2009, p. 86). Conversely, food *insecurity* exists when the food system is stressed so that one or more of the pillars of food security do not exist. Food sovereignty expands on food security by "including production, distribution and consumption of food with respect to their own cultures and their own systems of managing natural resources" (Meakin & Kurvits, 2009, p. 28; Declaration of Atitlán, 2002, p. 2). Within the Arctic context food sovereignty is focused on the ability to shape one's own diet in a way consistent with one's culture and includes local food systems, food distribution, and enhances community independence (Socha et al., 2012). While this aspect is not always explicitly stated as a goal within Arctic communities, ideas relating to food sovereignty are noted in communities' food security goals with the ability to access traditional foods as a high priority (Declaration of Atitlán, 2002; Skinner et al., 2013). Food security is a growing challenge for many Inuit living in the Canadian Arctic, as food insecurity rates for Inuit living in the Canadian Arctic (aged 15+) are much higher (41%) than those experienced in southern Canada (8%) (Huet, Rosol & Egeland, 2012; Wallace, 2014), and required diverse locally relevant solutions (Council of Canadian Academies, 2014).

Even though Inuit society has undergone profound changes in the last half century, placing new pressures on the subsistence food system, subsistence continues to be important in the lives of many Inuit. These changes include, but are not limited to, moving into permanent settlements, increasing populations, attendance in formal education, the rise of the wage economy, and the increasing cost of hunting. Residential schools in Canada contributed to changes in Inuit culture by removing Aboriginal (or Indigenous people of Canada) children (including Inuit) from their families, in part to weaken their culture and replace it with the culture of the Euro-Christian Canadian society (The Truth and Reconciliation Commission of Canada, 2015). These schools existed for more than 100 years in Canada, with successive generations of children attending them – thus removing Aboriginal children from their native language, culture, and family connections (Partridge, 2010). These impacts, along with younger generations spending more time in formal education, wage employment, and organized sport, has led to younger Inuit spending less time involved in subsistence activities compared to older generations (Pearce et al., 2011; Pearce et al., 2015a). Formal schooling and employment limit the amount of time youth and hunters can spend on the land, which results in less hands-on training of hunting and land skills, and can lead to a lack of skills and knowledge necessary to participate in subsistence harvesting activities (Pearce et al., 2011). In addition, the high costs associated with harvesting of country foods (i.e., foods that have been hunted, fished, or gathered locally) provide another barrier for participation in harvesting activities (Pearce et al., 2011; Hoover et al., 2013).

Even though households with active hunters are more food secure (Huet, Rosol & Egeland, 2012), most Inuit depend on imported foods to some degree, which tend to be nutrient poor and expensive to purchase (Kinlock, Kuhnlein & Muir, 1992; Pearce et al., 2010). This shift away from a subsistence-based diet consisting primarily of country foods to a diet high in store-bought foods has been identified as a key issue for food security in terms of the ability to access nutritionally adequate and culturally acceptable foods (Council of Canadian Academies, 2014; Pearce et al., 2010). In addition, country foods have been shown to significantly contribute essential vitamins and nutrients (e.g., folate; vitamins A, D, and E; essential fatty acids; pyridoxine; riboflavin; niacin; ascorbic acid) into the diet of Inuit (Geraci & Smith, 1979; Hidiroglou et al., 2008), with available store-bought foods often being inferior in terms of nutritional value.

The Nunavut Food Coalition, an organization addressing food security within the Nunavut Territory of the Canadian Arctic, has identified six key themes for improving food security: country food, store-bought food, local food production, life skills, programs and community initiatives, and policy and legislation (Nunavut Food Security Coalition, 2014). While broader policy and legislation changes are necessary to implement Arctic-wide changes to food security, here we propose ways to improve existing initiatives, in addition to highlighting locally based initiatives that have been shown to contribute to food security in addition to being culturally relevant. While these alone do not cover all possible avenues, they represent starting points to an increasingly important discussion on food security that must establish Inuit as key decision makers (Inuit Tapiriit Kanatami & Inuit Circumpolar Council Canada, 2014).

Top-down approach: Nutrition North

While federal and regional governments have a clear responsibility to ensure their citizens have access to appropriate and adequate foods, how these programs are administered is critical to their success. In Canada, federal programs are primarily responsible for food security initiatives that are delivered in the provinces and territories, as there is limited evidence of territorial or provincial programs that deal comprehensively with the issue of food security (Boult, 2004). Nutrition North Canada (NNC) was launched in 2011 "to bring healthy food to isolated Northern communities", and is the largest national food subsidy available in the Canadian Arctic (Nutrition North, 2016). It offers an airfreight subsidy directly to northern retailers in remote communities to help lower the costs of "healthy" foods (i.e., produce, dairy, cereals, meats, etc.) (Nutrition North, 2016). While the current subsidy works to reduce transportation costs to the retailer, it is unclear how many of these discounts are passed on to the consumer. Discounts only apply to certain items (both perishable items, such as milk, eggs, meat, cheese, vegetables, and fruit; and non-perishable items, such as grains, cereals, and infant formula) (Nutrition North Canada, 2013) that may be less culturally appropriate, while the cost of other food items and other grocery products remains high. The estimated weekly cost to feed a family of four is $360–$450 for northern residents, but the same foods would cost $200–$250 for southern Canadian residents (Nutrition North, 2016). Table 2.1 highlights the cost of select food items in Nunavut, noting some of these items may receive the NNC subsidy, yet the cost is still higher than in southern (urban) Canadian locations.

Lack of transparency within the system does not allow for confirmation of whether all subsidies make it to the consumer (Galloway, 2014; Office of the Auditor General of Canada, 2014.). In 2016, retailers began showing discounts received for food items under the NNC program to highlight savings (Office of the Auditor General of Canada, 2014); however, this initiative only shows savings to the consumer and not the subsidy received for the same item to the retailer. The NNC program helps alleviate the high costs for some food items, but taken alone, it can best be described as a "band-aid" solution. Rather, greater focus needs to be placed on people and cultures to better understand their food requirements and adjust current subsidies accordingly (Sanchez, 2009), with programs improving food security in the Arctic being driven by the communities with involvement from regional and national stakeholders (Council of Canadian Academies, 2014). Starting

TABLE 2.1 Comparison of select grocery prices from March 2015 in Nunavut compared to the Canadian average

Item	Size	Nunavut Average ($)	Canada Average ($)	Nunavut-Canada Ratio
Milk, 2%	1L	3.16	2.34	1.35
Butter, Salted	454g	7.20	4.59	1.57
Eggs	Dozen, Large	3.94	3.34	1.18
Frozen French Fries	650g–1kg	6.66	2.66	2.50
Evaporated Milk	385ml	3.33	1.88	1.77
Instant Coffee	200g	12.30	6.52	1.89
Tea Bags	72 × 227g	8.22	4.47	1.84
Soda Crackers	450g	7.09	2.80	2.53
Canned Baked Beans	398ml	4.30	1.30	3.31
Canned Tomatoes	796ml	5.29	1.62	3.27
Macaroni	500g	4.39	1.57	2.80
Cooking Oil	942ml–1L	9.17	4.18	2.19
Flour, All Purpose White	2.5kg	13.58	5.03	2.70
Sugar, White	2kg	8.72	2.81	3.10
Orange Juice	1L	5.57	2.07	2.69
Tomato Juice	1.36L	9.16	2.48	3.70
White Bread	675g	5.01	2.81	1.78
Bananas	per kg	4.61	1.73	2.66
Oranges	per kg	7.94	3.28	2.42
Carrots	per kg	6.17	1.98	3.12
Celery	per kg	9.26	2.57	3.60
Onions	per kg	4.12	1.68	2.45
Potatoes	4.54kg	12.15	5.56	2.19
Sirloin Steak	per kg	32.06	21.86	1.47
Stewing Beef	per kg	29.17	15.99	1.82
Whole Chicken	per kg	10.36	7.42	1.40
Sliced Bacon	500g	12.13	6.75	1.80

Source: Nunavut Bureau of Statistics (2016).

in May 2016, NNC began seeking input from communities and stakeholders to improve transparency, cost-effectiveness, and cultural appropriateness within the program (Government of Canada, 2016).

Bottom-up approaches: knowledge transfer, hunting equipment, community freezers, greenhouses, and herding

Of the previously identified themes for addressing food security – country food, store-bought food, local food production, life skills, programs and community initiatives, and policy and legislation (Nunavut Food Security Coalition, 2014) – only store-bought foods have been dealt with at the national level. Bottom-up approaches to address improving food security through other themes have been initiated in different capacities across the Arctic, and should be expanded to be included under federally derived funding, which currently favors a top-down approach. In addition, these approaches need to engage community members throughout the decision-making process, including the design of the program, implementation, monitoring, and review (Huet, Rosol & Egeland, 2012). We offer five examples of bottom-up approaches to increasing food security that would benefit communities across the Arctic: increase access for harvesting equipment and supplies (equipment), improve food storage options for high quality country foods (storage), reindeer herding to provide alternative food sources (herding), community Arctic greenhouses (greenhouse), and fostering knowledge sharing (knowledge). Figure 2.2 identifies how each of these five proposed solutions fit into the three components of food security: food access, food availability, and food quality (Gregory, Ingram & Brklacich, 2005; Ford, 2009).

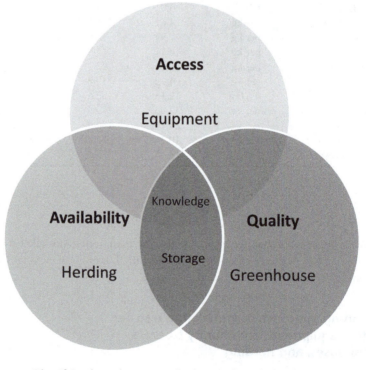

FIGURE 2.2 Identifying how the proposed solutions fit with the three components of food security: food access, food availability, and food quality

Source: Adapted from Gregory, Ingram & Brklacich, 2005; Ford, 2009.

Increase access for harvesting equipment and supplies

The financial cost of hunting equipment and supplies is a barrier to hunting for many Inuit (Ford, Smit & Wandel, 2006; Aarluk Consulting Incorporated, 2008; Hoover et al., 2013). Accessing the gear necessary to participate in harvesting activities requires a large financial investment, which can lead to country foods being more expensive to acquire than store-bought foods (Hoover et al., 2013). This cost discrepancy is made worse by the fact that store-bought foods receive federal subsidies (NNC) divided among national taxpayers, while country foods' costs fall only on the individual hunter, or on the immediate family. Willingness to pay for country foods is due to the cultural importance of hunting activities and consuming country foods (Condon, Collings & Wendel, 1995; Freeman, 2005). Even when hunters have access to equipment, repair costs and high prices of fuel (gas, oil, and naphtha or white gas) often prevent hunting trips (Hoover et al., 2013). Programs such as the Nunavut Harvester Support Program (Nunavut) and the Community Harvester Assistance Program (Inuvialuit Settlement Region or ISR, Northwest Territories) operate at territorial scales and provide some applicants with financial support to purchase large equipment (snowmobiles, boats, ATVs, motors) and small equipment (GPS, fishnets, sleeping bags, sewing machines, etc.) (Aarluk Consulting Incorporated, 2008; GNWT, 2014). However, even with these programs available, not all community members qualify for them, and navigation through the current programs can be difficult, resulting in less participation in harvesting (George, 2006).

Increasing funding support to hunter assistance programs is an important factor in reducing the high costs to individual hunters to allow participation in subsistence harvesting. Currently, funding resources determine the number of hunters supported, with some being denied funding. In addition, a lack of knowledge regarding programs combined with the difficulty of navigating the system prevents qualified hunters from applying (Aarluk Consulting Incorporated, 2008; Pearce et al., 2015b). Improving and expanding the existing programs by increasing awareness of the programs, increasing awareness of the program application process, and simplifying the application process – combined with increasing funding available – will help to reduce barriers to program participation and increase access for more hunters (Aarluk Consulting Incorporated, 2008; Pearce et al., 2015b).

Improve food storage options for high-quality country foods

Most harvesting activities take place in the spring and summer, with country foods being stored to last throughout the year when harvesting activities decrease. During the cold winter months, food may be stored outside or on the porch, so individual household freezers may be unplugged to save on high electricity costs. However, in warmer months, limitations on freezer space can lead to food wastage or the need to give food away to other families to make room for newly harvested foods. Community freezers may be more culturally appropriate than family freezers (which were widely distributed in the Inuvialuit Settlement Region when territorial funding was cut to community freezer programs) due to their role in facilitating food sharing and promoting country food consumption (Council of Canadian Academies, 2014). Whereas household freezers require family members and friends to ask for country food when they are in need, community freezers allow users to access country food without embarrassment. This serves to strengthen and perpetuate a cultural ethic of sharing (Searles, 2002).

As seasons are becoming warmer and temperatures fluctuate more, the length of time that freezer storage is required is becoming longer, leading to increased household energy costs and a limited ability to stock country foods for the less-active winter months. This may be remedied by various food-preparation techniques, such as drying, smoking, or fermenting meats, but cultural preferences also emphasize access to fresh (including raw) meats throughout the year.

> Yeah. Freezer space. Icehouse, walk-in freezer, it's a big issue. It was so nice to be able to get seals in the summer, freeze them whole in the walk-in freezer, in the icehouse without skinning them and then pick them up around Christmas during your family suppers and stuff and bring them in and skin it and it's not freezer burnt, it's like new because you froze it whole. It's so nice to be able to do that for the winter months.
>
> *(Emily Kudlak, Ulukhaktok, Northwest Territories,*
> *as quoted in Parker, 2016, p. 47)*

Community freezers have been built in a number of communities, as an alternative to household freezers and preservation, due in part to the melting of traditional icehouses (along with the permafrost they are encased in) (Organ et al., 2014). Community freezer programs exist in select communities across the Arctic, allowing harvesters to supply country foods to the freezer for access by the greater community. These programs depend on a variety of factors, including cost of operation, management structure, availability of country food, willing participants (hunters), and compensation for participants (i.e., equipment, money) (Organ et al., 2014; Council of Canadian Academies, 2014). Even though decision makers have identified freezers as a priority, the costs of powering a community freezer are a deterrent for many communities. Pilot projects for solar power community freezers are being used in Sanikiluaq, Nunavut. The freezer, designed by CanmetENERGY (Van Dusen, 2016), harnesses solar power during the summer when harvesting activities are high and the temperatures require country food preservation, until winter temperatures allow outdoor storage. The freezer unit, designed for local conditions, aims to be a model for other Arctic communities to help reduce power costs. Although community freezers are increasing across communities, they are not universal and require greater support for awareness and management (Organ et al., 2014). This culturally appropriate mechanism for food storage improves the quality of harvested foods and facilitates food sharing.

Reindeer herding to provide alternative food sources

In response to current and future changes in food availability, adaptations and knowledge transfer from other cultures can be useful in contributing to food security. Reindeer (the same species as caribou, but more easily domesticated) herding is an important subsistence food source to Sami (Indigenous people of Arctic Norway) (Riseth, 2003). In 1935, the federal government introduced roughly 3,000 reindeer into the Inuvialuit Settlement Region (ISR) to establish reindeer herding, in response to a decline in caribou numbers and harvesting (Scotter, 1972). Inuvialuit were taught to manage the reindeer herds, learning techniques from the Sami culture. Since that time, a tradition of herding has taken root within several families in the ISR, and indeed across the Canadian Arctic, with herds established in all four Inuit regions (Inuvialuit, Nunatsiavut, Nunavut, and Nunavik) until the 1970s. The ISR herd, now Inuvialuit owned, is the only one that remains and is available as a source of meat for residents of the region. The meat provides an alternative to caribou, but is viewed differently by some residents in terms of origin and taste. Reindeer meat can be purchased from the owner of the herd, either by private buyers or Inuvialuit organizations, for events and household distribution programs (Stern & Gaden, 2015). Although reindeer is not as highly valued as caribou (a country food), once purchased, reindeer is shared in the same manner as caribou or other harvested foods – as opposed to store-bought foods, which are not shared as widely (see Collings, Wenzel & Condon, 1998). This example is the closest alternative for providing a local source of protein to the communities that is shared in a manner similar to traditional country foods. While other ventures into farming and herding may be less culturally appropriate, the success of the ISR reindeer herd highlights opportunities for new potential ventures in the future, whereby Indigenous people in the Arctic can learn and adapt methods from other cultures.

Community Arctic greenhouses

Programs across the Arctic such as community greenhouses have strived to promote local food production (Northwest Territories Industry, Tourism and Investment, 2010). Large community greenhouses operate in Inuvik (NT), Iqalit (NU), and Kuujjuaq (NU), in addition to numerous others (30 established in the NWT alone) (Northwest Territories Industry, Tourism and Investment, 2010; Ramsay, 2015). These greenhouse initiatives allow communities to grow their own produce in areas where fresh fruits and vegetable are limited, of poor quality, and may not be traditionally grown due to climate limitations. As fresh produce has not historically been an important contribution to the Inuit diet, initiatives to teach and engage in agricultural techniques rely heavily on local leaders or champions within the community to engage community members, teach farming techniques, and maintain greenhouse activities (Skinner et al., 2013). Food production ranges from individual plots for members, to shared collective food production. While this solution improves food security and sovereignty, it does not share the same historical roots as the other solutions.

In productive greenhouses such as Inuvik, shared plots are used to grow extra food that is sold through community-supported agriculture (CSA) weekly produce boxes, or at the weekly local Arctic market (e.g., farmers market) (Ladik, 2016). A community garden in Whati, NT (a community of roughly 500), yielded over 1,000 pounds of potatoes in the summer of 2015 and was shared with over 50 families and individuals (Ramsay, 2015). The technology exists to grow food during the winter, and it is being done in Whitehorse (Yukon College) and in the community of Kuujjuaq (Nunavut), with more impressive operations at the Arthur Clarke Mars Greenhouse on Devon Island (Nunavut) led by the Canadian Space Agency. These initiatives highlight the ability of fresh foods to be grown year-round in extreme conditions, albeit with considerable costs. While community greenhouse programs are still being developed across the Arctic, their success very much depends on the support within each community. Fresh produce is still not fully integrated into the traditional Inuit diet, which is centered around hunted species. Inuit have proven to be highly adaptable in the face of changing environmental conditions (Ford, Smit & Wandel, 2006; Pearce et al., 2015b); however, changing one's diet to include more produce may not be easily accepted.

Fostering knowledge sharing

Historically, traditional knowledge and skills related to subsistence were passed down from one generation to the next through a process of cultural transmission, generally involving hands-on training and practice (Pearce et al., 2011). Given that subsistence involves the transmission of social norms and cultural values (Marks, 1997; Natcher, 2009), the destruction of Aboriginal culture associated with the residential school system has led to younger generations not learning the knowledge and skills important for safe and successful hunting (Aarluk Consulting Incorporated, 2008; Pearce et al., 2011). Knowledge sharing within and among Arctic communities provides an important opportunity for spreading knowledge about harvesting and food preparation, especially in cases where new species become available due to changes in migration or abundance. Subsistence skills such as navigation, hunting, and meat preparation are important factors in determining one's ability to participate in hunting, and subsequently in their ability to contribute to country food production (Pearce et al., 2015a). Hunting plays an important economic role domestically, but also allows for the continuation of traditional practices and supports the re-establishment of ties with the land (Condon, Collings & Wenzel, 1995). Hunting and food preparation programs need to receive consistent and widespread support in Inuit communities to foster inter-generational and inter-community knowledge transmission regarding the harvest and preparation of local foods.

To support younger generations, existing on-the-land programs have been developed to support the knowledge sharing within communities, to ensure this knowledge is passed down to the younger generation to support subsistence harvesting activities (Pearce et al., 2011). Programs in the Northwest Territories such as "Take your kid trapping and harvesting", community hunts, and other harvesting programs teach youth skills and knowledge about trapping, fishing, hunting, outdoor survival, boating skills, gun skills, on the land skills and preparation of food and animal skins (GNWT, 2014; Pearce et al., 2011). However, even with available programs, not all children and youth in the area have access to the same level of skill development and training. Furthermore, adequate training in the preparation of country foods is necessary to ensure foods are safe for consumption (Pearce et al., 2011). Therefore, on-the-land programs should also be linked to classroom programs that teach the hands-on skills necessary for country food harvesting and preparation. Examples of such programs include the nutrition education classes occurring in smaller Nunavut communities (led by the Nunavut Food Security Coalition) and pilot programs in the Inuvialuit Settlement Region (ISR), Northwest Territories (NT), that bring elders and hunters into the classroom.

Supporting the exchange of knowledge between communities is increasingly important, as species' distributions shift with the changing climate, to allow communities to adapt to changing resources. Inter-community hunter exchanges and community meetings are important methods for teaching hunting techniques and meat preparation to less experienced hunters. For example, changes in beluga migrations led to an increase in access for certain communities (Paulatuk, NT, 1980s; Kukgluktuk, NU, 2000s; Ulukhaktok, NT, 2014). Inter-community exchanges allowed traditional knowledge to be shared from more experienced beluga-hunting communities, where historically this traditional knowledge did not exist. Currently, costs and logistics are generally shared between federal, territorial, and local governments, depending on the program. However, universal programs and funds have not been established to support the transmission of knowledge within and between communities, contributing to what may be a mounting challenge for continued hunting in the face of climate change.

Technology is a useful tool to facilitate knowledge sharing, as resources are not always available in every community, and travel is expensive. Non-traditional avenues such as Internet technology and social media support the transmission of knowledge and already play a role in the Arctic. The Internet assists with the seamless transfer of data and knowledge, and has the ability to reach a large number of people (Eisner et al., 2012). Participatory web platforms, such as blogs, Facebook, Instagram, and WebGIS, can stimulate, structure, and enrich knowledge sharing (van Klaveren, 2015). Online databases, contributed to by local communities, benefit knowledge transfer by archiving environmental and food security knowledge. For example, researchers developed a web-based platform (Iñupiaq Web WebGIS) to display and store observations, and environmental knowledge, concerning landscape changes and processes of the Iñupiat communities indigenous to Arctic Alaska (Eisner et al., 2012). Other electronic platforms, such as the Inuit *siku* (sea ice) Atlas, was developed in part to respond to Inuit elders' and hunters' expressions of interest to share their knowledge with youth. Many components of the Atlas were incorporated into the school curriculum for Nunavut Schools through a partnership with the Government of Nunavut and the Department of Education.

Social media is used to communicate about harvesting activities and observations (e.g., the Facebook group NT Hunting stories of the day) and may play a role in supporting inter-community knowledge transmission. Further, public platforms can function as a meeting place where recipes, news items, thoughts, and facts and fiction related to Arctic food can be collected, mapped, shared (video messages, drawings, etc.), and discussed (van Klaveren, 2015). Greater accessibility and diversity of online programs, and further infrastructure development, are key to further strengthening online knowledge sharing in order to re-instill the skills and knowledge necessary to participate in harvesting activities. Additionally, successful mechanisms for returning knowledge back to the local community for future use as an educational and resource management tool will be needed.

Conclusions

Inuit are highly adaptable and continue to thrive in a challenging environment that is undergoing rapid change. In particular, the Inuit food system is sensitive to changing environmental conditions due to the reliance of many Inuit on subsistence hunting, fishing, and trapping, with many Inuit considered food insecure. The current top-down approach to improve food security lacks cultural relevance. We argue the need for a transition away from a singular top-down approach focused only on food security to multiple bottom-up approaches that not only improve food security, but also contribute to food sovereignty. Such a transition would support subsistence hunting, fishing, and trapping, which continue to play a vital role in providing culturally relevant solutions to improve food security. However, techniques borrowed from other cultures (herding, agriculture) have shown promise in the Arctic and provide alternatives to traditional methods. We suggest a re-evaluation of current top-down subsidies in favor of local-supported opportunities to empower communities with the ability to shape their own diets and control their own resources.

RECIPE: CARIBOU STEW

Caribou has been an important resource for many Canadian Inuit, with seasonal human movements tied to caribou migrations. This relationship is so innate that many Inuit identify as "caribou people", not just consuming the food, but also using hides for clothing and crafts. We chose this recipe, as it is still consumed often; and if there is no access to caribou, other meats can be substituted. For example, in the reindeer herding section of this chapter, we highlight how Arctic communities have learned different resource techniques from one another to contribute to food security by herding reindeer to supplement wild caribou resources. Reindeer can easily be used as a substitute in this recipe, but feel free to try beef, deer, or other meats.

Caribou stew ingredients

1 tbsp oil
1 lb stewing (cubed) caribou or reindeer
1/2 tsp garlic powder
1/2 tsp seasoning salt or 1 tsp steak spice
1 small (or 1/2 large) yellow onion (chopped)
4 cups water
1/2 small turnip (chopped)
2 medium russet potatoes (peeled, chopped)
1 large carrot (peeled, chopped)
5 mushrooms (stemmed, chopped)
1 tsp Italian spice
1 tsp seasoning salt
2 tsp paprika

Roux ingredients

2/3 cup water
4 tbsp flour

Stew cooking directions

1   In a large pot, heat oil and add meat to brown the edges.
2   Season meat with garlic powder and seasoning salt (1/2 tsp) or steak spice, and continue to brown (about 10 minutes).
3   Add onions and cook another 5 minutes.
4   Add 4 cups of water and bring mixture to a boil.
5   Add veggies: potatoes, turnips, carrots, mushrooms, and bring to a boil.
6   Add Italian spice, seasoning salt (remaining 1 tsp), and paprika.
7   Cover and let simmer for 1 hour.
8   Add roux (directions below) and cook stew another 5–10 minutes.
9   Serve with bannock (many recipes available online) or other bread of choice.

To make roux

1   Slowly add flour to water.
2   Mix until all flour is completely dissolved.
3   Add mixture to stew.

Recipe by Marjorie Hansen (Inuvik, Northwest Territories, Canada)

Research questions

1 What is the difference between food security and food sovereignty? Can you have food security without food sovereignty?
2 Which of these solutions will be the most important with climate change?
3 Is it appropriate to prioritize funding for programs that reflect the diets of people living in large cities outside of the Arctic in favor of country foods? Why or why not?
4 Country food markets have been established as an informal market whereby hunters can sell local foods to improve food security and share country foods. While these have been successful in other Arctic countries such as Greenland, it still remains a long-term goal for Canada, with some initiatives in place (Project Nunavut, 2013). But regulatory issues surrounding the commercialization of country foods remain a hurdle to implementing country food markets (Ford et al., 2010). Do you see this as a sound option to increase food security? Where in Figure 2.2 would this option fit best?

Acknowledgements

The authors would like to acknowledge ArcticNet for project funding (1.8 Knowledge Co-Production). In addition, we thank these additional funding sources and project partners: Fisheries and Oceans Canada, Natural Sciences and Engineering Research Council of Canada, W. Garfield Weston Foundation, Fisheries Joint Management Committee, Arctic Science Partnership, Northern Scientific Training Program, Environmental Studies Research Funds, Health Canada, Canadian Institute for Health Research (CIHR), and the Social Sciences and Humanities Research Council of Canada (OceanCanada Partnership). Thank you to our research partners from the communities of Tuktoyaktuk, Inuvik, Paulatuk, and Ulukhaktok (specifically Emily Kudlak, Adam Kudlak, Phylicia Kagyut, Susie Malgokak, Harold Wright, and Winnie Akhiatak), who are the source of many of the insights shared in this chapter. Finally, we would like to thank Kate Snow, John Iacozza, the reviewers, and the editors for their comments and suggestions.

References

Aarluk Consulting Incorporated. (2008) *A Consultation-Based Review of the Harvester Support Programs of the Government of Nunavut and Nunavut Tunngavik Inc.* Iqualit, Nunavut, Government of Nunavut and Nunavut Tunngavik Incorporated.
Boult, D. (2004) *Hunger in the Arctic: Food (In)security in Inuit Communities.* Ottawa, Ontario, Ajunnginiq Centre – National Aboriginal Health Organization.
Collings, P., Wenzel, G. & Condon, R. G. (1998) Modern food sharing networks and community integration in the central Canadian arctic. *Arctic.* 51 (4), 301–314.
Condon, R. G., Collings, P. & Wenzel, G. (1995) The best part of life: Subsistence hunting, ethnicity, and economic adaptation among young adult Inuit males. *Arctic.* 48 (1), 31–46.
Council of Canadian Academies. (2014) *Aboriginal food security in Northern Canada: An assessment on the state of knowledge.* Expert Panel on the State of Knowledge of Food Security in Northern Canada.

Declaration of Atitlán, Guatemala. (2002) *Indigenous peoples' global consultation on the right to food: A global consultation.* Available from: http://cdn5.iitc.org/wp-content/uploads/2013/07/FINAL_Atitlan-Declaration-Food-Security_Apr25_ENGL.pdf [Accessed: 23rd July 2016].

Eisner, W., Jelacic, J., Cuomo, C., Kim, C. & Hinkel, K. (2012) Producing an indigenous knowledge web GIS for Arctic Alaska communities: Challenges, successes, and lessons learned. *Transactions in GIS.* 16 (1), 17–37.

FAO. (2002) *The State of Food Insecurity in the World 2001.* Rome, Italy, Food and Agriculture Organization of the United Nations.

Ford, J. (2009) Vulnerability of Inuit food systems to food insecurity as a consequence of climate change: A case study from Igloolik, Nunavut. *Regional Environmental Change.* 9 (2), 83–100.

Ford, J., Pearce, T., Duerden, F., Furgal, C. & Smit, B. (2010) Climate change policy responses for Canada's Inuit population: The importance of and opportunities for adaptation. *Global Environmental Change.* 20 (1), 177–191.

Ford, J., Smit, B. & Wandel, J. (2006) Vulnerability to climate change in the arctic: A case study from Arctic Bay, Canada. *Global Environmental Change.* 16 (2), 145–160.

Freeman, M. (2005) "Just one more time before I die": Securing the relationship between Inuit and whales in the Arctic regions. *Senri Ethnological Studies.* 67, 59–76.

Friesen, T. M. (2002) Analogues at Iqaluktuuq: The social context of archaeological inference in Nunavut, Arctic Canada. *World Archaeology.* 34 (2), 330–345.

Galloway, T. (2014) Is the Nutrition North Canada retail subsidy program meeting the goal of making nutritious and perishable food more accessible and affordable in the North? *Canadian Journal of Public Health.* 105 (5), e395–e397.

George, J. (2006) Hunters need one-stop hunting shop. *Nunatsiaq News,* 31st March. Available from: www.nunatsiaqonline.ca/archives/60331/news/nunavut/60331_09.html [Accessed: 20th June 2016].

Geraci, J. R. & Smith, T. G. (1979) Vitamin C in the diet of Inuit hunters from Holman, Northwest Territories. *Arctic.* 32 (2), 135–139.

GNWT (Government of the Northwest Territories). (2014) *Guide to Government of the Northwest Territories Grants and Contributions Programs.* Yellowknife, NT, Government of the Northwest Territories.

Government of Canada. (2015) *Canadian climate normals 1981–2010 station data.* Available from: http://climate.weather.gc.ca/climate_normals/results_1981_2010_e.html?stnID=1789&lang=e&province=NT&provSubmit=go&dCode=0 [Accessed: 21st June 2016].

Government of Canada. (2016) *Nutrition North Canada engagement 2016.* Available from: www.nutritionnorthcanada.gc.ca/eng/1464190223830/1464190397132 [Accessed: 24th July 2016].

Gregory, P., Ingram, J. & Brklacich, M. (2005) Climate change and food security. *Philosophical Transactions of the Royal Society B: Biological Sciences.* 360, 2139–2148.

Hidiroglou, N., Peace, R., Jee, P., Leggee, D. & Kuhnlein, H. (2008) Levels of folate, pyridoxine, niacin and riboflavin in traditional foods of Canadian Arctic indigenous peoples. *Journal of Food Composition and Analysis.* 21 (6), 474–480.

Hoover, C., Bailey, M., Higdon, J., Ferguson, S. H. & Sumaila, R. (2013) Estimating the economic value of Narwhal and Beluga hunts in Hudson Bay, Nunavut. *Arctic.* 66 (1), 1–16.

Huet, C., Rosol, R. & Egeland, G. M. (2012) The prevalence of food insecurity is high and the diet quality poor in Inuit communities. *Journal of Nutrition.* 142 (3), 541–547.

Inuit Tapiriit Kanatami & the Inuit Circumpolar Council, Canada. (2014) *Inuit and the Right to Food: Submission to the United Nations Special Rapporteur on the Right to Food for the Official Country Mission to Canada.* Canada, Inuit Tapiriit Kanatami & the Inuit Circumpolar Council.

Kelly, R. (1983) Hunter-gatherer mobility strategies. *Journal of Anthropological Research*. 39 (3), 277–306.

Kinlock, D., Kuhnlein, H. & Muir, D. C. G. (1992) Inuit foods and diet: A preliminary assessment of benefits and risks. *The Science of the Total Environment*. 122 (1–2), 247–278.

Ladik, S. (2016) First vegetable bundles delivered. *Northern News Service*. Available from: www.nnsl.com/frames/newspapers/2016-07/jul14_16csaH.html [Accessed: 14th July 2016].

Marks, S. (1997) Hunting behavior and strategies of the Valley Bisa in Zambia. *Human Ecology*. 5 (1), 1–36.

Meakin, S. & Kurvits, T. (2009) *Assessing the impacts of climate change on food security in the Canadian Arctic*. Prepared by GRID-Arendal for Indian and Northern Affairs Canada.

Natcher, D. C. (2009) Subsistence and the social economy of Canada's aboriginal North. *The Northern Review*. 30, 83–98.

National Research Council Canada. (2015) *Sunrise/sunset calculator*. Available from: www.nrc-cnrc.gc.ca/eng/services/sunrise/index.html [Accessed: 23rd July 2016].

Northwest Territories Industry Tourism and Investment. (2010) *Growing forward: Small scale foods program community garden initiative*. Northwest Territories Industry Tourism and Investment. 2009/2010 Annual Report.

Nunavut Bureau of Statistics [online]. (2016) *2015 Nunavut Food Price Survey*. Available from: http://www.stats.gov.nu.ca/ en/Economic prices.aspx.

Nunavut Food Security Coalition. (2014) *Nunavut Food Security Strategy and Action Plan 2014–16*. Nunavut, Nunavut Food Security Coalition.

Nutrition North. (2016) *How nutrition North Canada works*. Available from: www.nutrition northcanada.gc.ca/eng/1415548276694/1415548329309 [Accessed: 23rd June 2016].

Nutrition North Canada. (2013) *Subsidized foods*. Minister of Aboriginal Affairs and Northern Development. Available at: www.nutritionnorthcanada.gc.ca/DAM/DAM-NUTRIN-NUTRIN/STAGING/texte-text/efn_2012_10_1369225959188_eng.pdf [Accessed: 23rd June 2016].

Office of the Auditor General of Canada. (2014) *Report of the auditor general of Canada*. Chapter Aboriginal Affairs and Northern Development Canada.

Organ, J., Castleden, H., Furgal, C., Sheldon, T. & Hart, C. (2014) Contemporary programs in support of traditional ways: Inuit perspectives on community freezers as a mechanism to alleviate pressures of wild food access in Nain, Nunatsiavut. *Health & Place*. 30, 251–259.

Parker, C. (2016) *Assessing Inuit food security in light of climate change and examining adaptation options: A case study of Ulukhaktok, NT*. MSc thesis, University of Guelph.

Partridge, C. (2010) Residential schools: The intergenerational impacts on Aboriginal peoples. *Native Social Work Journal*. 7, 33–62.

Pearce, T., Ford, J., Cunsolo Willox, A. & Smit, B. (2015a) Inuit Traditional Ecological Knowledge (TEK) subsistence hunting and adaptation to climate change in the Canadian Arctic. *Arctic*. 68 (2), 233–245.

Pearce, T., Ford, J., Duerden, F., Furgal, C., Dawson, J. & Smit, B. (2015b) Factors of adaptation – climate change policy responses for Canada's Inuit population. In: Stern, G. & Gaden, A. (eds.) *From Science to Policy in the Western and Central Canadian Arctic: An Integrated Regional Impact Study (IRIS) of Climate Change and Modernization*. Québec City, Québec, ArcticNet, pp. 403–427.

Pearce, T., Smit, B., Duerden, F., Ford, J. D., Goose, A. & Kataoyak, F. (2010) Inuit vulnerability and adaptive capacity to climate change in Ulukhaktok, Northwest territories, Canada. *Polar Record*. 46 (237), 157–177.

Pearce, T., Wright, H., Notaina, N., Kudlak, A., Smit, B., Ford, J. & Furgal, C. (2011) Transmission of environmental knowledge and land skills among Inuit men in Ulukhaktok, Northwest territories, Canada. *Human Ecology*. 39, 271–288.

Project Nunavut (2013). *Country food market*. Available from: www.projectnunavut.com/countryfoodmarket.html [Accessed 12th September 2016].

Ramsay, D. (2015) *Success of the small scale foods program in all regions*. Government of the Northwest Territories. Minister's Statement 248-17(5).

Riseth, J. A. (2003) Sami Reindeer management in Norway: Modernization challenges and conflicting strategies-reflections upon the co-management alternative. In: Jentoft, S., Minde, H, & Nilsen, R. (eds.) *Indigenous Peoples: Resource Management and Global Rights*. Delft, The Netherlands, Eburon Academic Publishers, pp. 229–248.

Sanchez, P. A. (2009) A smarter way to combat hunger. *Nature*. 458, 148.

Scotter, G. W. (1972) Reindeer ranching in northern Canada. *Journal of Range Management*. 25 (3), 167–174. doi: 10.1038/129609b0.

Searles, E. (2002) Food and the making of modern Inuit identities. *Food & Foodways*. 10 (1–2), 55–78.

Skinner, K., Hanning, R. M., Desjardins, E. & Tsuji, L. J. (2013) Giving voice to food insecurity in a remote indigenous community in subarctic Ontario, Canada: Traditional ways, ways to cope, ways forward. *BMC Public Health*. 13 (1), 427.

Socha, T., Zahaf, M., Chambers, L., Abraham, R. & Fiddler, T. (2012) Food security in a Northern first nations community: An exploratory study on food availability and accessibility. *Journal of Aboriginal Health*. 8 (2), 5–14.

Stern, G. & Gaden, A. (2015) From science to policy in the Western and Central Canadian Arctic: An Integrated Regional Impact Study (IRIS) of climate change and modernization. *ArcticNet*.

The Truth and Reconciliation Commission of Canada (2015). *Honouring the truth, reconciling for the future: Summary of the final report of the truth and reconciliation commission of Canada*. Available from: www.trc.ca/websites/trcinstitution/File/2015/Honouring_the_Truth_Reconciling_for_the_Future_July_23_2015.pdf [Accessed: 23rd June 2016].

Van Dusen, J. (2016) High-tech, made-for-Nunavut community freezer on its way to Sanikiluaq. *CBC News North*. Available from: www.cbc.ca/news/canada/north/sanikiluaq-nunavut-solar-powered-community-freezer-1.3665998 [Accessed: 6th July 2016].

Van Klaveren, R. (2015) Food Related: An Artistic approach towards knowledge sharing. *Ethnoscripts*. 17 (1), 138–158.

Wallace, S. (2014) *Inuit health: Selected findings from the 2012 aboriginal peoples survey*. Statistics Canada. Catalogue No 89-653-No.003, 1–26.

3

REBUILDING CONSUMERS' TRUST IN FOOD

Community-supported agriculture in China

Zhenzhong Si

Introduction

> I don't trust any of the food I eat, but I just eat it and hope for the best. I worry
> for my children, but it's what there is here in this country [China] (Mr. Feng,
> July 6, 2014).
>
> (in Regnier-Davies, 2015, p. 38)

People might be surprised by the desperation expressed by a Chinese shopper at a local food market in downtown Nanjing, China. It is ironic that in a country where food is ample, its citizens are so deeply frustrated by food safety risks. The story of Chinese food safety crisis largely began after a series of food safety scandals broke out in the millennium. In my explorations of China's changing food system, I often came across anxious consumers eagerly searching for safe food. Their concerns echoed those of Mr. Feng, quoted above. Pollution of air, soil and water; chemical residues; illegal additives in processed food; food adulteration and other similar stories have been staple news in Chinese media and daily conversations (FORHEAD, 2014; Xue & Zhang, 2013). Researchers have argued that rampant food safety problems have become a crisis that has contributed to the deterioration of general social trust in China (Yan, 2012) and to political tensions (Yang, 2013). Some have claimed that China has entered an "era when people are poisoning each other" (Hu, 2010, p. 1). In the meantime, the Chinese authority has been enforcing strict food safety laws and regulations and promoting standardization of the food industry (Jia & Jukes, 2013; Scott et al., 2014). For many ordinary citizens, trustworthy food sources have become a top pursuit, yet a pursuit that seems unattainable amidst the mixed sources of information. Consumers are gradually losing their trust in food producers and many other actors involved in the food supply chain. Lack of trust has become a major problem that hinders people's food security and safety in China.

The first facet of the story of the Chinese food safety crisis is associated with the various broad transformations of China's food system. Anxiety around food safety is one of the many representations of these transformations (Garnett & Wilkes, 2014). More than three decades after economic liberalization, China has not only accomplished remarkable economic growth but also witnessed significant changes in its food system. These changes, intimately felt by people in their daily lives, are mainly exemplified by the heavy pollution generated from the agricultural sector (Ongley, Xiaolan & Tao, 2010; Ellis & Turner, 2007), the food safety crisis (Yan, 2012), delocalization and elongation of food supply chains (Zhang & Pan, 2013), marginalization of smallholder farmers (Huang, Wang & Qiu, 2012; Schneider, 2015; Su et al., 2015), deterioration of food literacy among ordinary citizens, and a growing amount of food waste (Zhou, 2013; Leung, 2015, Si & Scott, 2016). These multifaceted changes are intertwined with and reinforce each other, while accompanied by broader socioeconomic trends of urbanization, marketization and industrialization.

Another facet of the story relates to the declining countryside amidst the remarkable urbanization process in the past few decades. China has become an urban nation, with an increase of the urbanization rate (the percent of permanent urban residents) from 20.43% in 1982 to 56.1% in 2015 (National Bureau of Statistics, 2016a). Meanwhile, smallholders in the countryside have undergone a dramatic decrease, as more than 2.7 million farmers have been driven by the high salaries of non-farming jobs and have become migrant workers in cities (National Bureau of Statistics, 2016b). The rural space in general faces a crisis of a collapsing economic base, environment, social relationships and culture viability (Pan & Du, 2011, Yan & Chen, 2013; FORHEAD, 2014).

Amongst these many socioeconomic changes that have created the trust problem in China's food system, a paradox emerges that deserves particular attention. On the one hand, against the backdrop of a rising middle class in Chinese society (Shi et al., 2011a, 2011b), anxious consumers spare no effort at securing access to safe food and pursuing trustworthy food of premium quality, largely for health concerns (Wang et al., 2015). On the other hand, many farmers, driven by the revenues from a higher yield, are overusing chemicals in commodity food production, while saving a plot to produce food with restricted or no chemical usage for self-consumption (Zhou & Fang, 2015). The knowledge and skills of sustainable agriculture, which characterizes China's thousand years' old traditional farming practices (King, 1911), are gradually being lost amongst its increasingly market-oriented and vertically integrated farmers. This contradictory situation reflects a breach of the market logic: consumers' growing demand for quality food does not feed into producers' willingness to supply it. This conundrum is driven by long supply chains that disconnect producers from consumers and prevent quality food attributes (e.g. restricted usage of chemicals in production) from being recognized and rewarded (Shi et al., 2011a).

Case study: the emergence and development of community-supported agriculture in China

It was precisely this food safety crisis and the urgent need for trust in China's food system that facilitated the emergence of community-supported agriculture (CSA) farms in China. CSAs, often discussed as a major type of Alternative Food Networks (Si, Schumilas & Scott, 2015), refer to a food venue based on direct consumer-producer relationships with trust and risk sharing. A group of consumers purchase "shares" of a farm's production prior to the growing season and become shareholders of the farm. The farmer commits to ecological farming and provides the shareholders with trustworthy food throughout the growing season, usually on a weekly basis. Consumers and producers share both the risk of farming (e.g. crop failure) and the harvest as well as the benefits. CSAs, as short food-supply mechanisms, redistribute values to farmers, support local economy development, reconvene trust between consumers and farmers, and contribute to environmental protection. CSAs embrace ideas of community building and empowerment. With strong embedded social and environmental values, CSAs constitute a critical component of the local food movement in the West and offer a place-based solution to many problems in industrialized food systems (Schnell, 2007; Sage, 2012).

CSAs were introduced to China by non-governmental organizations around 2006 and started to receive wide public attention after 2008, when food safety problems heightened, alongside the outbreak of the melamine milk scandal (Pei et al., 2011). In China, CSAs are normally found in peri-urban areas of large cities where potential customers are located. It was estimated that by 2015, there were about 500 CSA farms across China (Sinovator, 2016), and the number has been growing rapidly. Since 2010, Chinese CSAs have witnessed the formation of a national CSA network via the national CSA symposium organized annually by scholars from China Renmin University.

Despite the proliferation of CSA farms, the concept of CSA is rather obscure in Chinese descriptions, as the boundary of the definition is always fluid and elusive. What CSA means is being constantly redefined and reinvented by researchers, entrepreneurs and the media. It is now interpreted as an inclusive umbrella that embodies the enhancement of rural-urban interactions, the socialization of agriculture (re-embedding agriculture in social relationships), and the shortening of food supply chains. The Chinese translation of CSA therefore varies in different circumstances. Social agriculture, mutually supportive agriculture, and short-chain agriculture are some of the common translations used to refer to CSA farms. Based on different initiators, researchers have categorized Chinese CSA farms into various groups, including CSAs initiated by individual citizens, governmental organizations, academic institutions, non-governmental organizations, restaurants and organic farms, farmers' cooperatives and others (Shi & Cheng, 2015).

Chinese CSAs differ from their Western counterparts in various respects. Unlike in the West, where CSAs emerged with strong social and environmental values, the emergence of CSAs in China is more of a pragmatic response to the increasing demand for trustworthy and quality food among its growing middle class (Schumilas, 2014;

Si, Schumilas & Scott, 2015). Founders of CSAs in China were mainly entrepreneurs from an urban and non-farming background who have an agrarian dream and are dedicated to sustainability and social justice goals. A few peasants also established CSA farms with external supports from academic institutions or non-governmental organizations. Land is often accessed through leasing from farmers, while some have acquired land through their rural relatives. In most cases, instead of running the farm by themselves, farmers are hired on CSA farms as farm labor. Therefore, some researchers argue that there is a strong "elite capture" in the operation of Chinese CSAs, and thus the social justice that is a critical component in many western CSAs is always downplayed (Si, Schumilas & Scott, 2015). This "subjugates peasants and privileges entrepreneurs" (Schumilas, 2014, p. 182), and ties CSAs into the changing view of peasants as a social group in contemporary China – in particular, the distrust of peasants and the devalorization of peasants' role in development (Day, 2013; Schneider, 2015).

To better understand how CSAs in China address the urgent problem of consumer trust in food, I examine CSAs as spaces of participation and learning as well as ecological modes of food production by illustrating two cases in Chengdu and Beijing in China. Firstly, the participation and learning features of CSAs offer a specific food experience to consumers that conventional food venues fail to deliver. They enable more intense information and emotional exchange through enhanced personal connections between producers and consumers, thus fostering consumer trust. Secondly, the sustainable food production approaches adopted by these CSAs address consumers' health concerns closely associated with chemical residues. Therefore, it makes food channeled through CSAs both "good to eat" and "good to think", and in turn, contributes to consumer trust.

Case 1: Gao's CSA in Anlong village, Chengdu, Sichuan

In 2005, Chengdu Urban Rivers Association (CURA), a local non-governmental organization that promotes environmental protection, education and rural sustainable development in Chengdu, Sichuan province, launched its circular rural livelihood project in Anlong village in Pixian county near Chengdu city. This project strived to construct a zero-waste circle in the village by integrating crop cultivation and animal raising, transitioning to ecological agriculture and transforming household waste to farm inputs. The Gao family was one of the first few families in the village that adopted ecological farming, as they found the principle of sustainable agriculture corresponded with their Buddhist beliefs.

In 2006, a Hong Kong-based foundation called Partners in Community Development (PCD) partnered with CURA and introduced the concept of CSA to Anlong village. CURA facilitated the original visits of consumer groups to the village, many of whom were vegetarian or parents of students at the local Waldorf School. The Gao family started to establish its customer base in this process after 2007. Their CSA has been operating as a part of a local CSA network formed by five CSA farms in the village.

By 2015, the family farm was about 23 mu (1.5 hectares), producing vegetables and rice for about 80 shareholders (Chen, 2015). It has been promoting local varieties of seeds and growing produce suitable for the seasons, all without synthetic pesticides, herbicides, fertilizer or hormones. Intercropping and crop rotation are used to control pests and maintain soil fertility. Fermented slurry in methane tanks, diluted urine and treated human waste are used as fertilizer. The Gao family believes this is beneficial for the environment, and the health of both shareholders and producers.

On Gao's CSA farm in Anlong village, trust is forged mainly through its critical spirit of participation and learning. The learning process is for both producers and shareholders. Ms. Li, the mother of Mr. Gao, expressed how she developed a strong environmental ethic and knowledge through participating in lectures organized by CURA. When interviewed, Ms. Li demonstrated a rich knowledge of soil health and the various implications of ecological agriculture. She applied ashes of burned straw and leaves to the field to raise the pH level of the soil, which also helped to control pests. As Ms. Li said:

> Anlong village is a school of environmental protection, the environmental protection ideas it shows and the ecological knowledge it delivers is more important than the economic model.
>
> *(Ms. Li, 26 April 2012, Chengdu)*

When explaining the motivations of doing ecological farming, Ms. Li explained:

> Three basic concepts are supporting my family to keep growing ecological vegetables: environmental protection, health, and harmony. Ecological farming helped us to become friends with consumers. Some of my customers told me that although we are different, we are working towards some common goals . . . direct communication helps to foster the harmonious relationship among people.
>
> *(Ms. Li, 26 April 2012, Chengdu)*

The Gao family makes visiting the farm compulsory for potential customers before they apply to become shareholders. This strategy enables their customers to better understand the environmental and social values of participating in a CSA. It helps to ensure that farmers and their customers forge a solid base of trust. In an interview, Mr. Gao, the son of Ms. Li, was very blunt:

> You must visit our farm before placing your order . . . if people don't come here, they might be frustrated when receiving our vegetables. They will be unsatisfied by the limited varieties and their imperfect appearance compared to those vegetables in the market . . . this won't create any trust between consumers and us. It will easily destroy our reputation . . . the biggest challenge for us is the issue of trust.
>
> *(Mr. Gao, Chengdu, as quoted in and translated from Huang, 2011)*

For some customers, participation in the CSA was not confined to visits or becoming shareholders. Like most CSAs in China, Gao's CSA saved a certain proportion of the land for renting to companies or urban residents for recreational gardening. In 2015, they had about 10 families gardening on these plots. Normally, these families tend their plots on the weekend. The so-called "urban farmer plan" not only created more opportunities for direct communication between farmers and their customers, but also deepened consumers' understanding of ecological farming. Customers have also been involved in price setting. Every price rise in the past eight years received consent from most of the shareholders. Customers also ask questions on the farm's blog. While this style of direct participation results in a heavy workload for the Gao family, the process communicates a strong ethic to their customers. As customers explained, "they care about the farmland", "they care about our food safety and health" (Chen, 2015, p. 107). This ethic reflects one of the four basic principles of organic agriculture defined by IFOAM (n.d.), namely, the principle of health, the principle of ecology, the principle of fairness and the principle of care.

The value of CSAs in Anlong village is far beyond the benefits of ecological agriculture itself. Perhaps the more far-reaching value of it lies in the people – peasants who possess strong ecological and social values. Firstly, as peasants are generally disdained in China as a short-sighted and selfish social group (Schneider, 2015), CSA farmers in Anlong village offer a strong rebuttal to the entrenched bias. CSAs liberated these farmers from the market relations in conventional food supply chains and enabled them to rebuild a new market embedded in social relations. Although this challenging process would not have been possible without the assistance of CURA and PCD, peasants played a leading role in managing the CSA under ecological principles. Secondly, their vision of the future resembles the value "small is beautiful", which represents a strong alternative to the increasingly integrated and scaled-up agriculture sector in China (Chen, 2015).

Case 2: Shared Harvest Farm in Beijing

CSAs only started to attract public attention in China after 2008 when Little Donkey Farm – the most well known CSA – was founded by a few researchers from Renmin University in Beijing. One of them, the poster child of Chinese CSAs nowadays, is Shi Yan, a young and perseverant postdoctoral researcher with a strong commitments to Alternative Food Networks. The story of Shared Harvest Farm was unveiled in 2012 shortly after Shi Yan left Little Donkey Farm. The name "Shared Harvest" came from Elizabeth Henderson and Robyn Van En's book *Sharing the Harvest: A Citizen's Guide to Community Supported Agriculture* (Henderson & En, 2007). It implies a spirit of sharing, although risk sharing, an intimidating core value of CSAs, is hidden beneath the name.

When explaining the reasons why she left Little Donkey Farm, Shi Yan told the media that she could not agree with the CSA model that it has been operating, in which the company leased the land from peasants and then hired them as farm workers. In this way, the roles of peasants were reduced to simply farm workers. Rather, she envisioned peasants playing a much bigger role in management, sharing of profit and decision-making. Yet, it is very difficult for peasants to build a customer base on their own. Therefore, on its first production base in Tongzhou district in Beijing, Shared Harvest adopted a "company plus peasants" model in which the company manages the operation of the CSA (e.g. marketing, customer communication) and the peasants are in charge of the production.

By August 2016, Shared Harvest had about 660 shareholders and three production bases. The first production base was established in 2012 in Tongzhou in cooperation with a local vegetable farmer. Besides 60 mu (4 hectares) of vegetable production, it also had about 100 mu (6.7 hectares) of woods for raising free-run chickens and pigs. The second one was established in 2013 in Shunyi district with less than 50 mu (3.3 hectares) of vegetable production plus 230 mu (15.3 hectares) of orchard. Interestingly, due to various challenges they have encountered in working directly with peasants, the second production base in Shunyi district adopted the model of Little Donkey Farm and now is their major production base. Shi Yan explained the struggle during our interview:

> The model for this location is the same as Little Donkey Farm. Tongzhou is different . . . at the beginning we wanted to work with one farmer and encourage other farmers to join but later we found in Beijing that model is not [working] . . . actually because Beijing farmer's average income is already good so they don't want to put in four times as much work just to double their income . . . that's also the reason that in the second year we moved here . . . but to work with that farmer . . . some new varieties we want to grow, but that land is his and he doesn't want to try new varieties and techniques. That's also part of the challenges. . . . We used to try to be the bridge between farmers and consumers, now we think we have to be the farmers ourselves.
> *(Shi Yan, 24 August 2016, Beijing)*

The third production base was a rice farm operated by a local rice farmer in Wuchang, Heilongjiang province, an area well known for high-quality rice. Besides the three production bases, Shared Harvest also sells produce from several other farms that have passed their strict scrutiny and chemical-residue tests. Shared Harvest produces almost 30 varieties of vegetables and around 10 types of fruit throughout the year. In addition to delivering weekly to its CSA shareholders, they also sell their produce to local ecological farmers' markets (e.g. Beijing Farmers' Market, Farmers to Neighbor), buying clubs, their online store and a few restaurants.

Like many other CSAs in China, one of the major challenges confronting Shared Harvest Farm is to build and maintain trust among its customers. This is achieved through a strict control of production approaches and the creation of a participatory learning environment on the farm. The ecological production approaches of

Shared Harvest demonstrate its strong commitment to agroecology and the quality of food. As specified in its production standards,

> no chemical synthetic pesticides, fertilizer or hormone shall be used in production. The production follows the natural law and ecological principles, coordinates the balance across diverse varieties of crops, and maintains the balance of the production system with sustainable farming techniques.
>
> *(Shared Harvest, 2013)*

To cultivate trust in the first step, and to further demonstrate the results of their strict production control, Shared Harvest delivered third-party reports of soil test and chemical-residue tests of their products to customers with their shares. Although many requirements in its production standard resemble the standards of organic agriculture, Shared Harvest, like most CSA farms in China, is not certified organic. This is because of not only the high cost of certification, but also the limited value of certification in maintaining consumer trust. Instead of relying on third-party assurance, the trust comes from personal communications between the farm and its customers.

Shared Harvest has also provided a venue for participatory learning among its producers, customers and interns. The peasant farmer who converted to ecological farming and joined the production of Shared Harvest, and the 10 local farmers hired as farm workers, learned about the environmental, health and social consequences of conventional agriculture and the benefits of sustainable agriculture from Shi Yan. This knowledge was also communicated to Shared Harvest's customers and interns in various ways. Besides a WeChat (a widely used mobile app for instant communication) group and blogs, the farm has also been publishing a newsletter for its customers. It broadcasts recent changes and documents the work being done on the farm. It also includes personal reflections of workers and interns on the farm. By 2015, more than 20 interns had learned about CSA operation, and two of them have now started their own farms. The farm carries the dream of an alternative career for its interns and becomes an incubator for "new farmers" (*xin nongfu*).

Another group of activities that enhance trust among its customers leads to knowledge generation and dissemination from the farm. "Children of the Earth" (*dadi zhi zi*), a major educational program launched by Shared Harvest in 2014 on its production base in Shunyi district, has been providing food education to children and primary- and secondary-school students. Lectures on rooftop gardening are also being designed. These learning opportunities offered by Shared Harvest not only enable children to engage closely with agriculture and nature, but also to raise their awareness of sustainability. For example, through participating in farm work, children learn natural rules of farming, where their food comes from, how it is produced and what types of food are healthy. They also learn special techniques, such as making strawberry jam and drying tomatoes. This is a valuable complement to the formal curriculum in schools for many participants. The knowledge mobilization through these educational programs greatly enhances consumer trust.

Discussion

China's food system has faced a severe challenge in recent years: the deteriorated trust in food safety among consumers. The emergence and development of the trust crisis reflects various transformations in its broad food system and socioeconomic changes. These two cases of CSAs in China exemplify how place-based ecological farming and the creation of an open environment for learning and participation forge a solid base of trust in food relationships. The CSA model in this process bypasses the long intermediaries that distance consumers from producers and food production, and reconvenes trust between consumers and producers. It bridges the market breach so that consumers and producers both benefit from it. The approaches to rebuild and maintain trust revealed in these two cases include strict control of ecological farming approaches, effective communication with customers about the principles and operation of the farm, sufficient opportunities for customers to visit the farm, and educational programs for children and customers. Thus, CSAs provide a viable solution to the common challenge of building and maintaining trust confronting many food systems in the world.

In fact, the CSA model is far more than an alternative approach to building and maintaining trust in food; it also allows farmers to make a decent living from small-scale ecological farming through reconstructing a socially embedded relation with their customers. In contrast to the invisible peasants in modern, consolidated food supply chains, peasants in CSAs are revalorized for their role in producing healthy food. Although peasants are not the sole initiators in the establishment of these CSAs, they are the core figures in building and maintaining the relationship, especially in the Anlong village case. CSAs also redefine the relationship between human and nature, in that nature is no longer a resource to exploit; rather, it is Mother Nature that needs to be taken care of through sustainable farming approaches. Hence, CSAs exemplify a valuable solution to many of the urgent problems facing China and many other countries in the world.

The multidimensional value of CSAs does not negate the various challenges they face in the Chinese context. As Shi and Cheng (2015) and Fu and Ye (2015) noted, Chinese CSAs face a managerial challenge of motivating their often well-educated employees; a shortage of well-trained potential employees for small-scale ecological farming; a difficulty of conducting ecological farming amid the industrialized agriculture context; a lack of understanding of customers; and an unstable land supply under the collective farmland ownership. While the rapid development of CSAs in China mainly addresses food safety concerns of the middle class, the vast majority of smallholders have been excluded in this process. Yet the two cases presented in this chapter illustrate how these challenges can be partly overcome without compromising the ecological and social values of CSAs. Through ecological production and short food-supply chains, it not only addresses sustainability problems of our food system, but also sheds light on more profound social problems, such as the declining social trust and the marginalization of peasants. The development of CSAs in China has been and will be a winding but promising journey.

RECIPE: SCRAMBLED EGGS WITH TOMATOES

Tomatoes and eggs are common produce from the CSAs featured in this chapter. Plus, this is one of the most commonly eaten and well-known dishes in China.

Ingredients

2 medium-size tomatoes, cut into large pieces
3 eggs
4 tbsp of peanut oil (other cooking oil also works)
1 tsp of salt
1 tsp of sugar
1 tsp of Thirteen Spices (optional)

Method

1 Crack three eggs into a bowl and beat them well. Add a little bit of salt into it.
2 Heat a nonstick pan and put 2 tbsp of cooking oil in it. Pour egg mixture into the pan and stir gently until it forms soft curds; move it to a bowl.
3 Add 2 tbsp of cooking oil into the pan and put tomato pieces into the pan. Add Thirteen Spices and stir-fry for a few minutes until the tomato becomes a bit soft.
4 Add scrambled egg to the pan and mix them evenly; add salt and sugar.
5 Turn off the heat. Put them onto a plate, ready to serve.

Questions

1 What is community-supported agriculture? How is it different from conventional food-supply chains? What are some of its economic, social and environmental implications?
2 What do you think are the major reasons that led to the trust problem in China's food system?
3 How do Gao's farm and Shared Harvest Farm address the issue of trust? To what extent do their approaches concur with each other?
4 What are some other challenges in the industrial food system that community-supported agriculture can or cannot tackle? Why?

Acknowledgements

I would like to acknowledge funding from the Social Sciences and Humanities Research Council of Canada that made possible the fieldwork on which this chapter is based.

References

Chen, W. (2015) *The Vegetable Basket Revolution: Case Studies on Chinese Community Supported Agriculture*. Beijing, Economic Science Press. (in Chinese)

Day, A. (2013) *The Peasant in Postsocialist China: History, Politics, and Capitalism*. Cambridge, Cambridge University Press.

Ellis, L. J. & Turner, J. L. (2007) *Surf and turf: Environmental and food safety concerns of China's aquaculture and animal husbandry*. Woodrow Wilson International Center for Scholars. China Environment Series (CES) Feature Article no. 9.

Forum on Health, Environment and Development (FORHEAD). (2014) *Food safety in China: A mapping of problems, governance, and research*. Available from: http://webarchive.ssrc.org/cehi/PDFs/Food-Safety-in-China-Web.pdf [Accessed: 3rd March 2017].

Fu, H. & Ye, J. (2015) Rise and besieged: The development of community supported agriculture in China. *Chinese Rural Economy*. 6, 23–32. (in Chinese)

Garnett, T. & Wilkes, A. (2014) *Appetite for Change: Social, Economic and Environmental Changes in China's Food System*. Oxford, UK, Food Climate Research Network.

Henderson, E. & En, R. V. (2007) *Sharing the Harvest: A Citizen's Guide to Community Supported Agriculture*. White River Junction, USA, Chelsea Green Publishing.

Hu, Z. (2010) *The era of poisoning: Only conscience can light up food production*. Available from: http://finance.qq.com/a/20100925/001372.htm [Accessed: 3rd March 2017]. (in Chinese)

Huang, J., Wang, X. & Qiu, H. (2012) *Small-Scale Farmers in China in the Face of Modernization and Globalization*. Center for Chinese Agricultural Policy, Chinese Academy of Science.

Huang, Y. (2011) *CSA farms in Anlong village*. Available from: http://gengdu.baike.com/article-19479.html [Accessed: 3rd March 2017]. (in Chinese)

IFOAM. (n.d.) *Principles of organic agriculture*. Available from: www.ifoam.bio/en/organic-landmarks/principles-organic-agriculture [Accessed: 3rd March 2017].

Jia, C. & Jukes, D. (2013) The national food safety control system of China – a systematic review. *Food Control*. 32 (1), 236–245.

King, F. H. (1911) *Farmers of Forty Centuries*. Emmaus, PA, Rodale Press, Inc.

Leung, H. (2015) *No doggy bag please: Chinese attitudes on food waste*. Masters thesis, Royal Roads University.

National Bureau of Statistics. (2016a) *2015 Statistical report on national economic and social development*. Available from: www.stats.gov.cn/tjsj/zxfb/201602/t20160229_1323991.html [Accessed 3rd March 2017]. (in Chinese)

National Bureau of Statistics. (2016b) *2015 Report on migrant workers*. Available from: www.stats.gov.cn/tjsj/zxfb/201604/t20160428_1349713.html [Accessed 3rd March 2017]. (in Chinese)

Ongley, E. D., Xiaolan, Z. & Tao, Y. (2010) Current status of agricultural and rural non-point source pollution assessment in China. *Environmental Pollution*. 158 (5), 1159–1168.

Pan, J. & Du, J. (2011) The social economy of new rural reconstruction. *China Journal of Social Work*. 4 (3), 271–282.

Pei, X., Tandon, A., Alldrick, A., Giorgi, L., Huang, W. & Yang, R. (2011) The China melamine milk scandal and its implications for food safety regulation. *Food Policy*. 36 (3), 412–420.

Regnier-Davies, J. (2015) *'Fake meat and cabbageworms': Connecting perceptions of food safety and household level food security in urban China*. Masters thesis, University of Waterloo.

Sage, C. (2012) *Environment and Food*. New York, Routledge.

Schneider, M. (2015) What, then, is a Chinese peasant? Nongmin discourses and agroindustrialization in contemporary China. *Agriculture and Human Values*. 32 (2), 331–346.

Schnell, S. M. (2007) Food with a farmer's face: Community-Supported Agriculture in the United States. *Geographical Review*. 97 (4), 550–564.

Schumilas, T. (2014) *Alternative food networks with Chinese characteristics*. PhD thesis, University of Waterloo.

Scott, S., Si, Z., Schumilas, T. & Chen, A. (2014) Contradictions in state- and civil society-driven developments in China's ecological agriculture sector. *Food Policy*. 45 (2), 158–166.

Shared Harvest. (2013) The production standards of Shared Harvest. Weblog. Available from: http://blog.sina.com.cn/s/blog_a569abc901018kdx.html [Accessed: 3rd March 2017]. (in Chinese)

Shi, Y. & Cheng, C. (2015) *Opportunities and challenges of Chinese community supported agriculture*. Available from: www.kemir.net/news/2802/ [Accessed: 3rd March 2017]. (in Chinese)

Shi, Y., Cheng, C., Lei, P., Wen, T. & Merrifield, C. (2011a) Safe food, green food, good food: Chinese community supported agriculture and the rising middle class. *International Journal of Agricultural Sustainability*. 9 (4), 551–558.

Shi, Y., Cheng, C., Lei, P., Zhu, Y., Jia, Y. & Wen, T. (2011b) Correlation analysis of ecological urban agriculture development and the rise of urban middle class: A participatory study based on the operation of Little Donkey Farm CSA. *Guizhou Social Sciences*. 254 (2), 55–60. (in Chinese)

Si, Z., Schumilas, T. & Scott, S. (2015) Characterizing alternative food networks in China. *Agriculture and Human Values*. 32 (2), 299–313.

Si, Z. & Scott, S. (2016) *Approaching sustainable urban development in China through a food system planning lens*. Hungry Cities Partnership. Discussion Papers No.2. Available from: http://hungrycities.net/publication/hungry-cities-partnership-discussion-paper-no-2-approaching-sustainable-urban-development-in-china-through-a-food-system-planning-lens/ [Accessed: 1st March 2017].

Sinovator. (2016) *The developmental pathways of Chinese farms: Building good farms through "Good Farms" app*. Available from: www.ngocn.net/column/2016-04-19-2f2ab27b2cc7eec3.html [Accessed: 3rd March 2017].

Su, C. W., Liu, T., Chang, H. & Jiang, X. (2015) Is urbanization narrowing the urban-rural income gap? A cross-regional study of China. *Habitat International*. 48, 79–86.

Wang, R. Y., Si, Z., Ng, C. N. & Scott, S. (2015) The transformation of trust in China's alternative food networks: Disruption, reconstruction, and development. *Ecology and Society*. 20 (2), article 19.

Xue, J. & Zhang, W. (2013) Understanding China's food safety problem: An analysis of 2387 incidents of acute foodborne illness. *Food Control*. 30 (1), 311–317.

Yan, H. & Chen, Y. (2013) Debating the rural cooperative movement in China, the past and the present. *Journal of Peasant Studies*. 40 (6), 955–981.

Yan, Y. (2012) Food safety and social risk in contemporary China. *The Journal of Asian Studies*. 71 (3), 705–729.

Yang, G. (2013) Contesting food safety in the Chinese media: Between hegemony and counter-hegemony. *The China Quarterly*. 214, 337–355.

Zhang, Q. F. & Pan, Z. (2013) The transformation of urban vegetable retail in China: Wet markets, supermarkets and informal markets in Shanghai. *Journal of Contemporary Asia*. 43 (3), 497–518.

Zhou, L. & Fang, P. (2015) Multiple rationality: The motive of "one family, two systems" and social self-protection in food safety. *China Agricultural University Journal of Social Sciences Edition*. 32 (3), 76–84. (in Chinese)

Zhou, W. Q. (2013) *Food waste and recycling in China: A growing trend?* Available from: www.worldwatch.org/food-waste-and-recycling-china-growing-trend-1 [Accessed: 3rd March 2017].

4

PLACE-BASED FOOD SYSTEMS

"Re-valuing local" and fostering socio-ecological sustainability

Susanna E. Klassen and Hannah Wittman

Introduction

You might have noticed that the lexicon of "buy local" is increasingly visible at the supermarket, at the farmers' market, and in government marketing campaigns. Consumers today have access to more information than ever before about their food choices, including about animal welfare, greenhouse gas emissions, pesticide use, nutrition, and genetically modified foods. Consumers demand – and markets respond – with certification standards, an explosion of food labels, alternative food initiatives, and popular media on sustainable food. The advice to "eat local" was intended to support direct marketing from producer to consumer (Hinrichs & Allen, 2008) as a way of supporting sustainable local food economies, and is one of several proposed rules of thumb to facilitate better decision-making when it comes to food purchases. Promoted by activists and academics alike as a remedy to the dual problems of food insecurity and the ecological impacts of the global food system, the local food movement has gained significant momentum in recent years.

The complexity of the global food system seldom allows for simple answers, however. Local food initiatives vary in how "local" is geographically defined, and other important and multi-scalar dynamics affect how – and by whom – food is grown, distributed, and consumed. As a result, researchers have called for a "careful circumspection and greater clarity regarding how we delineate and understand the 'local'" (Feagan, 2007, p. 23). What defines a localized food system, and what are the key contributions of local food to creating a more sustainable and food-secure future? How might the concept of "place-based" food – with attention to the multi-scalar and networked constitution of distinctive agricultural and food practices and relationships – address the limitations of a local food approach?

What is "local food"?

The drive for localization is premised in part on the concept of "food miles", suggesting that reducing the distance food travels between farm (producer) and fork (consumer) will minimize the environmental impact of consumer food choices by reducing the energy used, and thus greenhouse gasses emitted, through transportation (Coley, Howard & Winter, 2009; Smith & Mackinnon, 2007; Pirog et al., 2001). However, food miles don't necessarily represent a substantial portion of the energy usage in the food system. There are other variables to consider when making food choices that may have more of an impact on diet-related greenhouse gas emissions.

For example, one study used Life Cycle Analysis of greenhouse gas emissions at different stages in the food chain in the United States to evaluate the contribution of "food miles" to total emissions, relative to other phases between production and consumption (Weber & Matthews, 2008). They found that the agricultural production stage was the largest contributor to overall emissions, and that this contribution varied significantly between food groups. The study also estimated that more than half of the emissions from food production are from non-CO_2 sources, including nitrous oxide (N_2O) emissions (from fertilizer application to crops, and soil and manure management) and methane (CH_4) emissions (from enteric fermentation in ruminants). The authors concluded that shifting diets away from red meat (the most greenhouse gas-intensive by energy content, mass, and household expenditure) could, on average, be a more effective means of lowering diet-related climate footprints than buying local to reduce transportation emissions. Other studies have highlighted the importance of considering seasonality of various foods in the calculation of energy or environmental footprint, as the energy required to store local products throughout the year may be greater than that of transporting the same product from a distant location (Canals et al., 2007). While there is a high degree of uncertainty and complexity involved with quantifying greenhouse gas emissions from different food products (Sim et al., 2007; Edwards-Jones et al., 2008), the conflation of food miles with environmental impacts has caused some to critique the localization trend for being a false solution to overall environmental degradation in the food system (Mariola, 2008; Fraser et al., 2015).

"Local" is also sometimes uncritically equated with "socially sustainable". While the geographic distance that food travels between farm and fork *could* be a partial indicator of environmental impact, a reduction in food miles does not translate directly to improving processes and outcomes that would qualify food as "sustainably produced", such as fair labor standards, improved livelihoods for farmers, and reduced environmental impact of particular production practices, such as a reduction in the use of pesticides that disproportionately affect farmworker health. Indeed, all food is local *somewhere*, regardless of the outcomes associated with its production and distribution.

Sustainability encompasses a larger range of social, economic, and environmental dimensions, including social equity and long-term farm economic viability (Schipanski et al., 2016). In addition to the broader consideration of the social aspects of sustainability, a comprehensive consideration of sustainability must also take a systems approach, which includes dynamics within and between multiple scales, including at farm-level production systems, across regional and global supply chains, and in relation to larger territories or landscapes (Wittman et al., 2016). Because the term "local" does not explicitly prescribe sustainability criteria, buying local does not automatically create transformative change in consumer consciousness (Winter, 2003). Along the same lines, personal interactions through direct marketing do not necessarily translate to improved social connectivity or increase social capital (Portes & Landolt, 1996; Hinrichs, 2000). Indeed, selective patronage campaigns like "buying local" and its various iterations can even undermine social equity by excluding certain groups, such as low-income or disadvantaged consumers (Hinrichs & Allen, 2008).

In summary, to focus exclusively on food miles as an indicator of a healthy and sustainable food system is to discount the importance of understanding how to support farmer livelihoods, the range of potentially sustainable farm management practices, the complex and multiple drivers of rural community resilience, and the urgent need to protect local farmland access and fair employment opportunities, all of which are integral components of a thriving food system.

From local to "place-based" systems

While food miles may be insufficient as a sole indicator of sustainable food, the local food movement has made some key discursive interventions into how to reshape the food system to be more connected to and reflective of its socio-ecological context in order to address ecological and social degradation.

While the concept of "local" may still be meaningful in generating discourse on how to address global food security challenges, the term "place-based" encompasses a broader conceptualization of scale and proximity beyond simple geography. Cresswell (2004) points out that "place" is not an esoteric term – it is commonly used in the English language – yet it has a rich and nuanced history. The concept of place encompasses social and relational meanings stemming from everyday practice, including trade between regions, with roots in historical and indigenous landscapes comprised of explicit relationships between people and their surrounding environment (Altamirano-Jiménez, 2013; Escobar, 2001). *Places* are multi-scalar, and networked (Escobar, 2001), actively constructed, and co-constituted through experience and relationships.

As such, while all food can be considered local *somewhere*, and is cultivated, gathered, and/or harvested by *someone*, the extent to which consumers are connected to the people and environments that produce and exchange food in particular places is partially mediated by the social and economic "distance" between production and consumption. Distance here is not necessarily restricted to the geographic or spatial sense – people are also removed from their food system through social separations in time, and through various institutions. For example, as a result of the globalization, deregulation, and financialization of the global food system, global commodity chains have been extended, obscuring connections and dissociating food from its context (Clapp, 2014). The increasing economic and discursive separation between regions where food is cultivated and where it is consumed – the "metabolic rift" between town and country (Wittman, 2009) – has also broken the socio-ecological cycle of nutrient cycling necessary to sustain the ecological functioning of food systems. Taking a closer look at food systems in particular places – as constituted and mediated by networked and multi-scalar social, economic, ecological, and political dynamics – can inform our understanding of "place-based" agriculture in relation to the international commodity networks in which they are embedded.

In order to advance the discussion on the role of scale and context in finding future solutions for a food-secure world, we explore the concept of a "place-based" food system to critically reconsider how to conceptualize the "value" of localized agricultural dynamics. We discuss the importance of social and ecological diversification and sustainable nutrient cycling as constitutive of a place-based agriculture that is reflective of and responsive to social, ecological, and economic contexts at multiple scales. Local food systems that are place-based can reduce negative environmental and social impacts by helping to foster ecological resilience, mitigate economic risk, facilitate the sustainable use of local resources, and create socially resilient connections to the landscape and within regional communities.

Blueberries in British Columbia

We use the export-oriented blueberry sector in British Columbia (BC) as a "case example" of a food that is significant in the local economy and culture, while also linked to global networks through trade and distant locales of consumption. The blueberry industry illustrates how local food systems are nested within larger social, political, and economic contexts. They are thus both subject to destabilizing forces emerging from the global economy, but also constitutive of socio-ecological relationships that can foster place-based resilience.

BC hosts the most diverse agricultural sector in Canada, with hundreds of economically important land- and sea-based foods traded in global and local markets. The cultivation of these foods is very regionally concentrated: distinct agricultural systems are clustered in different regions of the province based on bioregional characteristics and historical growing conditions. In the Lower Fraser Valley region (Figure 4.1), blueberry production is a prominent fixture on the landscape. Blueberries are one of the province's largest agri-food exports, with a total export revenue of $218 million in 2015 (BC Ministry of Agriculture, 2016). BC produces 95% of the country's highbush blueberries. The blueberry industry is not only important provincially – it is Canada's most significant fruit crop, both in cultivated area and market value.

Blueberry cultivation and harvesting has a significant natural history in the region, as one of the few major agricultural crops native to North America (Khoury et al., 2016). The small, fruit-bearing shrub (e.g. *Vaccinium ovalifolium*) was an important food source for Indigenous Peoples, who made use of the plant's leaves, roots, and the nutritious berries, and blueberries and their related huckleberries continue

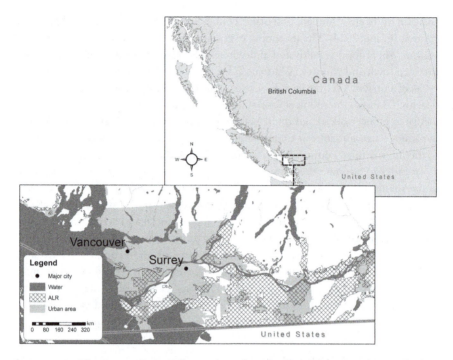

FIGURE 4.1 The Lower Fraser Valley region of southwestern BC, Canada. Prepared by the Sustainable Agricultural Landscapes Lab at the University of British Columbia using data from the BC Agricultural Land Commission

to be a culturally significant food crop today (Kuhnlein et al., 2012). Concerns about the commercialization of the berry industry in BC have been expressed by Indigenous elders related to the impacts of colonization and the loss of access to traditional territory for harvesting (Richards & Alexander, 2006). While Indigenous peoples have participated in commercial harvesting and trade of blueberries and huckleberries, nations are largely concerned with the preservation of traditional foodlands from agricultural encroachment.

The cultivated highbush blueberry (*Vaccinium corymbosum*) that is grown throughout the Lower Fraser Valley today was domesticated in New Jersey in the early 1900s, and was developed through artificial selection and natural breeding techniques (Charles, 2015). The first highbush blueberries were planted south of Vancouver, BC in the 1920s, and several of these original plants remain in production today, now having grown to seven feet tall (Van Baalen, 2009).

Despite the long history of the blueberry plant in North America, the substantial growth in the sector in BC has been relatively concentrated in the last decade. Between 2011 and 2013, the export value of blueberries grew by 20% (BC Ministry of Agriculture, 2014). Between 2006 and 2011, blueberry acreage grew by 77%, demonstrating the largest increase in land devoted to its production (BC Ministry of Agriculture, 2012). This growth was concentrated in the Lower Fraser Valley, now covering nearly 10% of total farmland area in the region, where 97% of the province's blueberry production takes place.

Export-driven specialization vs. diversification in place

The global agricultural landscape is increasingly characterized by industrial-scale food production shaped by comparative advantage, where regions specialize in particular agricultural commodities. In general, food production systems based on this model depend on export-oriented trade to sell crops. While specialized agricultural landscapes are still shaped by social and ecological characteristics of particular places (e.g. suitability to bio-physical landscape conditions, availability of labor, market infrastructure), they can also be created and structured to meet the needs of highly globalized supply chains. In turn, the environmental impacts of these globalized systems are felt locally.

For example, in the Lower Fraser Valley, an increasing proportion of productive land is devoted to growing blueberries, leading to a loss of diversification across crop species in the region. This is due in part to locally favorable soil and climatic conditions, as well as access to trade facilities in nearby coastal ports, including processing facilities and export channels to rapidly growing markets in Asia. The rapid expansion in blueberry production has resulted in a saturated local market and a reliance on these export channels to sell berries overseas.

A variety of interacting economic forces contributed to land-use change that resulted in the concentration of blueberry agriculture in the Lower Fraser Valley that we see today. First, BC farmers were under pressure due to increased competition for markets for a diverse range of field crops in both domestic and international markets, especially after the North American Free Trade Agreement (NAFTA) was signed in 1994. BC farmers found it difficult to compete with the field vegetables and strawberries produced in California and Mexico, where labor costs were lower, and which were now making their way into Canada. This economic stress on farmers occurred around the same time that blueberries began gaining international recognition for a variety of health benefits. Researchers found evidence that blueberry supplements could reverse age-related neurodegenerative disease because of their antioxidant content (Joseph et al., 1999). Following this discovery, an increasing number of studies and news articles were published that framed blueberries as a "super fruit". Consumer demand for blueberries increased as a result, and this, coupled with the economic decline of other crops driven by international markets, contributed to the specialization and rapid increase in blueberry production in the Lower Fraser Valley. Reflecting consumer demand, prices began increasing in the late 1990s to a peak in 2006, and then plummeted, partly as a result of the glut in the market. Not only were growers in the highly specialized industry vulnerable to the low market price, but they had made long-term investments in a perennial crop that takes a decade to mature. Despite the decline in market price, acreage devoted to blueberry production continued to increase.

While economic drivers in the global marketplace have played a role in the growth of the blueberry sector in the Fraser Valley, crop specialization and the loss of diversity within the regional agricultural landscape have also resulted in consequences for ecological resilience. Biological diversity in agricultural systems has been shown to increase resilience to disturbances at multiple scales, such as climatic fluctuations and pest threats (Kremen, Iles & Bacon, 2012). Depending on the type of crop, diversification is important for other biological elements of crop production, including pressure placed on pollinating insects, both managed and wild (Potts et al., 2010; Carvalheiro et al., 2010).

Currently, most blueberry farmers rely on managed honeybee colonies for the pollination of their crops (Klein et al., 2007). Yet, for many crops, including blueberries, honeybees are not the most efficient pollinator (Javorek, Mackenzie & Vander Kloet, 2002). Bumblebees are both more effective as pollinators for blueberries, and are more likely to perform this service despite poor weather conditions (Benjamin & Winfree, 2014) – an increasing concern with predicted climate change impacts in BC and around the world (Crawford & Beveridge, 2013). Moreover, honeybees around the world are increasingly vulnerable to diseases and stress (Gordon, Bresolin-Schott & East, 2014). As blueberries have come to dominate the landscape in the Lower Fraser Valley, demand for pollination services has been concentrated in both space and time, while agricultural biodiversity has been lost. The reliance on this single species of pollinator is a risk for the sector. This exemplifies how a lack of diversity driven by specialization has created precariousness and vulnerability in blueberry production systems, and threatens to undermine long-term production capacity.

In addition to the benefit of creating ecological resilience in local agricultural landscapes, diversification in crop varieties can also help reduce exposure to market fluctuations (Darnhofer, Fairweather & Moller, 2010). If a farmer or community is highly dependent on a single crop such as blueberries, they face significant economic risk from volatile global commodity prices. Moreover, specialization can also lead to market saturation, driving down the price of the crop, thus affecting the viability of farm businesses and the livelihoods of those producers that depend on that market for sales. By encouraging diversity, a regional food system could have a built-in buffer for adapting to changing markets, both locally and globally.

Finally, there is also an important relationship between agricultural diversity and demands on human labor systems (Otero & Preibisch, 2015). Agriculture is inherently a seasonal endeavor, but activities and crops (and different varieties within a single crop) tend to vary in their peak demands on labor. If producers distribute labor demand throughout the season, rather than concentrating it to a few months or even weeks, seasonal pressures on farmers and workers could decrease, creating conditions for a more socially just food system.

While the blueberry production systems showcased here are clearly embedded in the local landscape, they are also being shaped by international economic forces. This has enabled producers to access markets beyond local demand, but the resulting specialization and corresponding declines in agrobiodiversity have concentrated the ecological challenges of pest threats and pollination troubles. Market saturation and labor shortages are also spatially bounded in the Fraser Valley region. This case demonstrates the results of catering to global market demand at the expense of local socio-ecological system dynamics, and highlights the need to balance these considerations to ensure long-term sustainability of agricultural production.

Ecological extraction vs. closing the "metabolic rift"

While comparative advantage aims to increase efficiency through specialization, this can involve simply moving environmental problems "out of sight" and contribute to cycles of global environmental degradation and "unjust ecological exchange" (Jorgenson & Clark, 2009; Roberts & Parks, 2009). Alternatively, more localized food systems can bolster resource use efficiency through connectivity and complementarity, effectively "closing the rift" between cycles of production and consumption in the food system.

Nutrient management in blueberry production exemplifies this concept. The management of nutrient inputs to maintain soil fertility and achieve optimal crop yields is a challenge for farmers around the world. While the importance of nitrogen and phosphorus to plant growth is universal, the forms in which they are most available to producers (e.g. as synthetic fertilizer, manure, or aquatic plant matter) differ depending on a variety of contextual factors. For example, some blueberry growers access poultry manure as fertilizer through relatives or neighbors in the poultry sector, another significant industry in the region. However, the concentration in which each nutrient is needed in the environment differs based on biophysical parameters: different fields require different nutrient-management strategies based on crop type and soil conditions. As such, many blueberry farmers use custom fertilizer mixes of macro- and micro-nutrients for different times of the year based on soil tests, allowing them to adjust ratios to current soil nutrient content (e.g. if there are high levels of phosphorus in the soil already). This precision approach is one solution to major global problems with nutrient pollution where excess fertilizers from agricultural areas have leached into waterways. However, this practice does not address the need for importing nutrients from other places, or facilitate the recycling of farm waste as nutrient inputs. Particularly in the case of phosphorus, an essential nutrient required for plant growth and a non-renewable resource mined from rock phosphate deposits, addressing imbalances of too little and too much by recycling nutrients can help create more sustainable agricultural systems.

For example, where agricultural landscapes consist of both crop production and livestock operations in close spatial proximity, facilitating nutrient recycling between these systems could be more feasible than between geographically distant regions specializing in each of these commodities. Managing the flows of goods at an international scale in a global trade system presents its own challenges, but transporting manure is often not economically feasible, even at regional scales. Place-based systems can facilitate the redistribution of waste products as valuable inputs in order to ease the waste-disposal burden on farmers, reduce over-application, and meet nutrient input needs (Schreier, Bestbier & Derksen, 2003).

Food from nowhere vs. place-based agriculture

Perhaps one of the most significant yet undervalued benefits of a thriving local food system is the connection that it fosters to the local landscape and the food producers who steward it. This is referred to by some academics as the "re-spatialization" and "re-socialization" of food, and can be accomplished by shortening supply chains and re-embedding food production in the local landscape in order to increase proximity and connection between people and the farms (spatial) and farmers (social) that produce our food (Renting, Marsden & Banks, 2003). Yet, critical food-systems scholars recognize that face-to-face market exchanges do not necessarily foster constructive social relations, and that all supply chains (long and short) are embedded to some degree in a specific territorial context (Bowen, 2011).

BC's blueberry sector has provided an example of the multi-dimensional relationships of place-based food systems, including a dynamic and evolving multicultural social context. It has transitioned from a traditionally important Indigenous food crop, to a component of a diversified landscape, to a dominant, export-oriented commodity grown by members of an international diaspora, many of which are first- or second-generation Canadians. The multi-cultural nature of the sector is thus co-constituted with the cultivation of plant relatives of native ecological biota.

While the arguments in this chapter around diversification and nutrient cycling are presented as binaries, these artificial dichotomies are meant to illustrate two ends of a hypothetical continuum. Supporting the re-anchoring of a food system in a given locale does not erase the significance of global ties or propose the elimination of trade or specialization; instead, considerations of fossil-fuel efficiency should be balanced with an understanding of the far-reaching socio-ecological consequences of a highly specialized and globalized agricultural landscape. Local food systems cannot be separated from the influence of the global food system, but many outcomes of interest are spatially bounded and locally important. Moreover, food production cannot be de-coupled from the influence of local factors, such as pollinator declines and climate change (Lesk, Rowhani & Ramankutty, 2016). In other words, global forces may influence what a given region grows, but the consequences, such as pest threats, pollination pressures, labor demands, and market fluctuations, are experienced at the local level.

In order to facilitate a transition to place-based food systems, the connections to other places that are no longer so distant will need to be acknowledged, and the role of global economic integration as a driver of local socio-ecological changes needs to be recognized (Adger, Eakin & Winkels, 2009; Liu et al., 2007). If we are to successfully "re-socialize" our food systems, the multi-scalar and nested nature of these connections will need to be considered. Moreover, we will need to find ways to root our supply chains, and re-embed them to enhance transparency, stability, and resilience (Bowen, 2011). Institutions will have a central role to play in this at local and global scales.

Whether through farm management practices, institutional mechanisms, or consumer choices, developing thriving and diverse local food systems is an alternative to the inherent risk involved in specialization. Elucidating the precise benefits associated with supporting local food, as well as the challenges and trade-offs (Harrison & Getz, 2015; Johnson, Fraser & Hawkins, 2016), will be central to advancing the legitimacy of the local food movement. Considering the necessary transitions (and transformations) needed to achieve food security and sustainability, the solutions will need to be rooted in the contextual realities of place.

RECIPE: HEARTY SEASONAL SALAD

Description

This recipe for thoughtful eating parallels the approach to sustainable food systems explored in this chapter. This is not a recipe in the prescriptive sense, but, like the solution we present in this chapter, it's a set of guidelines to help inspire a delicious meal that suits *your* circumstances – gastronomic, economic, cultural, and (bio)regional. While it can be overwhelming to personally take on the ethical and environmental implications of every food choice, it is important to engage with food as a citizen, not just as a consumer. We encourage you to think through the different variables or dynamics implicated in this meal: the origin of chosen ingredients, the supply chains involved, the seasonal availability in your bio-region, or the methods of preservation that could extend the availability of locally sourced foods. But don't forget your personal needs and circumstances: How are you feeling? What is in your fridge already? Which flavors do you want to highlight?

Ingredients

Guidelines	Suggestion	Additional Inspiration
Salad		
1 cup uncooked grain, seed or pulse	farro	barley, millet, lentils, beans, quinoa, or rice
Water or broth	water (4 cups)	
1 pound vegetables	roasted zucchini	roasted tomatoes, fennel, winter squash, or root vegetables
1/2 cup nuts (toasted)	hazelnuts	walnuts, almonds, sunflower seeds

(Continued)

(Continued)

Guidelines	Suggestion	Additional Inspiration
Additional fresh vegetables	radish, diced arugula, torn	Whatever you have in the fridge or what looks good at the market/ store: grated carrots, grated beet, chopped pepper, lettuce, peas, beans, cucumber, or other greens
Allium (onion family)	spring onion, chopped	finely sliced shallot, caramelized onion, or chopped chives
Cheese	3/4 cup crumbled goat feta	Any cheese you can find, really – try a local dairy!
Fresh herb	1/2 cup basil, torn	Any herbs in the garden? Chopped dill, cilantro, mint, parsley. Try a mix if you're feeling adventurous.
Dressing		
5 tablespoons oil	olive oil	walnut, almond, sesame, or camelina oil
2–3 tablespoons vinegar	red wine vinegar	apple cider vinegar, balsamic vinegar, lemon juice. Have you ever tried making your own vinegar with juice or wine?
1 teaspoon sweetener	maple syrup	honey, agave, sugar, or skip altogether
Additional flavoring	mustard and 1 clove crushed garlic	miso, soy sauce, nutritional yeast, chili flakes, spices – anything really! This is where you can get creative.
Salt and pepper		

Instructions

Boil an appropriate amount of water for the desired grain that will serve as the base for the salad. Cook, following the instructions. For farro, rinse and drain the grains, and bring to a boil for 30 minutes (taste to determine when you think it's done – this is a matter of preference!). You can shorten the cooking time by soaking the farro overnight. Drain when you have deemed it cooked, and set aside in a large serving bowl.

Preheat the oven to 375 degrees Fahrenheit (or hotter, or cooler) and prepare vegetables for roasting. For the suggested variation above, slice zucchini into 1/2-inch thick slices, toss with olive oil, salt and pepper, and arrange on a baking sheet. Roast until golden brown, flipping or stirring part way through. For zucchini, this should take about 30 minutes, but allow 30–50 minutes depending on your oven, vegetable of choice, and size of pieces. Remove from the oven when finished, and add to the grain.

If you haven't toasted the nuts yet, do this while the vegetables are roasting. Chop the nuts to an appropriate size, place them on a baking sheet, and put the sheet in the oven for 5–7 minutes at first; check every minute or so to be sure they don't burn. This happens fast.

While these things are cooking, you can prepare the remaining ingredients. Chop the vegetables into bite-size pieces, tear/chop the herbs, crumble/grate the cheese, and add everything to the farro and roasted vegetable mixture.

Mix the ingredients together for the dressing. I like the "shake everything in a jar" method, or the blender if you're making a large batch that you want to be well incorporated.

Dress the salad, taste, and season to your preference. Serve warm or cool. Store in the fridge for up to 5 days – leftovers make the best lunches!

Questions

1 What are potential trade-offs faced by farmers in making choices about what crops to grow? Consider how local and regional market structures (including cultural food practices and preferences), business viability, and ecological dynamics interact.
2 How can globalized food systems be integrated with place-based food landscapes without negative consequences?
3 What are some methods/approaches that can enable production efficiency, while building diversity and resilience into the system?
4 Spatial proximity and short supply chains can help create more place-based and socially embedded food systems, but they do not guarantee it. What are some mechanisms that could help build social connectivity and facilitate the "emplacement" of food production and commodity sectors?

Acknowledgements

This research was supported by the Canadian Institutes for Health Research, and the Social Sciences and Humanities Research Council of Canada. The authors would also like to thank the BC Blueberry Council and the blueberry growers who shared their valuable perspectives, and to Dr. Navin Ramankutty and the editors for helpful comments.

References

Adger, N. W., Eakin, H. & Winkels, A. (2009) Nested and teleconnected vulnerabilities to environmental change. *The Ecological Society of America.* 7 (3), 150–157.

Altamirano-Jiménez, I. (2013) *Indigenous Encounters with Neoliberalism: Place, Women, and the Environment in Canada and Mexico.* Vancouver, BC, UBC Press.

BC Ministry of Agriculture. (2012) *2011 Census of Agriculture: British Columbia District Highlights.*Victoria, BC.

BC Ministry of Agriculture. (2014) *2013 Export Highlights: British Columbia Agrifoods.*Victoria, BC.

BC Ministry of Agriculture. (2016) *2015 Export Highlights British Columbia Agrifood and Seafood.*Victoria, BC.

Benjamin, F. E. & Winfree, R. (2014) Lack of pollinators limits fruit production in commercial blueberry (vaccinium corymbosum). *Environmental Entomology.* 43 (6), 1574–1583.

Bowen, S. (2011) The importance of place: Re-territorializing embeddedness. *Sociologa Ruralis.* 51 (4), 325–348.

Canals, L. M., Mclaren, S., Sim, S. & Basson, L. (2007) Comparing domestic versus imported apples: A focus on energy use. *Environmental Science and Pollution Research – International.* 14 (5), 338–344.

Carvalheiro, L. G., Seymour, C. L., Veldtman, R. & Nicolson, S. W. (2010) Pollination services decline with distance from natural habitat even in biodiversity-rich areas. *Journal of Applied Ecology.* 47 (4), 810–820.

Charles, D. (2015) *How New Jersey tamed the wild blueberry for global production.* Available from: www.npr.org/sections/thesalt/2015/08/04/428984045/how-new-jersey-tamed-the-wild-blueberry-for-global-production [Accessed: 2nd March 2017].

Clapp, J. (2014) Financialization, distance and global food politics. *The Journal of Peasant Studies.* 41 (5), 794–814.

Coley, D., Howard, M. & Winter, M. (2009) Local food, food miles and carbon emissions: A comparison of farm shop and mass distribution approaches. *Food Policy.* 34 (2), 150–155.

Crawford, E. & Beveridge, R. (2013) *Strengthening BC's Agriculture Sector in the Face of Climate Change.*Victoria, BC, Pacific Institute for Climate Solutions.

Cresswell, T. (2004) *Place: A Short Introduction.*Cambridge, Wiley-Blackwell.

Darnhofer, I., Fairweather, J. & Moller, H. (2010) Assessing a farm's sustainability: Insights from resilience thinking. *International Journal of Agricultural Sustainability.* 8 (3), 186–198.

Edwards-Jones, G., Milà i Canals, L., Hounsome, N., Truninger, M., Koerber, G., Hounsome, B., Cross, P., York, E. H., Hospido, A., Plassmann, K., Harris, I. M., Edwards, R. T., Day, G. A. S., Tomos, A. D., Cowell, S. J. & Jones, D. L. (2008) Testing the assertion that "local food is best": The challenges of an evidence-based approach. *Trends in Food Science and Technology.* 19 (5), 265–274.

Escobar, A. (2001) Culture sits in places: Reflections on globalism and subaltern strategies of localization. *Political Geography.* 20 (2), 139–174.

Feagan, R. (2007) The place of food: Mapping out the "local" in local food systems. *Progress in Human Geography.* 31 (1), 23–42.

Fraser, E., Legwegoh, A., KC, K., CoDyre, M., Dias, G., Hazen, S., Johnson, R., Martin, R., Ohberg, L., Sethuratnam, S., Sneyd, L., Smithers, J., Van Acker, R., Vansteenkiste, J., Wittman, H. & Yada, R. (2015) Biotechnology or organic? Extensive or intensive? Global or local? A critical review of potential pathways to resolve the global food crisis. *Trends in Food Science and Technology.* 48, 78–87.

Gordon, R., Bresolin-Schott, N. & East, I. J. (2014) Nomadic beekeeper movements create the potential for widespread disease in the honeybee industry. *Australian Veterinary Journal.* 92 (8), 283–290.

Harrison, J. L. & Getz, C. (2015) Farm size and job quality: Mixed-methods studies of hired farm work in California and Wisconsin. *Agriculture and Human Values.* 32 (4), 617–634.

Hinrichs, C. C. (2000) Embeddedness and local food systems: Notes on two types of direct agricultural market. *Journal of Rural Studies.* 16 (3), 295–303.

Hinrichs, C. C. & Allen, P. (2008) Selective patronage and social justice: Local food consumer campaigns in historical context. *Journal of Agricultural and Environmental Ethics*. 21 (4), 329–352.

Javorek, S. K., Mackenzie, K. E. & Vander Kloet, S. P. (2002) Comparative pollination effectiveness among bees (Hymenoptera: Apoidea) on lowbush blueberry (Ericaceae: *Vaccinium angustifolium*). *Annals of the Entomological Society of America*. 95 (3), 345–351.

Johnson, R., Fraser, E. & Hawkins, R. (2016) Overcoming barriers to scaling up sustainable alternative food systems: A comparative case study of two Ontario-based wholesale produce auctions. *Sustainability*. 8 (4), 328.

Jorgenson, A. K. & Clark, B. (2009) Ecologically unequal exchange in comparative perspective: A brief introduction. *International Journal of Comparative Sociology*. 50 (3–4), 211–214.

Joseph, J., Shukitt-Hale, B., Denisova, N. A., Bielinski, D., Martin, A., McEwen, J. J & Bickford, P. C. (1999) Reversals of age-related declines in neuronal signal transduction, cognitive, and motor behavioral deficits with blueberry, spinach, or strawberry dietary supplementation. *The Journal of Neuroscience: The Official Journal of the Society for Neuroscience*. 19 (18), 8114–8121.

Khoury, C. K., Achicanoy, H. A., Bjorkman, A. D., Navarro-Racines, C., Guarino, L., Flores-Palacios, X., Engels, J. M. M., Wiersema, J. H., Dempewolf, H., Sotelo, S., Ramírez-Villegas, J., Castañeda-Álvarez, N. P., Fowler, C., Jarvis, A., Rieseberg, L. H. & Struik, P. C. (2016) Origins of food crops connect countries worldwide. *Proceedings of the Royal Society B: Biological Sciences*. 283, 20160792.

Klein, A.-M., Vaissière, Cane, J. H., Steffan-Dewenter, I., Cunningham, S. A., Kremen, C. & Tscharntke, T. (2007) Importance of pollinators in changing landscapes for world crops. *Proceedings of the Royal Society B: Biological Sciences*. 274 (1608), 303–313.

Kremen, C., Iles, A. & Bacon, C. (2012) Diversified farming systems: An agroecological, systems-based alternative to modern industrial agriculture. *Ecology and Society*. 17 (4), 44.

Kuhnlein, H. V., Erasmus, B., Spigelski, D. & Burlingame, B. (eds.) (2012) *Indigenous Peoples' Food Systems and Well-Being: Interventions and Policies for Healthy Communities*. Rome, Italy, Food and Agriculture Organization (FAO) of the United Nations.

Lesk, C., Rowhani, P. & Ramankutty, N. (2016) Influence of extreme weather disasters on global crop production. *Nature*. 529 (7584), 84–87.

Liu, J., Dietz, T., Carpenter, S. R., Alberti, M., Folke, C., Moran, E., Pell, A. N., Deadman, P., Kratz, T., Lubchenco, J., Ostrom, E., Ouyang, Z., Provencher, W., Redman, C. L., Schneider, S. H. & Taylor, W. W. (2007) Complexity of coupled human and natural systems. *Science*. 317 (5844), 1513–1516.

Mariola, M. J. (2008) The local industrial complex? Questioning the link between local foods and energy use. *Agriculture and Human Values*. 25 (2), 193–196.

Otero, B. G. & Preibisch, K. (2015) *Citizenship and Precarious Labour in Canadian Agriculture*. Vancouver, BC, Canadian Centre for Policy Alternatives.

Pirog, R., Van Pelt, T., Enshayan, K. & Cook, E. (2001) *Food, fuel, and freeways: An Iowa perspective on how far food travels, fuel usage, and greenhouse gas emissions*. Leopold Center Pubs and Papers. 3.

Portes, A. & Landolt, P. (1996) The downside of social capital. *The American Prospect*. 26, 1–4.

Potts, S. G., Biesmeijer, J. C., Kremen, C., Neumann, P., Schweiger, O. & Kunin, W. E. (2010) Global pollinator declines: Trends, impacts and drivers. *Trends in Ecology & Evolution*. 25 (6), 345–353.

Renting, H., Marsden, T. K. & Banks, J. (2003) Understanding alternative food networks: Exploring the role of short food supply chains in rural development. *Environment and Planning A*. 35 (3), 393–411.

Richards, R. T. & Alexander, S. J. (2006) *Social history of wild huckleberry harvesting in the Pacific Northwest*. U.S. Department of Agriculture. General Technical Report PNW-GTR-657.

Roberts, J. T. & Parks, B. C. (2009) Ecologically unequal exchange, ecological debt, and climate justice: The history and implications of three related ideas for a new social movement. *International Journal of Comparative Sociology*. 50 (3–4), 385–409.

Schipanski, M. E., MacDonald, G. K., Rosenzweig, S., Chappell, M. J., Bennett, E. M., Kerr, R. B., Blesh, J., Crews, T., Drinkwater, L., Lundgren, J. G. & Schnarr, C. (2016) Realizing resilient food systems. *BioScience*. 66 (7), 600–610.

Schreier, H., Bestbier, R. & Derksen, G. (2003) A quantitative assessment of agricultural intensification and associated waste-management challenges in the lower fraser valley. *Georgia Basin/Puget Sound Research Conference*.

Sim, S., Barry, M., Clift, R. & Cowell, S. J. (2007) The relative importance of transport in determining an appropriate sustainability strategy for food sourcing. *The International Journal of Life Cycle Assessment*. 12 (6), 422–431.

Smith, A. & Mackinnon, J. B. (2007) *The 100-Mile Diet: A Year of Local Eating*. New York, Vintage Canada.

Van Baalen, L. (2009) *The history of blueberries in British Columbia*. Available from: www.bcblueberry.com/site/industry.html [Accessed: 20th September 2016].

Weber, C. L. & Matthews, S. H. (2008) Food-miles and the relative climate impacts of food choices in the United States. *Environmental Science & Technology*. 42 (10), 3508–3513.

Winter, M. (2003) Embeddedness, the new food economy and defensive localism. *Journal of Rural Studies*. 19 (1), 23–32.

Wittman, H. (2009) Reworking the metabolic rift: La Vía Campesina, agrarian citizenship, and food sovereignty. *The Journal of Peasant Studies*. 36 (4), 805–826.

Wittman, H., Chappell, M. J., Abson, D. J., Kerr, R. B., Blesh, J., Hanspach, J., Perfecto, I. & Fischer, J. (2016) A social–ecologicall perspective on harmonizing food security and biodiversity conservation. *Regional Environmental Change*. 17, 1291–1301.

5

RECOVERING FARMLAND COMMONS

Jamie Baxter

Introduction: food and farmland tenure insecurity

Farmland tenure – the set of property rights available to farmers in relation to the land they use to produce food – is insecure when those rights are undefined or unclear; when they are clearly defined but inconsistently enforced by the state or through social norms; and/or when they are impermanent, persisting only for a limited and perhaps indeterminate period of time. Separately or together, each of these aspects of farmland tenure insecurity introduces an element of uncertainty into decisions about land use and food production, thereby reducing farmers' incentives and capacities to invest in practices and material improvements that would achieve better ecological, economic and social outcomes. While our understanding of the causal relationship between land insecurity and food security remains incomplete (Holden & Ghebru, 2016), there is reliable evidence to suggest that insecure tenure negatively impacts several aspects of food security, including soil quality and farmland biodiversity (Gebremedhin & Swinton, 2003), farmland productivity (Deininger & Jin, 2006), and access to farmlands for marginalized persons and groups (Ali, Deininger & Goldstein, 2014).

The challenges associated with land tenure insecurity have mainly been studied in development contexts – namely, in the global South and in post-Soviet Eastern Europe – where extensive state-driven land reform programs have been implemented over the past few decades to formalize and regularize informal and customary land regimes (Trebilcock & Veel, 2008; Meinzen-Dick & Mwangi, 2009). By comparison, because the legal institutions needed to define, record and enforce private property and contractual rights are well developed in wealthy industrialized countries, farmland tenure in these contexts is generally assumed to be secure and therefore of little relevance to the broader challenges of food insecurity. But changing farmer demographics in North America, Australia and Europe have recently thrown the spotlight onto an emerging set of challenges that may be undermining the security of farmland tenure. Declining rural economies and changing social norms around participation in family farm enterprises appear to be causing large numbers of retiring farmers to exit the agricultural sector without family successors, while new entrant farmers from non-farm backgrounds face unaffordable farmland prices and other market constraints that make land access a predominant barrier to entry (Baxter, 2012; Michel, 2014; Bigelow, Borchers & Hubbs, 2016; Wheeler et al., 2012; Zagata & Sutherland, 2015). This situation raises the specter of a generational gap over the coming decades in which new farmers increasingly participate in precarious short-term leasing arrangements or adopt informal "handshake" agreements with existing owners in order to access the farmlands they need in order to produce food (Jacobi & Andersen, 2016, p. 187). Such trends may risk institutionalizing tenure insecurity for an entire generation of new farmers, even as farmland ownership becomes simultaneously more concentrated and more readily repackaged as a financial asset for foreign direct investment (Magnan, 2015; Magnan & Sunley, 2017).

From the perspective of farmers, there are at least two general dynamics linking food and farmland insecurity suggested by the double meaning of "security" as both an antidote to uncertainty and as a financial instrument used in collateralized lending (Besley, 1995; Brasselle, Gaspart & Platteau, 2002). First, insecure land rights are more likely to erode farmers' incentives to invest money, time and effort in practices and infrastructure that contribute to ecologically and economically sustainable land use, especially when these investments entail high up-front costs and yield significant returns only in the long term. Where farmers' precarious tenures make it highly uncertain that they will be able to realize the benefits of sustainable land use in the future, they will be unlikely to allocate their scarce resources to such investments today (Cox, 2011). For example, by comparing soil management practices on leased versus owned farmlands in British Columbia, Fraser (2004) found that farmers who owned their lands were more likely to engage in sustainable practices that required investments with low short-term returns, such as planting perennial crops and forage legumes. Similar results have been observed in studies of land tenure in the United States (Soule, Tegene & Wiebe, 2000) and Europe (Sklenicka et al., 2015). Likewise, insecure tenure has been found to discourage knowledge-based, technological and other investments that would increase the productivity and economic resilience of farmlands (Place, 2009). There is also evidence that insecure farmland tenure may disproportionately impact women (Carter, 2016). Second, when farmers are tenure insecure, their lands are less valuable for use as financial security on loans, thereby limiting the availability, or increasing the cost, of utilizing farm capital to finance new investments (Feder et al., 1990). The uncertainty generated by insecure land tenures can lead potential lenders to perceive either a higher risk of default or an inability to enforce their security, causing significant constraints on agricultural credit markets. Thus, even when farmers have good reasons to make long-term investments in sustainable land uses, insecure land rights may make it impossible for them to access the capital resources needed to put these plans into practice.

The conventional suite of legal and policy responses to farmland tenure insecurity as a cause of food insecurity have, unfortunately, tended mainly to reproduce farmers' precarity rather than offer lasting solutions. One set of strategies has tried to increase farmers' access to private landownership by enacting land use regulations and tax policies to suppress land market values, and by creating new fiscal programs to improve farmland credit flows (Michel, 2014). But either because political commitments to such initiatives are difficult to sustain (Michel, 2014) or because getting private incentives right in these circumstances raises a host of practical and informational challenges (Katchova & Ahearn, 2015), such market-assisted interventions are likely to be limited in their impact. Alternatively, some jurisdictions have experimented with increasing farmers' access to publicly owned farmlands. Throughout the 1970s, for example, the Province of Saskatchewan undertook an ambitious plan to operate Canada's first public land bank through which a provincial agency purchased nearly 1.2 million acres from retiring farmers on the open market and offered to lease these lands back to young farmers with guaranteed leasehold tenure until age 65, and the option to purchase the title after an initial five-year term (Gidluck, 2003). Ultimately, however, few participants in this decade-long experiment made the transition to private ownership, and it seems that the outcome was, at best, to benefit a small cohort of retiree and new entrant farmers in the short term while leaving the majority of new entrants no better off (Gidluck, 2003).

More worrying than the respective limitations of policies that aim to support private and public farmland ownership are the ways in which market-state failures may be emerging as cyclical and collaborative (Mattei, 2014; Friedmann, 2015). This has been the lesson from several development contexts, where state-driven, market-assisted land reforms to address tenure insecurity have improved access to both private and state-held land title, only to see ownership and control flow away from local food producers and into the hands of corporate investors and land market speculators (De Schutter, 2011; Löhr, 2012). Some of these same worries have, more recently, begun to register in the agricultural sectors of industrialized countries as well (Heminthavong & Lavoie, 2015), raising the crucial question of how law and policy might envision new alternatives to address farmers' land insecurity in ways that are not contingent on the connected market and state failures that have exacerbated this insecurity in the past.

Farmland commons

There are thus two dimensions to the problem linking land tenure and food insecurity as I have described them above: one flowing from demographic changes in farmland ownership and control, leading to the threat of new insecure tenure arrangements on the ground, and another arising from the limitations of seeing the market (as private farmland ownership) and the state (as public farmland provision) as the only possible institutional alternatives for addressing that insecurity. Fortunately, recent thinking and practice has started to clear the way for us to envision the "farmland commons" (Rioufol & Wartena, 2015) as a serious alternative to addressing both dimensions of this problem. The remainder of this chapter explores this emerging alternative as a solution to the challenges of tenure insecurity and the limitations of conventional legal and policy responses described above. At the same time, I also try to unpack some of the competing perspectives on the commons that have recently evolved, noting that contemporary movements advocating for commons solutions have started to encounter several points of divergence from within. For some, farmland commons are a "workable property regime" (Huron, 2015, p. 965), a practical alternative to conventional forms of private or public ownership that can be effectively implemented among small groups of individuals for localized governance of agricultural production. For others, farmland commons rise to the level of a social ideal and a social process through which members of the commons – or "commoners" – are called to recapture control over collective resources as the shared inheritance of all citizens derived from historical investments of labor (Linebaugh, 2008). The brief overview and comparison below suggests that farmland commons (i) might best be understood as an evolving and contested set of ideas and practices, but (ii) are nonetheless offering a diversity of practical approaches that usefully illuminate next steps for addressing solutions to food and farmland insecurity.

Defining farmland commons

The term "farmland commons" describes an institutional structure for collective action, i.e., a set of rules, norms and strategies for shared access, use and management of farmland resources. The commons distinguishes itself from private ownership as a regime of *shared* access to farmlands, and from public ownership or control as a *self-governing* system with finite membership, to the exclusion of outsiders (Dagan & Heller, 2001). But within that fairly broad definition, real-world farmland commons can take multiple forms and will more often than not implicate multiple or hybrid forms of property (Cole & Ostrom, 2011). Some farmland commons involve small, decentralized groups of farmers who band together to share access to farmlands, the title to which remains vested in private owners. While research has yet to explore the extent and diversity of these arrangements, the Tamara Ranch Project in Red Deer, Alberta, serves as one illustrative example. Tamara Ranch is a small farmland commons comprised of two independent farm enterprises who rent land jointly as part of a long-term leasehold agreement with the ranch's private landowners (who are themselves retired farmers still living on the land) (Hall, 2016). These two farm enterprises – members of the commons, along with the landowners – are designed to operate symbiotically: one produces pastured beef and other meats, while the other produces vegetables for a Community-Supported Agriculture (CSA) and restaurant supply business. From an agroecological standpoint, the farmers collaborate to rotate pasturing and horticultural production to mutually support and enhance soil quality and other components of the farm ecosystem. Most significantly from a legal standpoint, the members of this commons have used formal contracts to establish a set of rules governing land access, use and management – such as the maximum number of grazing animals, the timing of field rotations, and the upkeep of farm infrastructure (Hall, 2016). As with other kinds of natural resource commons (Ostrom, 2005), this institutional structure identifies the authorized participants in the commons and their roles, the choices available to each participant, the provision and exchange of information, and the benefits and sanctions associated with different actions (e.g., "You break it, you fix it") (Hall, 2016).

We might understand the Tamara Ranch Project as one version of the farmland commons that partially transforms spaces of private ownership into spaces of shared access, use and management among, and to the benefit of, a small, local, decentralized group of individuals. Other commons, by comparison, are broader in scale and scope, and perhaps best described as an alternative to public ownership – one that secures the collective value of farmlands as a shared societal resource outside the conventional mechanisms of the state. A prominent example of this version of the farmland commons is Terre de Liens, a French civic organization established in 2003 to preserve farmland and support land access for a new generation of French farmers (Rioufol & Wartena, 2011). Terre de Liens operates as a direct purchaser of farmlands in private land markets and as a collective landlord to individual farmers who farm its lands under negotiated long-term lease agreements. The organization now owns more than 100 farmland properties across France, has attracted more than 12,000 shareholders and manages millions in investment savings and donations from participants in its different corporate and charitable arms (Terre de Liens, 2016).

Superficially, the Terre de Liens model recalls Saskatchewan's land banking experiment from the 1970s, discussed above, whereby a provincial agency acquired lands for lease to individual farmers. But while Saskatchewan's land bank was centrally controlled and held farmlands in state ownership, the Terre de Liens commons is defined and implemented through the use of two legal entities that mark it as an alternative to the state: a limited-share corporation and a statutory land trust. By putting these conventional corporate and private law forms to creative use, the idea of the farmland commons has been expanded by Terre de Liens to encompass the French citizenry as commoners with concrete legal remedies to enforce their collective interests in managing and maintaining French farmlands over the long term. La Foncière, the investment company of Terre de Liens, extends membership in the farmland commons to each of the company's shareholders, and therefore to any member of the public who can afford or who is willing to pay the roughly 100 euro share price as a form of "solidarity savings" with zero investment return (Rioufol & Wartena, 2011). Each shareholder, in turn, participates directly in collective decision-making about the farmland commons to the extent made possible by the company's charter and the strictures of French corporate law. Likewise, La Fondation, the land trust established by Terre de Liens in 2013, affords formal decision-making control over the farmlands held within the trust to its trustees and the foundation's directors, but vests entitlements to the collective benefits from the trust in its beneficial owners – here, the members of the French public (Rioufol &

Wartena, 2011). As beneficial owners of the trust property, the Terre de Liens commoners have standing to enforce their rights and ensure that farmlands held under the land trust are managed in accordance with the trust's established purposes or objectives. In essence, both the investment company and public trust forms of Terre de Liens provide concurrent avenues for large numbers of dispersed commoners to participate in decision-making about, and control over, the French farmlands that comprise these commons.

In practice, farmland commons thus come in a range of shapes and sizes that combine different forms of land tenure and make use of conventional legal vehicles such as contracts, corporations and trusts to define institutional structures for self-governance. Depending on their form, different farmland commons also tend to understand their scope of membership and their entitlements to individual or collective benefits from the commons in different terms. What links these arrangements together as farmlands commons is that each establishes a means for collective action and collective decision-making directly among members of the group, and therefore provides the basis for an alternative logic to market and state regimes for the governance of farmland resources.

Addressing tenure insecurity

Of course, as structures for collective decision-making, commons raise a host of their own uncertainties and insecurities, not the least of which is the pervasive threat of collective action problems in which the interests and aims of individual commoners diverge from those of the group as a whole (Olson, 1965). Decades of both empirical and theoretical research on longstanding common-pool resource governance regimes in fisheries, forests, pasture lands and irrigation systems has supplied many deep insights into the institutional structure of both successful and unsuccessful commons, yielding lessons for institutional design that address the insecurities that can plague collective decision-making (Ostrom, 1990). We now know that, under the right conditions, groups of resource users can sustainably self-govern, suggesting farmland commons as one feasible response to the interconnected problems of tenure and food insecurity in certain contexts. Against the challenges of precarious short-term or informal leasing arrangements faced by new entrant farmers, commons regimes may provide innovative options for pooling resources when needed to access collective land ownership through private land markets or create longer-term leasehold interests. Such resource pooling, combined with good coordinating institutions, may also provide the basis for constructing farm enterprises at larger and more sustainable "landscape scales" that are better suited to economic diversification and better matched to farmland ecologies (Perfecto, Vandermeer & Wright, 2009; Friedmann, 2015). From the perspective of farmlands as a collection of natural systems (Holden & Ghebru, 2016), farming at such landscape scales may be needed to best coordinate soil, water, forest and other systems. Collective action of this sort also offers new opportunities for risk-spreading among members of the group as a form of insurance against economic and environmental shocks (Dagan & Dagan, 2014). To the extent that farmland commons make secure farmland access more achievable for new entrants, they may also do so in ways that promote social justice and inclusion – depending, of course, on the community's own rules governing both entry/exit and the distribution of benefits and costs from production. Finally, because collective action within a commons will require the explicit definition of rules for decision-making and action, the process of "commoning" may itself improve land tenure security by improving the clarity of participants' respective roles, rights and obligations.

Farmland commons thus present a range of exciting possibilities to address the connected problems of food and tenure insecurity. At the same time, advocates of this solution may also benefit from some of the more cautious lessons to be drawn from the last few decades of research on the commons, especially leading work by Elinor Ostrom and her colleagues at the Workshop in Political Theory and Policy Analysis. Perhaps the most significant of these cautions was Ostrom's firm resistance to the existence of panaceas to social problems and her commitment to the value of institutional diversity adapted to local needs and conditions (Ostrom, 2005). Ostrom was dogged in her assertion that commons regimes always implicate a range of costs as well as benefits, all of which need to be weighed in light of a resource community's socio-ecological setting. A key next step for advocates of farmland commons will therefore be to engage with questions of institutional design, and more specifically to take stock of the legal infrastructures and resources that are needed for commoners to design successful regimes for self-governance. For example, the specific form of a farmland trust that enables Terre de Liens to designate all members of the public as beneficial owners is made possible by French statute, but access to this kind of legal infrastructure will likely require dedicated legal reforms in other jurisdictions (Bailey, 2013). Likewise, the capacity of members of localized commons like the Tamara Ranch Project to draft contractual agreements that are sufficiently tailored to their needs and goals will likely require access to knowledgeable legal advice – itself not an insignificant cost for new farmers with limited resources. A full analysis of these questions surrounding institutional design will no doubt be taken up by future research, but the final portion of this chapter explores briefly how evolving understandings of the commons at the level of a social ideal may help to motivate the legal and political reforms necessary to support and grow farmland commons in the future.

Conclusion: the farmland commons as a social ideal

Ostrom's (2010) rejection of panaceas led her to understand the commons as a means to move beyond strict binary thinking about the range of institutional possibilities available to address social problems – and thus a means to "move beyond markets and states" as the only possible alternatives for resource governance. But this same orientation also led her to carefully avoid claims that the commons was itself better suited than other institutional forms to achieve particular normative goals such as social justice, democratic participation or economic efficiency. A recent line of thinking has emerged to challenge this approach – one that attempts to associate the commons more closely with a set of normative commitments, to reposition the commons as a foundation for transforming economic relations (Harvey, 2011; Bailey, 2013). This latter work makes a radical break with Ostrom's rationalist political economy by attempting to reimagine resources such as climate, water and land as common goods implicating a set of inter-relationships between commoners, rather than a set of market relationships mediated by the state. Such arguments respond more directly to the challenge, described above, that market and state are not merely limited substitutes, but increasingly aligned in ways that continue to reproduce the linked problems of farmland and food insecurity. In other words, these arguments have presented the commons as "not a third way but a challenge to the alliance between private property and the state" (Mattei, 2014, p. 1389/11127). Here, the commons stands apart from relations of hierarchy and commodification "in a world increasingly governed by capitalist economies intermeshed with state regulation" (Huron, 2015, p. 965). This characterization also presents another way to distinguish the two examples of farmland commons described above: Tamara Ranch as a pragmatic, localized solution to the micro-foundations of land access and tenure insecurity, and Terre de Liens as an aspirational and emancipatory social project or social movement in pursuit of broader political aims (Bailey & Mattei, 2013).

Ostrom's critics may ultimately come to recognize that there is less distance between their two approaches than initially thought. Both, for example, have embraced the idea that real-world commons are not static entities but evolving social processes, and both have been closely attentive to the role of trust and communication in successful commons regimes. Ostrom, for her part, became increasingly focused on the dynamics of institutional change (Ostrom & Basurto, 2011), while the historian Peter Linebaugh has written extensively on "commoning" as a social process, observing that "[t]he practice of commoning can provide mutual aid, neighborliness, fellowship, and family with their obligations of trust and expectations of security" (Linebaugh, 2008, p. 59).

Nevertheless, recognizing that the commons is linked to a set of political discourses about the neoliberal state is an important insight, and advocates of commons-based solutions to the linked problems of land tenure and food insecurity should contemplate the kinds of strategic alliances necessary to motivate social, political and legal change in this context. By thinking about farmland commons and farmland commoning as part of a social movement in the register of Terre de Liens, other successful social movements offer themselves as models, such as the recent Italian commons (ben comuni) movement organized to confront the enclosure of that country's water and other natural resources (Bailey & Mattei, 2013). But as the Terre de Liens example also makes clear, even where farmland commons present themselves as an institutional alternative, they remain heavily dependent on the mechanisms of both market and state for their proper functioning – something we might ultimately embrace as both a challenge and a tribute to the creative potential of collective action.

RECIPE: FRESH COLLARD WRAPS WITH QUICK PICKLED ONION AND GREEN TOMATO SALSA

This recipe encapsulates for me the prospect and the promise of the commons. Feeling somewhat disconnected and distracted after two years in law school, I had convinced my family to experiment with a small Community-Supported Agriculture enterprise on our farm a few hours from Toronto. Each week, I was shuttling a new carload of fresh produce into the city, and over time, the inevitable extras became the basis for a weekly dinner party, an easy excuse to cook and eat with friends and neighbors. The humble collard green was the vehicle to incorporate whatever assortment of vegetables was in season that week. Most importantly, this dish can and should be prepared (and of course consumed) in common, as the collective effort of many hands peeling, chopping, stuffing, sampling, holding and folding produce a different but delicious result each time.

Ingredients

1 dozen large collard leaves

For the paste

4 sweet potatoes
2 onions, quartered
4 large carrots, peeled
4 cloves garlic, peeled
1/2 cup tahini
Salt to taste

For the filling

1/2 head red cabbage, thinly sliced
2 red onions, halved and sliced
1 bunch cilantro, roughly chopped
2 cups apple cider vinegar
2 tbsp olive oil

For the salsa

1 lb green tomatoes
1 serrano pepper
1 medium white onion
1/4 cup of cilantro
Pinch of raw sugar
Salt to taste

Directions

1 Preheat the oven to 400° F.
2 Trim the collard leaves and blanch them in a large pot of boiling water for 30 seconds, then submerge immediately in a large bowl of cold water to stop them from over-cooking. Once cool, remove and pat dry.
3 Roast the sweet potatoes, onions, carrots and garlic on a large baking sheet lined with parchment paper for about 1 hour. The sweet potatoes should be fully soft inside, and the other vegetables should be well roasted but not burnt. After they have cooled, peel the sweet potatoes and combine with the other roasted vegetables, tahini and salt in a bowl. Using a potato masher or a hand blender, mix and mash until you have a smooth paste.
4 Heat a dry cast iron skillet on medium high and dry roast the tomatoes, turning until the skins are blackened all over (alternatively, you can do this step in the oven with the other vegetables while they are roasting). Remove the skins from the tomatoes and combine with the other salsa ingredients in a blender. Blend on high until roughly chopped.
5 While the vegetables are roasting, set the red onions in a colander and poor a full kettle of boiling water over them. Submerge the onions in a bowl with the vinegar for about 20 minutes. Combine the onions with the rest of the ingredients and toss with olive oil.
6 Lay a collard leaf open on a flat surface, slather with a few tablespoons of the paste, add a handful of the filling and top with the salsa. Folding one end of the collard leaf up toward center, close the wrap by folding one side over another and fasten with a toothpick.

Critical questions

1 What are the different conceptions of farmland commons identified in this chapter? What are the different objectives and values associated with each of these? Do you think they can be reconciled?
2 Does the type of resource at stake matter for the success or failure of a commons? In what ways are farmlands similar to or different from some other resources like fisheries, air or water in this respect?
3 Some critics have noted that it can be especially difficult for members of a commons to "exit" these regimes in a way that fully respects the rights and obligations of all parties. What challenges might this pose in terms of food security, and how might members of a farmland commons attempt to resolve these challenges?

Acknowledgements

I am grateful to the Social Sciences and Humanities Research Council of Canada for their support for this research. Jimmy Bray and Jenna Khoury-Hanna provided invaluable research assistance for this chapter and the broader research project of which it is a part.

References

Ali, D. A., Deininger, K. & Goldstein, M. (2014) Environmental and gender impacts of land tenure regularization in Africa: Pilot evidence from Rwanda. *Journal of Development Economics*. 110, 262–275.

Bailey, S. (2013) The architecture of commons legal institutions for future generations. In: Bailey, S., Farrell, G., & Mattei, U. (eds.) *Protecting Future Generations Through Commons*. Strasbourg, Council of Europe Publishing, pp. 107–140.

Bailey, S. & Mattei, U. (2013) Social movements as constituent power: The Italian struggle for the commons. *Indiana Journal of Global Legal Studies*. 20 (2), 965–1013.

Baxter, J. (2012) Legal institutions of farmland succession: Implications for sustainable food systems. *Maine Law Review*. 65 (2), 381–408.

Besley, T. (1995) Property rights and investment incentives: Theory and evidence from Ghana. *Journal of Political Economy*. 103 (5), 903–937.

Bigelow, D., Borchers, A. & Hubbs, T. (2016) *U.S. farmland ownership, tenure, and transfer. United States Department of Agriculture*. Economic Information Bulletin Number 161.

Brasselle, A-S., Gaspart, F. & Platteau, J.-P. (2002) Land tenure security and investment incentives: Puzzling evidence from Burkina Faso. *Journal of Development Economics*. 67 (2), 373–418.

Carter, A. (2016) Placeholders and changemakers: Women farmland owners navigating gendered expectations. *Rural Sociology*. doi: 10.1111/ruso.12131.

Cole, D. & Ostrom, E. (2011) The variety of property systems and rights in natural resources. In: Cole, D. & Ostrom, E. (eds.) *Property in Land and Other Resources*. Cambridge, MA, Lincoln Institute of Land Policy, pp. 37–66.

Cox, E. (2011) A lease-based approach to sustainable farming, part II: Farm tenancy trends and the outlook for sustainability on rented land. *Drake Journal of Agricultural Law*. 16, 5–30.

Dagan, H. & Dagan, T. (2014) *Facilitating the commons inside out*. Tel Aviv University Law Faculty Papers. Working Paper 183.

Dagan, H. & Heller, M.A. (2001) The liberal commons. *The Yale Law Journal*. 110 (4), 549–623.

De Schutter, O. (2011) How not to think of land-grabbing: Three critiques of large-scale investments in farmland. *The Journal of Peasant Studies*. 38 (2), 249–279.

Deininger, K. & Jin, S. (2006) Tenure security and land-related investment: Evidence from Ethiopia. *European Economic Review*. 50 (5), 1245–1277.

Feder, G., Lau, L. J., Lin, J.Y. & Luo, X. (1990) The relationship between credit and productivity in Chinese agriculture: A microeconomic model of disequilibrium. *American Journal of Agricultural Economics*. 72 (5), 1151–1157.

Fraser, E. (2004) L and tenure and agricultural management: Soil conservation on rented and owned fields in southwest British Columbia. *Agriculture and Human Values*. 21 (1), 73–79.

Friedmann, H. (2015) Governing land and landscapes: Political ecology of enclosures and commons. *Canadian Food Studies*. 2 (2), 23–31.

Gebremedhin, B. & Swinton, S. M. (2003) Investment in soil conservation in northern Ethiopia: The role of land tenure security and public programs. *Agricultural Economics.* 29 (1), 69–84.

Gidluck, L. (2003) The Saskatchewan land bank: An experiment in land reform, 1971–82. In: Diaz, H., Jaffe, J. & Stirling, R. (eds.) *Farm Communities at the Crossroads: Challenge and Resistance.* Regina, University of Regina Press, pp. 149–164.

Hall, B. (2016) *Running a herdshare on rented land.* [Land Testimonials Webinar Series] 17 February 2016.

Harvey, D. (2011) The future of the commons. *Radical History Review.* 109, 101–107.

Heminthavong, K. & Lavoie, A. (2015) *Farmland grabbing in Canada.* Library of Parliament, Ottawa, Canada. Publication No. 2014-101-E.

Holden, S. & Ghebru, H. (2016) Land tenure reforms, tenure security and food security in poor agrarian economies: Causal linkages and research gaps. *Global Food Security.* 10, 21–28.

Huron, A. (2015) Working with strangers in saturated space: Reclaiming and maintaining the urban commons. *Antipode.* 47 (4), 963–979.

Jacobi, D. & Andersen, C. (2016) Agriculture and the law: Can the legal profession power the next green revolution? *Drake Journal of Agricultural Law.* 21, 177–263.

Katchova, A. & Ahearn, M. (2015) Dynamics of farmland ownership and leasing: Implications for young and beginning farmers. *Applied Economic Perspectives and Policy.* 38 (2), 334–350.

Linebaugh, P. (2008) *The Magna Carta Manifesto: Liberties and Commons for All.* Berkley, University of California Press.

Löhr, D. (2012) The failure of land privatization: On the need for new development policies. In: Bollier, D. & Helfrich, S. (eds.) *The Wealth of the Commons: A World Beyond Market and State.* Amherst, Levellers Press.

Magnan, A. (2015) The financialization of agri-food in Canada and Australia: Corporate farmland and farm ownership in the grains and oilseed sector. *Journal of Rural Studies.* 41, 1–12.

Magnan, A. & Sunley, S. (2017) Farmland investment and financialization in Saskatchewan, 2003–2014: An empirical analysis of farmland transactions. *Journal of Rural Studies.* 49, 92–103.

Mattei, U. (2014) First thoughts for a phenomenology of the commons. In: Bollier, D. & Helfrich, S. (eds.) *The Wealth of the Commons: A World Beyond Market and State.* Amherst, Levellers Press.

Meinzen-Dick, R. & Mwangi, E. (2009) Cutting the web of interests: Pitfalls of formalizing property rights. *Land Use Policy.* 26 (1), 36–43.

Michel, K. (2014) Landless: Legal and policy tools for transferring Vermont farmland to the next generation of stewards and food producers. *Vermont Law Review.* 39, 461–488.

Olson, M. (1965) *The Logic of Collective Action: Public Goods and the Theory of Groups.* Cambridge, Harvard University Press.

Ostrom, E. (1990) *Governing the Commons: The Evolution of Institutions for Collective Action.* Cambridge, Cambridge University Press.

Ostrom, E. (2005) *Understanding Institutional Diversity.* Princeton, Princeton University Press.

Ostrom, E. (2010) Beyond markets and states: Polycentric governance of complex economic systems. *American Economic Review.* 100, 641–672.

Ostrom, E. & Basurto, X. (2011) Crafting analytical tools to study institutional change. *Journal of Institutional Economics.* 7 (3), 317–343.

Perfecto, I., Vandermeer, J. & Wright, A. (2009) *Nature's Matrix: Linking Agriculture, Conservation and Food Sovereignty.* New York, Earthscan.

Place, F. (2009) Land tenure and agricultural productivity in Africa: A comparative analysis of the economics literature and recent policy strategies and reforms. *World Development*. 37 (8), 1326–1336.

Rioufol, V. & Wartena, S. (2011) *Terre de Liens: Removing land from the commodity market, and enabling organic and peasant farmers to settle in good conditions.* Available from: www.access toland.eu/Terre-de-liens-France [Accessed: 20th January 2017].

Rioufol, V. & Wartena, S. (2015) Terre de Liens: Experiencing and managing farmland as commons. In: Bollier, D. & Helfrich, S. (eds.) *Patterns of Communing*. Amherst, Levellers Press.

Sklenicka, P., Molnarova, K., Salek, M., Simova, P., Vlasak, J., Sekac, P. & Janovska, V. (2015) Owner or tenant: Who adopts better soil conservation practices? *Land Use Policy*. 47, 253–261.

Soule, M., Tegene, A. & Wiebe, K. (2000) Land tenure and the adoption of conservation practices. *American Journal of Agricultural Economics*. 82 (4), 993–1005.

Terre de Liens. (2016) *The Foncière*. Available from: www.terredeliens.org/la-fonciere. [Accessed: January 18, 2017].

Trebilcock, M. & Veel, P.-E. (2008) Property rights and development: The contingent case for formalization. *University of Pennsylvania Journal of International Law*. 30, 397.

Wheeler, S., Bjornlund, H., Zuo, A. & Edwards, J. (2012) Handing down the farm? The increasing uncertainty of irrigated farm succession in Australia. *Journal of Rural Studies*. 28 (3), 266–275.

Zagata, L. & Sutherland, L. (2015) Deconstructing the 'young farmer problem in Europe': Towards a research agenda. *Journal of Rural Studies*. 38, 39–51.

PART II

Enhancing participation

6

THE POLITICAL ECONOMY OF CUSTOMARY LAND RIGHTS IN MOZAMBIQUE

Lessons from a food sovereignty movement

Helena Shilomboleni

Introduction: competing interests in land-use rights

How can it be that some countries in Sub-Saharan Africa with the strongest legal provisions recognizing customary-based land rights face significant problems with land grabs and associated negative side-effects? These countries include Mozambique, Tanzania, Ethiopia and Zambia (LandMark, 2016). Their governments have undertaken comprehensive land reform measures to welcome foreign and domestic investors to their agriculture sectors, while at the same time protecting and/or formalizing community land rights. But there are important questions to consider. Should states formalize tenure rights in order to transfer land to the most efficient producers through privatized markets? Can land reform measures protect non-monetized community land use, which in some contexts contributes directly and indirectly to livelihood and food security? How can communities that are most affected by land dispossession be involved in land governance processes in a meaningful way?

These questions are especially pertinent to Mozambique, where the process of allocating land-use rights is increasingly characterized by competing interests. On one hand, the country's land law seeks to guarantee secure and equitable access to land for rural populations who produce a significant proportion of the country's food. On the other hand, the state aims to foster greater economic growth in the agricultural sector by attracting commercial investors. The result is a land-use tension between government policy for economic development and farmers' rights to utilize land for various livelihood purposes. There is a need for more systematic and participatory land governance measures that safeguard peasant land-use rights.

Tensions surrounding land-use rights have increased in parts of Sub-Saharan Africa, especially following the 2007–2008 global food crisis, due to a rise in the demand for land from foreign and domestic investors who wish to grow crops for global markets. The subsequent displacement of populations and loss of livelihoods have prompted an international outcry, compelling global and regional institutions to introduce initiatives that promote responsible investments in land transfers (Collins, 2014). These initiatives include the Principles for Responsible Agricultural Investment developed by the UN Conference on Trade and Development (UNCTAD); the Food and Agriculture Organization of the United Nations (FAO); the International Fund for Agricultural Development (IFAD) and the World Bank; the Voluntary Guidelines on the Responsible Governance of Tenure of Land, Fisheries and Forests developed by the Committee on World Food Security; and the African Union's Land Policy Initiative.

Global and regional land reform initiatives recognize the importance of protecting and formalizing community-based land rights, such as those that exist under traditional tenure systems (United Nations Human Rights: Office of the High Commissioner, 2008; AUC-ECA-AfDB Consortium, 2010; FAO, 2012; Byamugisha, 2013). The end goal of formalizing land rights for some institutions, notably the World Bank and the African Union, is to clarify property rights under a variety of existing tenure systems so that land can be transformed into a commodity that stimulates growth in the agricultural sector ((AUC-ECA-AfDB Consortium), 2010, p. 16). Byamugisha (2013, p. 36) argues that formalizing tenure systems in Africa would improve the "fluidity of land markets" and increase productivity as "land moves from less efficient to more efficient producers through rental and sales markets." The author also supports demarcating community property rights as a way to avoid and effectively manage land-related conflicts.

Extensive empirical evidence from different regions of Sub-Saharan Africa, however, demonstrates that market-based tenure systems result in the transfer of land to the highest bidder, under unequal terms (Paul & Steinbrecher, 2013; UNAC and GRAIN, 2015). For the most part, privatized tenure systems fail to recognize the multiple forms of land use by communities, such as grazing, sourcing forest foods and engaging in cultural practices and rituals. In Mozambique, peasants' legal rights to land use are increasingly violated as the government faces pressure to allocate land to private investors. Over the last ten to fifteen years, authorities have welcomed investors to the agriculture sector as a means of increasing productivity and rural development. But land transfers are happening quickly and at a large scale: in a period of just four years, 2004–2009, official estimates show that 2.7 million hectares were leased to land developers in the country (Cotula, 2013). The process has displaced a large number of peasants, and others face pressure to give up their land occupancy (Matavel, Dolores & Cabanelas, 2011).

Under Mozambique's land law, land is the property of the state, and as such it cannot be sold or mortgaged. However, individuals and communities can occupy or use land based on one of three conditions outlined in the land law (GoM, 1997). Each of the provisions represents a state-granted land right, referred to as a "direito de uso e aproveitamento dos terras" or DUAT. The first is that people can occupy land based on customary norms or practices. This entails settling on land that has been passed down (or inherited) from one generation to the next.

The second condition is occupation based on "good-faith" for a period of at least ten years. This provision addresses an important historical event. Mozambique was affected by a fifteen-year civil war (1977–1992) that created more than three million refugees and internally displaced people (Andersson, 1992). Therefore, the land law offers land-use rights to citizens who ended up in a new part of the country. Customary and good-faith occupancy-based DUATs are recognized automatically, and individuals and communities are not required to register their lands with local authorities.

The final condition upon which individuals can gain land-use rights is through applying for a lease from the state. Such leases are commonly known as investor-based DUATs, and are predominantly reserved for private investors, including foreign companies. Investors seeking to obtain such a lease must also undertake community consultations to identify lands that are not occupied and/or negotiate their use with communities (Hanlon, 2004). If there are no counterclaims, the state can approve the DUAT for up to 50 years, and can renew it once for another 50 years. In the vast majority of cases, however, land deals have not worked in the public's best interest; they are often characterized by corruption and by improper to no community consultations (Cotula, 2013).

An example of such a case is the district of Marracune, Maputo province, located 35 km south of Maputo city in the Incomati river basin. Farmers in Marracune are regularly intimidated by authorities over their land occupancies. During the colonial era, this region was under intensive agriculture, farmed by Portuguese settlers who owned large-scale farms, growing rice and other crops to feed Maputo. At the time of independence in 1975, most Portuguese farmers fled the country. Peasants who were farm laborers on settlers' plantations occupied those lands, forming cooperatives under the new government, led by the Front for the Liberation of Mozambique (FRELIMO) party, whose Marxist-Leninist ideology sought to establish a socialist state (Ottaway, 1988). Under the country's *socialization of the countryside program*, agricultural production was collectivized through a three-tier system, comprised of state farms, communal villages and cooperatives. The purpose of the program was to raise productivity and to implement state-run marketing networks in the agricultural sector (see Ottaway, 1988; Manning, 2002). The state cooperative system, however, was unable to generate sufficient food to meet domestic needs or to export (Hanlon, 1996). The result was perennial trade deficits, which became increasing difficult to finance amidst a civil war that further drained the government of scarce resources (Hanlon, 1996).

While Mozambique's state-run cooperatives were unsuccessful, they generated strong peasant mobilization at the grassroots. In Marracune, some peasants continued to work together, and in 1987, they came together with other peasant associations to form the National Union of Mozambican Peasants (UNAC, 2014). This peasant movement emerged in the era of market-liberalization policies that the country adopted starting in 1987 as a result of the International Monetary Fund's structural adjustment policies (UNAC, 2014). UNAC was established as a national platform to mobilize agricultural resources for rural communities and to advocate for peasants' livelihood interests (Nhampossa, 2009). In 2004, UNAC officially became a food sovereignty movement upon joining La Via Campesina. Today, UNAC is active in the country's ten provinces and in over 50 districts, representing over 100,000 Mozambican peasants.

FIGURE 6.1 Members of an UNAC farmers association water their land in the early morning hours

Photo credit: H. Shilomboleni

In Marracune, over 5,000 UNAC farmers organized into 28 associations belong to its union's branch in the district, the *Uniao de Cooperativas Agrricolas de Marracune* (UCAM) (see Figure 6.1). However, some farmers in this district are under pressure to give up their land occupancy. Members of one UNAC farmers association explain that

> now the government comes here and wants to take away this land – arguing that we do not have legal papers that state that this land is ours. Authorities told us that if we want to keep the land, we must pass through a bureaucratic process to properly claim the land . . . so we feel obligated to go through [such a process] in order to obtain legal papers.
>
> *(male and female study participants, 12 June 2014, Marracune)*

Such legal documentation is technically not required because farmers have occupied the land for over ten years, and thus have achieved their DUAT based on good-faith occupancy. However, many rural populations are unfamiliar with the law and their rights. UNAC and other civil society organizations frequently lobby the government to uphold communities' land rights and to improve the administration of land transfers (Paradza, 2011), but such efforts have seen little success.

Teaching practices to (re)claim land rights

A majority of rural Mozambicans use land to directly produce their food and for various subsistence purposes, such as collecting wild foods (Hanlon, 2004). UNAC's struggle for peasants' land rights, therefore, comes from an understanding that land is central to food security – both at the household and national levels. According to an UNAC staffer:

> We cannot talk about food security in Mozambique when people who live and work the land do not have secure access to it. Peasants conserve our traditional food systems – the place where our national food security will come from – and those at its center cannot be dispossessed of land.
>
> *(male study participant, 26 May 2014, Maputo)*

The looming threat of land dispossessions in Mozambique has prompted UNAC and its member unions to take proactive measures to safeguard community land rights through education and skills training. In Marracune, the movement teaches its farmers about their legal rights to land use and assists them in formalizing their DUATs (by registering their land with the public land registry services). Community awareness of the land law and use of its legal framework offer a solution to slowing down the pace of land transfers and potentially preventing the worst forms of land dispossession.

The land law trainings target the movement's farmers at the association level. This means that farmers learn the information collectively with their peers through a series of workshops. In gaining a comprehensive understanding of the land law, UNAC farmers learn several strategies to help them exercise their land-use rights more effectively. Farmers can a) refuse land deals, b) address internal land conflicts and c) negotiate better terms of engagement, including compensation in land transfers. UNAC activists, however, place greater emphasis on refusing land deals. Although land investors commonly promise attractive compensation packages, employment opportunities and infrastructure projects, the likelihood of such benefits materializing is far from clear (Aabø & Kring, 2012). UNAC has watched helplessly as many of its peasant members in other regions lost their land to large-scale agro-investors, such as in northern Mozambique, where vast areas have been transferred to "a number of foreign companies, some in collaboration with local businesses linked to members of [the country's] ruling FRELIMO party" (UNAC & GRAIN, 2015, p. 5). The land is expected to be used for various purposes, including investments in mining, transportation, resource extraction, and production of export crops (UNAC & GRAIN, 2015).

Those farmers who received training about the land law in Marracune articulated the experience of empowerment that comes with understanding their rights. Members of one association explain that:

> the land law training . . . has helped us so much because every day we are fighting against authorities and people who want to take our land. We have copies of the land law so we are able to invoke the articles that protect us.
>
> *(male and female study participants, 12 June 2014, Marracune)*

UNAC farmers who received the land law training are now well aware that they have legal occupancy of their land and no one is allowed to take it away without adhering to the law. This newly acquired knowledge has given them a voice to engage with authorities and the outside world to (re)claim their rights.

UNAC farmers in Marracune also appreciate the important role that land has for food security. One farmer explains that:

> the land law training has opened our eyes to say no to land dispossession. For example, government officials brought an investor who wanted to take our land in order to plant sugar cane. They told us we would get jobs as farm laborers on the plantations. This is not sustainable – because you are going to go there as a worker and receive MT 3,000.[1] If you have four children, how will you feed them with [that money]? But if you have your own land and grow your food, you can have something to eat and something to sell.
>
> *(female study participant, 23 June 2014, Marracune)*

While the land law training has empowered peasants to push back on land grabs, the process has not stopped authorities from intimidating communities over land claims. This is why UNAC also assists farmers to formalize their DUATs. The technical process of formalizing a DUAT is known as "delimitation" and involves a (verbal) testimony from a community leader about the applicant's customary or good-faith occupancy, and registering that DUAT with the government's land registry services (Norfolk & Tanner, 2007). This step offers further protection from land dispossession, as land that is visible to authorities in government databases is less likely to be targeted for investment purposes. In the event that land under a formalized DUAT becomes the target of investment, the investors are actually forced to negotiate its use with communities (The Oakland Institute, 2011).

Farmers who are well-informed about their land occupancy rights are more likely to be better prepared to engage in discussions with investors and authorities, and to be in a good position to negotiate favorable terms on their land leases, for example, by demanding fair compensation. Thus, land rights training as a participatory action can help improve land governance – by giving marginalized people a real voice and capacity to engage with authorities and the outside world.

There are several important distinctions to make about UNAC's support for formalized land rights. As mentioned earlier, the movement's farmers face pressure from the government to formalize their DUATs. Thus, UNAC's activities are partially a response to such an official mandate. Moreover, considering that the legal system does not protect farmers' land rights against powerful interests, formalizing customary DUATs may be a safeguard that does, and as such might be desirable.

As a food sovereignty movement, UNAC's underlying motive behind formalized tenure systems is also quite distinct from the land reform initiatives of mainstream governance institutions identified above. Institutions like the World Bank seek to "make land a productive and investible resource" (Silva-Castaneda, 2016, p. 688) – by turning it into an equity asset. In contrast, UNAC is concerned with safeguarding land for social reproduction purposes. In Marracune, an UCAM activist explained that the government claims to bring economic development to the area, but forgets about the human rights issue (to land). He argued that authorities do not follow the law – they come and take the land without prior community consultation about investment projects. In the process, peasants are obliged to abandon their way of life, and their traditional linkages to their ancestor's graves, just to satisfy someone's interest. This, in his view, is what actually undermines the life of peasants (male study participant, 17 June 2014, Marracune).

Indeed, the global food sovereignty movement, under the leadership of La Via Campesina, is against land reform policies that privatize land under a neoliberal agenda. This position can be traced back to 1999, when La Via Campesina launched the Global Campaign for Agrarian Reform (GCAR). The purpose was to mobilize a "human rights-based approach" to land, which recognizes its multiple functions and distinction as a "common community resource" instead of a commodity (Borras, 2008, pp. 262–265). While the GCAR campaign has influenced global land reform debates to at least consider the various functions (and meanings) of land, governance institutions still predominately take a privatization approach to land reform, particularly to Sub-Saharan Africa (Borras, 2008). In recent years, La Via Campesina, in response to shifting global land initiatives and debates, has reformulated its strategy to the issue, adopting the concept of *territory* whereby the purpose of land is to "reconstruct and defend community" (Rosset, 2013 in Claeys, 2015, pp. 49–51).

In Marracune and other parts of Mozambique, UNAC's land rights trainings use the tactics of food sovereignty to raise awareness among the movement's farmers about the political importance of land. In particular, trainers help farmers to appreciate the multidimensional functions of land. This emphasis on the different values of land serves to dissuade farmers from ceding their land occupancy to authorities and private investors even when compensation packages are offered – as mentioned, such benefits scarcely materialize. The land law trainings also seek to give value to traditional food systems, because authorities often expropriate land from peasants on the basis that they do not use it efficiently, "in ways that maximize production" (male study participant, 17 June 2014, Marracune). Thus, the movement helps farmers to increase their food productivity, using traditional farming practices as a way to give visibility to their land occupancies.

Limitations and challenges

Some of UNAC strategies to re(claim) community land rights, particularly persuading farmers to refuse land deals, raises some challenges. As mentioned, the land law trainings target the movement's peasant members. Non-members are largely left out, and there has not necessarily been a systematic sharing of information at a broader community level. The impact of not scaling-up land rights trainings to a wider rural population base is that communities' disparate interests in land deals go unresolved, which in some cases can exacerbate internal land conflicts (c.f. Shilomboleni, 2017). In Manica province, Mozambique, UNAC members affected by land grabs take issue with non-member farmers who negotiate land

deals with investors, including ceding communal land, in return for compensation offers (Shilomboleni, 2017). As UNAC members increasingly embrace the
tactic of refusing land deals, they can come in conflict with other community
members who do not necessarily share their position and/or are unfamiliar with
the land law.

UNAC's inability to scale-up land law trainings is due to both resource constraints and contextual difficulties, that is, working in a policy environment that
is unsupportive of politicized land rights activities. The movement operates on a
relatively small budget – about US $3.8 million per annum over a five-year period
(male study participant, 15 April 2015, Maputo), and relies on various development partners for agricultural assistance. Partners include Action Aid International,
the Norwegian People's Aid, the Swedish International Development Cooperation
(SIDA), the Mozambican government, and the Southern African Confederation of
Agricultural Union (SACAU). UNAC's budget is inadequate to assist all its farmers, and as a result, resources are inconsistently distributed (male study participant,
15 April 2015, Maputo). While some development partners, notably Action Aid, are
highly supportive of the movement's land rights issues, others are not, and tend to
earmark their resources for technical assistance. For example, the Ministry of Agriculture's District Service of Economic Activities (SDAE) in Marracune periodically
supports UNAC farmers, as well as other farmers in the district, to gain access to
agricultural inputs, commercial maize seeds and fertilizers at subsidized rates (male
study participant, 4 June 2014, Marracune).

Funding constraints, moreover, hinder UNAC's efforts to adequately support
traditional food systems in order to increase food productivity and to give visibility
to farmers' land occupancies. As a result, UCAM in Marracune tends to assist only
the most organized associations, shown by members' ability to work collaboratively
and to adopt agricultural technologies. An UCAM staffer explains that allocating
scarce resources based on a performance track-record seeks to ensure (and encourage) high-quality outcomes, e.g., in production and in sales (male study participant,
17 June 2014, Marracune). Associations not selected for assistance must cover the
cost of inputs themselves. One association leader summarizes the predicament that
comes with organizational financial constraints:

> farming is difficult here because peasants do not receive sufficient assistance
> from the government. Peasants need inputs as well as equipment such as
> tractors to work the land. They are poor and cannot afford to buy [these] on
> their own. As UCAM, we fight to help them improve their production and
> to diversify their farming activities. However, the movement does not have a
> lot of resources to assist farmers. We rely on donors to help us but we do not
> get enough support from them either.
>
> *(female study participant, 3 June 2014, Marracune)*

Those farmers who are unable to access improved inputs, either through the
union or purchase, express frustration at being unable to expand their crop output

(male study participant, 9 June 2014, Marracune). One farmer articulates that "our goal is to grow food to eat at home as well as to market widely in the country. But for this we need resources – and we are ready to produce" (male study participant, 18 June 2014, Marracune).

Improving land law trainings and participatory land governance

Despite the challenges associated with UNAC's efforts to (re)claim peasant land rights, there are some practical suggestions that the movement can consider to improve its land law trainings. To minimize or prevent internal land conflicts between UNAC members who lean towards refusing land deals and non-members who tend to embrace them, the movement must adopt a more systematic strategy of disseminating land law information to the wider community. A dissemination strategy needs to target the most vulnerable individual farmers – those with productive land that is likely to be sought after by authorities and/or private investors, but who are unfamiliar or have limited knowledge about the land law and their tenure rights. UNAC would have to identify and partner with existing community leaders who can serve as liaisons to disseminate land law trainings to a broader rural population base.

Whereas community leaders do not necessarily have to adopt a tactic of dissuading vulnerable inhabitants to refuse land deals, it is important to equip farmers with knowledge about the legitimacy of their land occupancy rights as enshrined in the national law and international frameworks. Such skills can help farmers to understand that they, too, are important stakeholders in land affairs, and thus can make better-informed decisions in negotiations with authorities and investors should they choose to do so. As land law trainings reach a wider segment of the rural population, the process could steadily catalyze the broad-based political pressure needed to prompt the state to establish greater transparency and equity in land governance over time.

What is important to emphasize in land law trainings as well as in policy discussions on improving land governance is a need to clarify the purpose of formalizing customary-based tenure rights in specific contexts. Rather than transforming land into an equity asset, formalization should serve to protect farmers against powerful interests while maintaining communities' multiple land-use functions. As mentioned, market-based tenure systems in many parts of Sub-Saharan Africa rarely address the livelihood needs of the rural poor, including issues of gender inequality in tenure allocations (Paul & Steinbrecher, 2013; Collins, 2014; Milgroom, 2015). In the context of Mozambique, non-commercialized and protected community-based tenure systems are best poised to mitigate negative effects, such as land conflicts, and enhance potential benefits, e.g., sustainable land-use practices and equity in resource use. UNAC's land law practices in Marracune provide timely lessons for rural communities elsewhere that are similarly struggling against privatization interests in customary-based land-use rights.

RECIPE: MOZAMBICAN COCONUT CHICKEN

My local homestay family in Marracune made this meal frequently. It's really delicious when prepared with fresh coconut and raw peanuts.

Ingredients

2 pounds chicken breasts
2 tablespoons garlic, chopped
1 onion, diced
1/2 cup red/green peppers
2 cups raw peanuts (can be substituted with peanut paste)
2 fresh coconuts (can be substituted with canned coconut milk)
1 tablespoon of cilantro, chopped, to garnish
2 teaspoons of salt

Directions

1   Break the coconuts and blend the flesh in 1–2 cups of hot water; drain and put the coconut milk aside.
2   Blend the raw peanuts in 1–2 cups of hot water; drain and pour the peanut milk together with the coconut milk.
3   Place the coconut and peanut milk in a large pot on medium heat for 20 minutes.
4   In a frying pan, sauté onion and garlic. Season with salt.
5   Add chicken, onion and garlic to the pot; cook for 35 minutes.
6   Add peppers and cook for another 5–10 minutes.
7   Once done, garnish with cilantro and serve with white rice.

Questions to consider

1   In what ways do participatory land governance measures help to improve community land-use rights?
2   How might states reconcile the competing interests present in land reform measures, i.e., between market-based tenure systems and non-monetized community forms of land use?
3   What role can global governance institutions play to ensure greater transparency in transnational land transfers?

Acknowledgements

This chapter is based on the author's PhD field research conducted in Mozambique for a period of seven months in 2014 and 2015. Research in Marracune was carried out in the period of May to June 2014. I would like to thank Jennifer Clapp for her helpful feedback on earlier drafts, and the editors for their helpful suggestions.

Note

1 Mozambique's currency exchange rate was US $1 = MT 32 in 2014 when this field research was conducted.

References

Aabø, E. & Kring, T. (2012) *The political economy of large-scale agricultural land acquisitions: Implications for food security and livelihoods/employment creation in rural Mozambique.* United Nations Development Programme: Regional Bureau for Africa. Working Paper 2012-004: January 2012. Available from: www.undp.org/content/dam/rba/docs/Working%20 Papers/Agriculture%20Rural%20Mozambique.pdf [Accessed: 15th June 2015].

African Union, African Development Bank & United Nations Economic Commission for Africa (AUC-ECA-AfDB Consortium) (2010). *Framework and guidelines on land policy in Africa: A framework to strengthen land rights, enhance productivity and secure livelihoods.* Available from: www.uneca.org/sites/default/files/PublicationFiles/fg_on_land_policy_eng. pdf [Accessed: 3rd August 2015].

Andersson, H. (1992) *Mozambique: A War Against the People.* New York City, St. Martin's Press.

Borras, S. (2008) La Vía Campesina and its global campaign for Agrarian reform. *Journal of Agrarian Change.* 8 (2–3), 258–289.

Byamugisha, F. (2013) *Securing Africa's Land for Shared Prosperity: A Program to Scale Up Reforms and Investments.* Washington DC, World Bank. Available from: http://elibrary.worldbank. org/doi/book/10.1596/978-0-8213-9810-4?queryID=74%2F3925125& [Accessed: 26th May 2015].

Claeys, P. (2015) *Human Rights and the Food Sovereignty Movement: Reclaiming Control.* London, Routledge.

Collins, A. (2014) Governing the global land grab: What role for gender in the voluntary guidelines and the principles for responsible investment? *Globalizations.* 11 (2), 189–203.

Cotula, L. (2013) *The Great African Land Grab? Agricultural Investments and the Global Food System.* London, Zed Books.

Food and Agriculture Organization of the United Nations (FAO) (2012) *Voluntary guidelines on the responsible governance of tenure of land, fisheries and forests in the context of National Food Security.* FAO. Available at: www.fao.org/docrep/016/i2801e/i2801e.pdf [Accessed: 11th June 2015].

Hanlon, J. (1996) *Peace Without Profit: How the IMF Blocks Rebuilding in Mozambique (African Issues).* Oxford, James Curry.

Hanlon, J. (2004) Renewed land debate and the 'cargo cult' in Mozambique. *Journal of Southern African Studies.* 30 (3), 603–625.

LandMark. (2016) *Global platform of indigenous and community lands.* Available from: www. landmarkmap.org/map/#x=-15.98&y=8.66&l=3 [Accessed: 25th July 2016].

Manning, C. (2002) *The Politics of Peace in Mozambique: Post-Conflict Democratization, 1992–2000.* Westport, Praeger Publishers.

Matavel, N., Dolores, S. & Cabanelas, V. (2011) *Lords of the land – preliminary analysis of the phenomenon of land grabbing in Mozambique.* Justiça Ambiental & União Nacional de Camponeses (UNAC). Available from: http://landwise.resourceequity.org/record/2192 [Accessed: 11th June 2015].

Milgroom, J. (2015) Policy processes of a land grab: At the interface of politics 'in the air' and politics 'on the ground' in Massingir, Mozambique. *The Journal of Peasant Studies*. 42 (3–4), 585–606.

Mozambique (Government of) (GoM) (1997). Decree No. 19/1997. Approved by the Council of Ministers on 1 October 1997.

Nhampossa, D. (16 January 2009). Organizing food sovereignty in Mozambique. *Motion Magazine*. Available from: www.inmotionmagazine.com/global/d_nhampossa_int.html [Accessed: 10th July 2015].

Norfolk, S. & Tanner, C. (2007) *Improving tenure security for the rural poor: Mozambique – country case study*. Food and Agriculture Organization of the United Nations (FAO). LEP Working Paper #5 (Workshop for Sub-Saharan Africa). Available from: www.fao.org/3/eeb28104-4b4f-55a9-988f-487ad3afe2ac/k0786e00.pdf [Accessed: 3rd June 2015].

The Oakland Institute (2011) *Understanding land investment deals in Africa – country report: Mozambique*. Available from: www.oaklandinstitute.org/sites/oaklandinstitute.org/files/OI_country_report_mozambique_0.pdf [Accessed: 14th June 2015].

Ottaway, M. (1988) Mozambique: From symbolic socialism to symbolic reform. *Journal of Modern African Studies*. 26 (2), 211–226.

Paradza, G. (2011) *Mozambique land grabs expose hypocrisy of large scale land transfers to private investors*. Available from: www.plaas.org.za/blog/mozambique-land-grabs-expose-hypocrisy-large-scale-land-transfers-private-investors#sthash.eTlXIJno.dpuf [Accessed: 8th June 2015]

Paul, H. & Steinbrecher, R. (2013) *African agricultural growth corridors and the new alliance for food security and nutrition: Who benefits, who loses?* EcoNexus. Available from: www.econexus.info/sites/econexus/files/African_Agricultural_Growth_Corridors_&_New_Alliance_-_EcoNexus_June_2013.pdf [Accessed: 14th January 2016].

Rosset, P. (2013) Re-thinking Agrarian reform, land and territory in La Via Campesina. *Journal of Peasant Studies*. 40 (4), 721–775.

Shilomboleni, H. (2017) *The African green revolution and the food sovereignty movement: Contributions to food security and sustainability: A case-study of Mozambique*. PhD thesis, University of Waterloo.

Silva-Castaneda, L. (2016) In the shadow of benchmarks: Normative and ontological ussues in the governance of land. *Environment and Planning A*. 48 (4), 681–698.

União Nacional de Camponeses (UNAC) (2014) *Who we are: Aims, mission and members*. Available from: www.unac.org.mz/english/index.php/2014-11-05-15-16-45/our-aims [Accessed: 16th May 2015].

União Nacional de Camponeses (UNAC) and GRAIN (2015) *The land grabbers of the Nacala corridor: A new era of struggle against colonial plantations in Northern Mozambique*. Available from: www.grain.org/article/entries/5137-the-land-grabbers-of-the-nacala-corridor.pdf. [Accessed: 16th May 2015].

United Nations Human Rights: Office of the High Commissioner (2008) *United Nations Declaration on the Rights of Indigenous Peoples (UNDRIP)*. Available from: www.ohchr.org/EN/Issues/IPeoples/Pages/Declaration.aspx [Accessed: 15th July 2015].

7

SMALL-SCALE AQUACULTURE IN THE BOLIVIAN AMAZON

A contextually-based solution for positive social and economic outcomes

Tiffanie Rainville, Sean Irwin, Verónica R. Hinojosa Sardán, Cintya Castellón Antezana, and Widen Abastoflor Sauma

Introduction

Every morning, Doña Victoria leaves her house, in rural Bolivia's Amazon region, and walks to a large pond 200 m away to feed 2,000 small fish who eagerly come to the surface. This is one of the many tasks she and her family fit into their day, though it forms part of a relatively new livelihood activity undertaken to complement or replace a vulnerable rice agriculture practice which had left her family impoverished eight years ago.

Bolivia, one of two landlocked countries in South America, is characterized by six regions, including the tropical lowlands of the Parana and Amazon basins. In the lower Amazon region, where much of the tropical aquaculture is taking place, agriculture is the backbone of the local economy and small-scale farming is the primary economic activity for over half of all households (INE, 2012). Farms tend to be small, between 30 and 50 hectares, and often include widespread livestock farming as a secondary livelihood activity. Crop prices, especially for rice, have become increasingly volatile and often depressed over the past 20 years, and this has also increased vulnerability for farmers. The problem has been further compounded by climate change and environmental degradation, both of which increase crop yield volatility, and thus erode income. Farmers have therefore become increasingly interested in livelihood diversification or change. Despite widespread land ownership and agricultural livelihoods, many households are food insecure, with access to food and poor nutritional quality being the leading problems. Poverty has been on the decline in the aquaculture production region, but two-thirds of people still live below the national poverty line (INE, 2012). A challenge has been to identify agricultural activities that fit within the existing resource base of the region, the skill-sets of farmers, and current livelihood portfolios.

Although tropical aquaculture has been promoted nationally as an economic development activity since the 1980s, it has lagged behind neighboring countries due to a lack of technical and organizational support, fluctuating access to inputs (feed and fingerlings), and an under-developed domestic market. This chapter discusses how family-based aquaculture can be a timely development "solution" to Bolivia's prevalent rural poverty, food insecurity, and gender inequality by responding to some of the previous bottlenecks which have inhibited its development. We delve into the details of a case, supported by a local non-governmental organization (NGO) and international project to further describe the process and how this success story has influenced gender, livelihoods, and food security, including through spin-off activities. We then describe how navigating the national and local context within Bolivia has been (and continues to be) critical to the development and implementation of aquaculture activities. Finally, this chapter outlines some of the contextually-derived challenges that remain, and the opportunities that have yet to be fully explored in Bolivia and in development projects in general.

Understanding the Bolivian context

Bolivia is a country of wealth and poverty, both in terms of people and resources. Its history is rooted in colonialism, exploitation, and inequality, and this has bred a social and political pattern of conflict and unrest. In recent years, many grievances have been tempered by the arrival of an indigenous-led socialist government that claims to put social welfare on par with economic development. However, while the country has undergone many noteworthy changes, considerable inequality remains. This has complicated efforts at development, particularly for the poor in rural areas.

Bolivia is ecologically diverse, mostly tropical, and has a large endowment of natural resources. These factors can be problematic for growth and development in developing countries (Gallup, Gaviria & Lora, 2003). Bolivia's resources have complicated its development by attracting colonialists, initially, and foreign and domestic economic elites subsequently, all of whom sought enrichment at the expense of natural resources and the indigenous peoples. This "resource curse" plagued the country for centuries and undermined broader social development (Auty, 1994). The colonialism it provoked generated massive inequality that falls along a complex mixture of ethnic, geographical, and economic lines (Van Cott, 2000).

Bolivia has a higher percentage of Indigenous People than any other country in the Americas. Throughout history, they have been regularly exploited and oppressed. During the years of Spanish colonialism, many were pressed into slavery working in the silver mines that fed the Spanish crown. After independence in 1825, land tenure became quasi feudal under the minority white ruling elite, and Indigenous People were coerced into deplorable working conditions on plantations or forced to toil on remote marginal lands (Klein, 1982). It wasn't until the 1950s and the Bolivian National Revolution that universal suffrage was introduced, and rural Indigenous peasants began to receive political attention. Indigenous identity and empowerment began to grow but developed slowly, complicated by marginalization and conflict and/or racism between different Indigenous communities, which continues to this day. The rocky relations have complicated economic and social development and poverty reduction, particularly in rural areas, by creating friction in policy formation, projects, and programs that must, by nature, involve various groups (Pila, 2014). Nonetheless, the election of the country's first Indigenous president in 2006 led to significant reconciliation between groups, and served as a watershed moment for indigenous identity, rights, and empowerment.

The combination of cultural friction, social problems, and competing visions of development have presented many challenges to development practitioners in Bolivia, especially around a livelihood activity such as aquaculture. However, within the fabric of Bolivian society, there currently exists several opportunities. Political and governmental stability has increased thanks to the new socially-oriented indigenous-led government, which has led to a marked decline in civil strife and upheaval. The country has enjoyed one of the highest growth rates in the world over the past decade, and has made notable strides towards poverty reduction, food security, and overall social development (World Bank, 2016). Small but meaningful steps have been made towards reorienting resource revenues towards generating social benefits. This combination of social and economic progress has done much to support development work, trickling down into the local contexts where agriculture, and now aquaculture, take place.

Aquaculture development in Bolivia

Globally, fish is extremely important. It contributes to over 10% of global livelihoods through fish value chains and is an important source of protein and nutrition, especially for people in the developing world (Bené et al., 2015). Aquaculture is currently the fastest-growing food sector globally and made up nearly half of total fish production (44.1% of total production, including for non-food uses, from capture fisheries and aquaculture in 2014 (FAO, 2016)). Bolivia has over 700 identified species of freshwater fish, though wild stocks are declining due to pollution and overfishing. This makes aquaculture a highly promising alternative, though the growth of the aquaculture sector in Bolivia has been very slow until quite recently.

Bolivia has one of the lowest per-capita rates of fish consumption in the world, largely due to being landlocked but also due to the development of a diet that favours poultry and beef. However, demand is on the rise. In a recent market study, the demand for fish in Bolivia's four main cities and in the core aquaculture producing region was 1,505 tonnes per year, nearly 300 tonnes higher than current supply in the same regions, demonstrating a growing interest in its consumption (QUATRIM S.R.L. & IMG S.R.L., 2016). In fact, recently, in an effort to capture developmental benefits associated with aquaculture, the government began providing logistical and financial support for aquaculture producers, and is focused on increasing national fish consumption from approximately 3.5 kg of fish per person per year to 5.2 kg over the next few years.

In 2008, the NGO "Center for the Promotion of Peasant Agriculture" (CEPAC) began to tackle the prevalent problems of rural poverty, food insecurity, and gender inequality by searching for a new livelihood strategy that would address vulnerability to market fluctuation and environmental stressors affecting the large population of small-scale rice farmers in the Southern Amazonian region of Central Bolivia. The idea of fish farming partially emerged from a study on Territorial Development in Yapacaní, which showed that 25% of rural rice-farming families had high vulnerability, and 65% had intermediate vulnerability to climate extremes (flooding and droughts) and market fluctuations (Carazas et al., 2006). Many families had high debt loads due to dependency on rice production, and women were increasingly pushed out of participating in the manual labour due to the incorporation of new technologies, such as tractors, which were predominantly driven and managed by men. Using a participatory approach, and analyzing the socioeconomic and environmental factors prevalent in the region, they – both farmers and CEPAC – found fish farming to be a promising livelihood diversification solution.

CEPAC's focus was on "Productive Family Units", which were generally small-scale family farms where women could hold leadership roles. To achieve this model, CEPAC supported the creation of a women-led aquaculture association named Association of Producers of the Integrated North of Yapacaní (APNI); this model emphasized livelihood diversification, sustainability, and gender equality – three strategies that aim to increase the social and economic benefits of aquaculture while minimizing context-specific risk and vulnerability.

Fifteen families from APNI began to diversify their livelihoods to incorporate farming of the native Amazonian fish pacú (*Colossoma macropomum*) and tambaqui (*Piaractus brachypomus*), or their hybrids, in ponds located near their rural homes. These fish are predominantly herbivorous, thus requiring only low-cost soy-based feed. They are fast growing, resistant to water temperature fluctuations, and can survive in low-oxygen conditions. Their ponds require only minimal maintenance and are excavated mostly on soils unsuitable for other agricultural activities. Ponds are typically filled with rainwater, which lessens the impact on nearby rivers and watersheds. It is estimated that the 450 ponds in the region generate an extra mosquito-free water surface of 90 hectares (as the fish eat mosquito larvae), diversifying habitat and making it both a socially and environmentally beneficial activity.

In 2012, the work was recognized by the *Peces Para La Vida* (PPV or Amazon Fish for Food) project partners as a positive solution and "success story" in Bolivian aquaculture, leading to the incorporation of CEPAC and APNI's work as a core component and partner of the three-year follow-up PPV project in 2015, funded by the government of Canada. The PPVII project's objective has been to utilize the aquaculture solutions to scale-up aquaculture production and benefits in the Bolivian Amazon and to increase fish consumption nationally. The CEPAC approach prioritizes small-scale farmers, and particularly women-led initiatives, so that access and control of benefits are more equitably distributed.

The work of CEPAC and the PPV projects (I and II), and the development of small-scale aquaculture, has not been without its challenges and complexities;

the unique cultural and social conditions in the country and in the target region have required a nuanced and creative approach. Outcomes thus far have included poverty reduction amongst aquaculture value-chain actors, improvements in gender equality, and increased food security for producers and consumers, though manoeuvring political instability continues to be a challenge. CEPAC and APNI's holistic approach to the development sector focused on engaging not only with producers, but also with other actors along the value chain, which helped ensure that actions had net benefits, and that market outlets for new fish products existed.

The local context

For people in Yapacaní, a municipality of 52,587 inhabitants (INE, 2014) in the Southern Amazonian region of Bolivia where APNI producers reside, poverty, food insecurity, gender inequality, and social unrest are common problems. Indigenous Peoples collectively called Chanes initially inhabited the region. However, during the 1940s to 1960s, many people from the Andean region migrated to the area in search of land, and they now constitute the majority (PDM, 2003). Their presence has been a contributing factor to inter-Indigenous and inter-cultural racial tension that has been present in the region for decades. This continues even though many of the former Andeans have broken their ties with their communities of origin; although some of the older generation speak their traditional language of *Quechua*, 95% speak Spanish as their first language.

These agricultural families produce crops such as rice, soybeans, bananas, corn, beans, citrus, and cassava, and farm livestock (dairy, beef, pork, and poultry). Their diversified livelihood activities also include hunting wild animals (the main game species are the painted agouti, tropero pig, collared peccary, and tapir), and fishing (chad, surubí, and wild pacú), though these resources are becoming scarce due to indiscriminate extraction. Aquaculture has been adopted relatively easily as an additional or replacement livelihood activity which complements their current mixed activities, and fits into the lifestyle and livelihood activities of men and women, and their families.

Gender equality for productive family units

Not only has Bolivia struggled with civil tension and unrest rooted in economic inequality and race, but it has also struggled with the marginalization of women. Women are important actors in development as they tend to re-invest new time and income into productive activities such as child care and education, and improved household diets (FAO, 2011). Bolivian women, unfortunately, face a number of barriers to greater social and economic prominence. A culture of *Machismo*, a stereotype that emphasizes hyper-masculinity of the Latin American male along with aggression, strength, physical power, and sexual exploitation, is present (Ingoldsby, 1991; Hardin, 2002). With it comes a history of female servitude, and the country has one of the highest rates of domestic abuse towards women in Latin America (Bott et al., 2013).

Traditionally, *campesina* and Indigenous women seldom participated in positions of decision-making and leadership within their organizations, and were often not official members, which inhibited their ability to access capacity-building opportunities, and financial services. This, along with low control over natural and productive resources and laws which inhibited women's property rights, created a continuous cycle of disempowerment and gender-based limitations. Women in Yapacaní tend to still be a marginalized group. Though they make significant contributions to agricultural activities, they are also frequently tasked with cooking for working men, caring for children, and maintaining the household. This heavy workload – in productive, reproductive, and community realms – is a critical contribution to well-functioning, small-scale family farms and households, yet tends to be undervalued and under-appreciated. This regional, and often national, situation perpetuates gender-based marginalization and vulnerability.

The socioeconomic model developed in Yapacaní not only focuses on the family as productive units ("Productive Family Unit") but also embraces a gender-equality lens, which, although not the only factor contributing to success, has shown significant positive impacts for women and their families. In the past, attempts at aquaculture development by government and international NGOs included subsidies meant to kick-start aquaculture, such as free pond construction, free production inputs, and/or construction of community ponds. The subsidization approach (in some cases to encourage alternative production away from the coca leaf; see USAID, 2007) generally failed to produce sustainable adoption of aquaculture. Currently this form of development continues, but is now typically carried out by local and regional governments, who are meant to be more in tune with local wants and needs. The CEPAC and PPVII model seeks to complement these efforts by incorporating a focus on individual investment in and ownership of ponds (including access to new, innovative financial mechanisms, such as leasing and loans), business training and market development, specialized technical assistance, and facilitating links with input providers. This has been a key piece in the development puzzle, recognizing the successes and tendencies towards Productive Family Units as opposed to the more communal ownership previously seen, while also addressing gender equality head-on through female entrepreneurship support.

Although hesitant initially, women increasingly gravitated to aquaculture because of the opportunities it afforded them to maintain their traditional household responsibilities while also making them key contributors to household income. Aquaculture has provided an opportunity for women to adapt to climatic and social changes, address their vulnerabilities (for example, from rice culture), by taking on more active leadership in family income generation, and building resilience to a changing environment. Fish culture was a relatively easy social transition, fitting into a familiar social context of animal rearing and presence in the home. This extension of women's domestic tasks integrates with childrearing and household chores (Brugere et al., 2001). This is similar to regions in Asia, where aquaculture can be socially accepted because it is not labor- or time-intensive, and ponds are typically located in proximity to households, making it fit well with women's traditional household responsibilities (Kelkar, 2001). Incorporating aquaculture has also allowed families to continue previously established livelihood activities.

Recently, a study in the pilot region of the PPV project demonstrated that women are predominantly responsible for fish feeding and processing, though entire families often participate collectively in the remaining production tasks. Women's leadership roles in fish production has resulted in less suffering (in terms of decreasing challenging field conditions), more family time, and improved household welfare, all of which has contributed significantly to women's empowerment and gender equality in the region. As one female producer puts it:

> Life is much easier now. We no longer suffer working under the hot sun, fighting bugs and being away from home. Now with aquaculture my children are close by and help feed the fish, and my husband works with me.
>
> *(female producer, 31 January 2013, Yapacaní, Bolivia)*

Increasingly, male partners have joined in the work, though access and control over income has remained in the hands of women or in partnership. One of the most important factors has been the recognition of women's productive role, changing the stereotype of women as "helpers" in agriculture to one in which they are "leaders" in economic initiatives. Many women have become notable aquaculture entrepreneurs and producers; the importance of this cannot be understated. Recently, during a peer-to-peer training course led by APNI women, they stated to current and potential funders "we don't only want to be great fish farmers, we also want to be businesswomen!" (female producer – APNI, 8 December 2016, Cascabel, Bolivia).

The CEPAC model is strongly rooted in improving one's capacity for self-determination (as in Moser, 1993) and an ability to make strategic life choices, aspects which are key to women's empowerment (Kabeer, 1999). Greater family income, control over this income, and decision-making power over the pond is evident. As one person said, "I wanted to contribute, to be able to have money for our family. Now, I can buy clothes for my children, put them in better schools, and make sure they eat well" (female producer – APNI, 20 March 2013, Yapacaní, Bolivia). In APNI households, for example, 94% of female producers participate in household decision-making, and between 24% to 63% of household decisions are now made exclusively by women (PPV, 2014; OXFAM, 2015).

Recently, though, women have experienced empowerment and seen improvements in their role in society, especially at the political level. In fact, Bolivia now has the second highest rate of female legislative representation in the world, and gender equality has been enshrined into the country's constitution (Constitute Project, 2009). At a local level, this translates to participation in municipal councils and local associations, such as APNI. One female farmer describes the situation before aquaculture:

> The woman used to be always relegated, in the background. They didn't participate in meetings, or those that did gave the name of their husbands [as members]. Women participated secondarily, not as people, the women didn't speak out. Now our situation has changed a tonne.
>
> *(female producer and technical staff, 31 January 2013)*

The changes in gender gaps within APNI are demonstrated in Figure 7.1, including levels of female and male participation in the organization and board of directors, their roles within the organization, and their access and control over the organization's resources and in management. The spider chart demonstrates a comparison between men and women from an APNI association after approximately eight years, since the beginning of fish farming, where initially female participation would have been very low. Evidently, in APNI there has been a much stronger development of female leadership, and this has been reflected in organizational

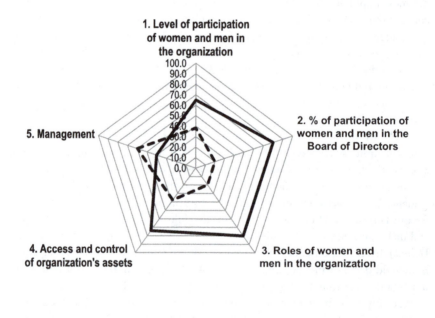

FIGURE 7.1   Gender gaps in APNI organization (2016)

Source: CEPAC-PPVII (2016)

strength, as APNI is now a reference and leader in the region and able to access additional funding – for example, to create a side business, ACUAPEZ, for fish feed production.

The benefits of spin-offs through nutrition and employment

The emergence of aquaculture in the region has also contributed to empowerment of rural indigenous peoples. Most farmers are descendants from Indigenous Peoples 73% of households in Yapacaní currently identify as *Quechua* (CEPAC-PPVII, 2016), many of whom were oppressed by the country's economic elite. As noted above, the history of colonialism runs deep in the area, but holding power over economic activities is one way in which indigenous peoples are becoming increasingly empowered and overthrowing their marginalization. As an inclusive livelihood activity that is forming new linkages between actors in the value chain, aquaculture is also contributing to inter-Indigenous cooperation.

Aquaculture has generated significant multiplier effects as well. Producing families hire workers during harvest periods, who receive a wage and retain fish products that they can incorporate into their own households' diets (for example, leftover fish fat). Restaurants serving the locally-produced fish have turned the barbecued fish into a local specialty food, popular with visitors and locals alike. Restaurants in the region currently have a demand of 61 tonnes/year (QUATRIM S.R.L & IMG S.R.L., 2016). These businesses generate employment for cooks, servers, and cleaners, and engender a culture of entrepreneurship. Input businesses have grown in tandem with aquaculture production, and they, too, have become sources of employment in the region. These results are similar to findings from recent studies that show that employment, spin-off industries, and cheap fish protein help achieve poverty reduction and food security benefits (Allison, 2011). The involvement of rural women in aquaculture can contribute to improving family nutrition and household income (as in Seila, Kwasek & Tsatsaros, 2016). Female farmers commented that fish farming "gives to the pot", meaning "aquaculture provides food" for the family sustenance. In Asia, similarly, households reported using a fish pond like a "refrigerator" as an alternative to fishing (Seila, Kwasek & Tsatsaros, 2016).

Fish is a critical food source; it contains high-quality protein in addition to essential fatty acids and micronutrients, and is a particularly valuable food for nutritionally vulnerable people throughout the world (Bené et al., 2016; HLPE, 2014). Unfortunately, fish has received little attention in food security and nutrition strategies thus far (HLPE, 2014). Fish farming in Yapacaní has directly influenced producer food security by increasing home consumption from 3.8 kg/year in 2008 to 6.6 kg/year in 2014 (PPV, 2014). The availability of fish in the region has resulted in the creation of over 10 new fish-based restaurants, thus elevating consumption in the municipality to 5.4 kg/person/year (QUATRIM S.R.L. & IMG S.R.L., 2016). Family-based aquaculture, and access to fish, is thus aiding in the fight against micronutrient deficiencies, chronic malnutrition, and overall food insecurity in the region.

Aquaculture production has also led to more indirect food security benefits through increased income to purchase other foods. From the $3,000 USD gained annually from traditional livelihood strategies (2007), incorporating fish farming has added an additional $6,000 USD per pond of income for APNI families. The farmers average 4.7 ponds each, and have an average gross income of $10,610 USD/year (CEPAC-PPVII, 2016; Colque & Hinojosa, 2016). For 54% of fish farming families in APNI, aquaculture is now their main source of income.

Fish farming, as a socially and environmentally sustainable initiative, has a key role to play for Bolivia in terms of adapting to a changing environment and building resilience. Considerable climatic changes, such as variability in seasonal rain, drought, and flooding, have created greater challenges for traditional agricultural activities, whereas aquaculture ponds tend to be less vulnerable to these seasonal changes. Interestingly, farmers have also noticed the creation of micro-climates due to the concentration of several bodies of water in a previously drought-prone area.

Aquaculture, when properly adapted to local contexts, has shown to be effective at generating sustainable rural livelihoods and poverty reduction (Edwards, 2000; Brummett, Lazard & Moehl, 2008; Little et al., 2012). The solution presented here was devised and based on experiences of CEPAC and PPV in Yapacaní, and an appreciation for the history, opportunities, and challenges that were present in Bolivia. The context and development knowledge was a critical key to success.

Context and development

The focus of international development has evolved significantly over the past 50 years. Once narrowly concerned with macroeconomic growth, it is now far more nuanced and complex (Ascher et al., 2016). Widespread failure of "one size fits all" development approaches to reduce poverty and improve well-being has led researchers to explore questions of how development projects and policies could do better (see, for example, Chambers & Conway, 1992 or Sen, 1999). Invariably, the successes and failures in these projects were attributable to elements of the context in which they were operating. The diversity of peoples, cultures, environments, economies, and social conditions played critical roles in mediating development efforts. By the late 20th century, it was widely acknowledged that understanding national and local contexts, and incorporating this understanding into solutions, was indeed necessary for success (Crossley, 2010; UNDP, 2012).

However, incorporating contextual factors into development work, or spending enough time understanding the context, is no easy task, and remains one of the leading challenges for development practitioners. The dynamic and complex nature of the interaction between society, culture, the economy, and the environment is often not only challenging to understand, but additionally makes it difficult for development interventions to generate equitable socioeconomic improvements. Context reveals both opportunities and challenges, and effectively navigating these is often what lies at the core of successful development solutions. Learning from the successes of others, in terms of their process in utilizing and implementing place-specific contextual factors, is one of the most effective ways to improve our contextual navigation skills.

Conclusion

The initial 15 families which began in APNI and shifted to aquaculture production has now grown to more than 200 families in the region (157% growth since 2008), with 376 ponds producing approximately 450 tonnes of fish per year (43–54% of national production) (Colque & Hinojosa, 2016). Although challenges remain, important achievements have been made in terms of diversifying livelihoods to include aquaculture, and improving economic and social benefits. The adoption of new technologies and best practices in this new activity is slow, and there is a growing need to focus on creating and improving markets. These market and technology solutions must first consider the local and national realities, with their many nuances and complexities, as they aim to address increases in production and demand, and to find adequate solutions to current issues in this budding livelihood activity. Care must be taken to continue working with men and women on gender equality aspects, so that access and control over resources doesn't shift away from women. Though neighboring countries offer many lessons learned from their advanced fish farming, these lessons must first be adapted and adjusted in a participatory exercise with farmers, and key actors in the value chain, in order to increase rates of acceptance and use. The PPVII project is working with the producers of this "solution" to scale-up this successful experience to other geographic regions. This experience is contributing to the international body of knowledge that is looking at whether and how small-scale enterprises are more effective than medium-scale enterprises at addressing poverty reduction and food security.

RECIPE: BOLIVIAN PACÚ FROM YAPACANÍ

FIGURE 7.2   Serving suggestion

Photo credit: L. Cordova

Ingredients

1 kilo of fresh pacú, recently harvested, gutted, and scaled (scales removed)
2 fresh lemon-oranges, or lemons
1 teaspoon of salt or sea salt (or to taste)
Charcoal or gas for barbecue

Directions

1   Clean the recently harvested, gutted, and scaled pacú fish.
2   Cut in half, lengthwise, to create a butterfly cut. Place both pieces flesh-side up.
3   Squeeze the juice from the lemon-oranges and pour over fish flesh.
4   Sprinkle the salt on each piece of fish.
5   Place on hot barbecue for 10 minutes, meat-side down.
6   Flip to skin-side down for 3 minutes.
7   Serve with rice, yucca, and salad.

Questions

1   How do traditional gender roles influence the adoption of aquaculture as a livelihood?
2   What social barriers may inhibit the adoption of a new livelihood strategy?
3   How does cultural context influence how new livelihood strategies or technologies are taken up or scaled-up?

Acknowledgements

This work was carried out with the aid of a grant from Canada's International Development Research Centre (IDRC), www.idrc.ca, and with financial support from the Government of Canada, provided through Global Affairs Canada (GAC), www.international.gc.ca, through the Canadian International Food Security Research Fund (CIFSRF). The authors would also like to acknowledge Ayuda en Acción for their support in the beginning phases of aquaculture development. Finally, we thank APNI producers for being so open and genuine in our work together and the PPVII team.

References

Allison, E. H. (2011) Working Paper 2011-65. Penang, Malaysia, The WorldFish Center. 60 pp. Available from: http://pubs.iclarm.net/resource_centre/WF_2971.pdf [Accessed: 2nd November 2015].
Ascher, W., Brewer, G. D., Cheema, G. S. & Heffron, J. M. (2016) *The Evolution of Development Thinking: Governance, Economics, Assistance, and Security*. New York, Palgrave Macmillan.

Auty, R. (1994) The resource curse thesis: Minerals in Bolivian development 1970–90. *Singapore Journal of Tropical Geography*. 15 (2), 95–111.

Bené, C., Arthur, R., Norbury, H., Allison, E. H., Beveridge, M., Bush, S., Campling, L., Leschen, W., Little, D., Squires, D. & Thilsted, S. H. (2016) Contribution of fisheries and aquaculture to food security and poverty reduction: Assessing the current evidence. *World Development*. 79, 177–196.

Bené, C., Barange, M., Subasinghe, R., Pinstrup-Andersen, P., Merino, G., Hemre, G-I. & Williams, M. (2015) Feeding 9 billion by 2050 – Putting fish back on the menu. *Food Security*. 7 (2), 261–274.

Bott, S., Guedes, A., Goodwin, M. & Mendoza, J. (2013) *Violence against women in Latin America and the Caribbean: A comparative analysis of population-based data from 12 countries*. The Pan American Health Organization.

Brugere, C., Felsing, M., Kusakabe, K. & Kelkar, G. (2001) *Women in aquaculture*. Asia Pacific Economic Cooperation Project, FWG 03/99.

Brummett, R., Lazard, J. & Moehl, J. (2008) African aquaculture: Realizing the potential. *Food Policy*. 33 (5), 371–385.

Carazas, D., Saldaña, J. C., Hinojosa, V. R. & Valverde, J. (2006) *Estudio de medios de vida, Área de Desarrollo Territorial Yapacaní*. Santa Cruz, Bolivia, Centro de Promoción Agropecuaria Campesina (CEPAC) y Ayuda en Acción. 107 pp.

CEPAC-PPVII. (2016) *Baseline study for producer and non-producer families in Yapacaní, Entre Rios, Ivirgarzama, San Juan and San Carlos Municipalities, Bolivia*. IDRC, GAF, Canada.

Chambers, R. & Conway, G. (1992) *Sustainable rural livelihoods: Practical concepts for the 21st century*. Institute for Development Studies. IDS Discussion Paper 296.

Colque, P. & Hinojosa, V. R. (2016) *Actor map for Productive Chain in 5 municipalities from Peces para la Vida Project*.

Constitute Project. (2009) *Bolivia (plurinational state of)'s constitution of 2009*. Available from: www.constituteproject.org/constitution/Bolivia_2009?lang=en [Accessed: 5th March 2017].

Crossley, M. (2010) Context matters in educational research and international development: Learning from the small states experience. *Prospects*. 40 (4), 421–429.

Edwards, P. (2000) Aquaculture, poverty impacts and livelihoods. *Natural Resource Perspectives*. 56, 1–4. Available from: http://dlc.dlib.indiana.edu/dlc/bitstream/handle/10535/3704/56-aquaculture-poverty-impacts-livelihoods.pdf?sequence=1&isAllowed=y [Accessed: 10th November 2016].

Food and Agriculture Organization (FAO). (2011) *The state of food and agriculture 2010–11: Women in agriculture closing the gender gap for development*. Available from: www.fao.org/docrep/013/i2050e/i2050e.pdf [Accessed: 10th November 2016].

Food and Agriculture Organization (FAO). (2016) *The state of world fisheries and aquaculture 2016. Contributing to food security and nutrition for all*. Available from: www.fao.org/3/a-i5555e.pdf [Accessed: 11th December 2016].

Gallup, J., Gaviria, A. & Lora, E. (2003) *Is geography destiny? Evidence from Latin America*. Palo Alto, CA, Stanford University Press.

Hardin, M. (2002) Altering masculinities: The Spanish conquest and the evolution of the Latin American Machismo. *International Journal of Sexuality and Gender Studies*. 7 (1), 1–22.

High Level Panel of Experts on Food Security and Nutrition (HLPE). (2014) *Sustainable fisheries and aquaculture for food security and nutrition: A report by the high level panel of experts on food security and nutrition*. Committee on World Food Security.

Ingoldsby, B. (1991) The Latin American family: Familism vs. machismo. *Journal of Comparative Family Studies*. 22 (1), 57–62.

Instituto Nacional de Estadística de Bolivia (INE). (2012) *Censo de Poblacion y Vivienda 2012.* Available from: http://censosbolivia.ine.gob.bo

Instituto Nacional de Estadísticos (INE). (2014) *Annual statistics Bolivia.* Available from: www. ine.gob.bo/indice/visualizador.aspx?ah=PC20103.HTM [Accessed: 1st November 2015].

Kabeer, N. (1999) Resources, agency, achievements: Reflections on the measurement of women's empowerment. *Development and Change.* 30 (3): 435–464. Available from: doi: 10.1111/1467-7660.00125 [Accessed: 1st November 2015].

Kelkar, G. (2001) Gender concerns in aquaculture: women's roles and capabilities. In: Kusukabe, K. & Kelkar, G. (eds.) *Gender Concerns in Aquaculture in Southeast Asia.* Bangkok, Asian Institute of Technology, pp. 1–10.

Klein, H. (1982) *Bolivia: The Evolution of a Multi-Ethnic Society.* Oxford, Oxford University Press.

Little, D. C., Barman, B. K., Belton, B., Beverdige, M. C., Bush, S. J., Dabaddie, L., Demaine, H., Edwards, P., Haque, M. M., Kibria, G., Morales, E., Murray, F. J., Leschen, W. A., Nandeescha, M. C. & Sukadi, F. (2012) Alleviating poverty through aquaculture: progress, opportunities and improvements. In: Subasinghe, R. P., Arthur, J. R., Bartley, D. M., De Silva, S. S., Halwart, M., Hishamunda, N., Mohan, C.V. & Sorgeloos, P. (eds.) *Farming the waters for people and food: Proceedings of the Global Conference on Aquaculture 2010, 22–25 September 2010, Phuket, Thailand.* FAO, Rome and NACA, Bangkok, pp. 719–783.

Moser, C. O. N. (1993) *Gender, planning and development: Theory, practice and training.* London and New York: Routledge.

OXFAM. (2015) *Baseline for Proyecto ECV "Empresa ACUAPEZ."* Santa Cruz, Bolivia.

PDM. (2003) *Municipal development plan 2003–2007 for Yapacaní municipality.* Santa Cruz, Yapacaní, Ichilo.

Peces para la Vida (PPV) (2014) *Appendix, Final report.* Report No. 6.

Pila, E. (2014) "We don't lie and cheat like the *Collas* do." Highland lowland regionalist tensions and indigenous identity politics in Amazonian Bolivia. *Critique of Anthropology.* 34 (4), 429–449.

QUATRIM S.R.L. & IMG S.R.L. (2016) *Baseline report on fish market and consumption in Bolivia.* Peces para la Vida Project. IDRC, GAC. Bolivia, p. 129.

Seila, C., Kwasek, K. & Tsatsaros, J. (2016) The role of gender in the development and adoption of small-acale aquaculture: Case study from Northeast Cambodia. Gender in aquaculture and fisheries: The long journey to equality. *Asian Fisheries Science Special Issue.* 29S, 111–126.

Sen, A. (1999) *Development as freedom.* New York, Oxford University Press.

UNDP. (2012) *Institutional and Context Analysis Guidance Note. United Nations Development Programme.* New York, UNDP.

USAID. (2007) *Informative bulleting from the Embassy of the United States of America.* Bolivia, La Paz.

Van Cott, D. (2000) *The friendly liquidation of the past: The politics of diversity in Latin America.* Pittsburg, U Pittsburg Press.

World Bank. (2016) *The World Bank data: Bolivia.* Available from: http://data.worldbank.org/ country/bolivia [Accessed: 1st December 2016].

8

BUILDING 'A WORLD WHERE MANY WORLDS FIT'

Indigenous autonomy, mutual aid, and an (anti-capitalist) moral economy of the (rebel) peasant

Levi Gahman

Introduction: prelude to a rebellion

> *Another world is not only possible, she is on her way.*
> *On a quiet day, I can hear her breathing.*
>
> – Arundhati Roy-

> *And it is clear that in the colonial countries the peasants alone are revolutionary, for they*
> *have nothing to lose and everything to gain.*
>
> – Frantz Fanon-

We need not turn any further than the words of Arundhati Roy (2003) and Frantz Fanon (1963) to gain insight into what most threatens life and dignity on this planet, as well as where the ground is most fertile for decolonization and transformative change. Whether it be mutually recognizing the inherent worth of others, decentralizing governance, fostering communities of care, co-creating cultures from below, engaging in emancipatory violence, or effecting food justice, both Roy (2003) and Fanon (1963) rightfully suggest that we just might have something to learn from rural Indigenous peasants in identifying what lies at the roots of structural social problems, as well as how to intelligently confront and solve them. One of the greatest threats the world currently faces, particularly regarding food security, is neoliberalism. The logic of neoliberalism, which has become status quo over the past half-century and valorizes global 'free market' capitalism, is made manifest through economic policies that facilitate privatization, deregulation, economic liberalization, and reductions in social spending (Mohanty, 2013). In addition to strings-attached contracts and socially fragmenting agendas that are part and parcel to its purported 'open border' trade agreements, neoliberalism is also a discourse that promotes entrepreneurialism (defining one's identity/existence on capitalism's terms), individualism (placing oneself ahead of the community/collective whole), and self-capitalization (structuring relationships around potentials for earning profit, accumulating wealth, and acquiring social status) (Springer, Birch & Macleavy, 2016). Despite rarely being criticized or even mentioned by state officials and mainstream media, neoliberal programs, practices, and rhetorics continue to give rise to unprecedented levels of poverty, anxiety, and anguish.

The consequences of neoliberalism are so acutely visceral that the Zapatistas (predominantly Indigenous Ch'ol, Tseltal, Tsotsil, Tojolobal, Mam, and Zoque rebels in Chiapas, Mexico) called the 21st century's most highly touted free trade policy, the North American Free Trade Agreement (NAFTA), a 'death certificate' for Indigenous people (Marcos & de Leon, 2002). This is because, under the agreement, imported surplus commodities (largely subsidized corn from the U.S.) would flood Mexican markets and devalue the food products of the country's rural *campesinos* (agrarian peasants). The socio-spatial fallout from the 'agricultural dumping' (exporting commodities to other countries at prices below those of the domestic products in recipient markets in order to eliminate local competition) that ensued displaced millions of working class/poor food producers from their homes in the Mexican countryside. Rapid urbanization followed as dispossessed farmers sought employment in *maquiladoras* (industrial factories where working conditions are often highly exploitative and dangerous) that were growing in number due to increases in foreign direct investment and the presence of multi-national corporations (Jordaan, 2012; Matsushita et al., 2015). Other Mexican growers rendered precarious by NAFTA were forced to try to cross borders to scratch out livings in family-fracturing temporary worker programs (e.g. Canada's Seasonal Agricultural Worker Program [SAWP]), or risk peril, border agent hostility, police aggression, indeterminate detention, incarceration, and dehydration/hypothermia in the Sonoran Desert by trekking to the United States as undocumented workers (Walia, 2010).

Free-market agricultural dumping exposes Indigenous people in Mexico to more intense degrees of vulnerability than others in Mexico, largely because they are typically less socio-economically and geographically mobile since: 1) they experience higher rates of systemic oppression, racist exclusion, and classist discrimination within the country (i.e. they are less likely to be hired for the degrading work that is available in urban sweatshops); and 2) they are less likely to leave their ancestral territories given that their kinship ties, origin stories, and living histories are situated within the geographies where they reside. In light of these realities, the Zapatistas responded to the impossible circumstances that had been levied against them 'with fire and blood' (EZLN, 2012). While the ratification of NAFTA appeared to be the direct cause of their uprising, the roots of their rebellion actually stem from over 500 years of colonial persecution and capitalist exploitation (see Table 8.1). Their revolt in 1994 was thus only one part of a historical (and ongoing) response to the unjust subjugation Indigenous people have faced as a result of

TABLE 8.1 Abbreviated timeline of events that led to the Zapatista Uprising

- 1492: Widespread European imperialism and the colonization of the Americas begins with the arrival of Christopher Columbus in the Caribbean.

- 1519–1521: Colonizers, under the command of the Spanish Crown, direct the dispossession, enslavement, and execution of Maya communities throughout the Yucatan region.

- 1528: Spanish colonizers arrive in Chiapas to seize territory and establish the *encomienda* system, private plantation-like land holdings whose owners demand "tribute" (coerced theft of peasant resources and goods) from enslaved Indigenous people. The city of *Villa Real de Chiapa* (now San Cristobal de las Casas) is founded so that Indigenous populations can be monitored, disciplined, and controlled.

- 1528: Indigenous Maya revolt against land theft, colonial occupation, and dehumanization. The Spanish occupiers respond with military force.

- 1712: The Tzeltal Revolt of 1712 in Cancuc (Chiapas) occurs and is brutally repressed.

- 1821: The Mexican War of Independence ends Spanish rule.

- 1847: The Caste War of Yucatán begins as Maya people confront colonial hierarchies of race and class. After half a century, the Mexican Government eventually gains control.

- 1867: Indigenous rebellion in Chamula, a Tzotzil stronghold in the Chiapas Highlands, ensues due to colonially imposed taxes, market control, and lack of religious freedom.

- 1910: The Mexican Revolution begins. Emiliano Zapata leads the Liberation Army of the South under the rallying cry: *Tierra Y Libertad* ("Land and Freedom").

- 1917: The Mexican Constitution is drafted. Article 27 sets out provisions calling for land reform and the distribution of *ejidos* (communally held lands).

- 1919: April 10. Emiliano Zapata is assassinated.

- 1920s–1980s: The land reforms set by the constitution runs idle and languishes. Indigenous communities continue to be displaced and forced into de facto indentured servitude.

- 1979: Indigenous communities in Chiapas amplify their calls for independence.

- 1982: The state of Chiapas, with support from the federal government, cracks down on Indigenous resistance. The imprisonment, forced disappearance, and murder of Indigenous organizers ensues. Military and security forces anchor themselves in rural Chiapas to surveil and intimidate.

- 1983: The EZLN is formed in Chiapas and begins to clandestinely mobilize.

- 1992: Article 27 of the constitution is modified to promote the privatization of land, ending the government's commitment to land reform and the distribution of *ejidos*.

- 1993: Zapatista Women's Revolutionary Law is announced.

- 1994: January 1. NAFTA takes effect. The Zapatista Uprising occurs. The EZLN declares war on the Mexican Government and global capitalism, thereby publicizing its struggle "For Humanity, Against Neoliberalism."

*Sourced from the Zapatista Rebel Autonomous Spanish and Maya Languages Center (CELMRAZ), Mexico Solidarity Network, Schools for Chiapas, Bats'il K'op, and personal interviews.

accumulation by dispossession, cultural ignorance, state repression, and, at that given moment, neoliberal incursions that were further privatizing once communally held lands (*ejidos*).

A brief genealogy of the EZLN

> *We, the Zapatistas of the EZLN, rose up in arms in January of 1994 because we saw how widespread had become the evil wrought by the powerful who only humiliated us, stole from us, imprisoned us, and killed us – and no one was saying anything or doing anything.*
>
> (EZLN, 2005)

The emergence of the Zapatista Army of National Liberation (EZLN) in its contemporary form dates back to November 17, 1983, when six university-educated militants (three *mestizo* and three Indigenous, including one woman) journeyed into the Lacandon Jungle of Chiapas (Mexico's most impoverished state) to establish a guerrilla vanguard. Upon arriving, their efforts – which were being supported by an intricate network of sympathizers with links to Marxist radicals, Catholic liberation theologists, and grassroots socialists – were subsequently transformed by the Indigenous communities they encountered (Marcos, 2005). What ensued thenceforth was over a decade of rural clandestine organizing, reciprocal learning, and community discernment.

Once prepared, upon the dawn of New Year's Day 1994 (the day NAFTA was ratified), insurgents from the EZLN threw down the gauntlet against capitalism. Under the cover of mask and fog, armed Zapatistas stormed out of the shadows to declare '*¡Ya Basta!*' (Enough!) to the violence that had been historically imposed upon them. During the insurrection, the EZLN laid siege to six cities, occupied government buildings, freed political prisoners, burned fabricated arrest records that criminalized Indigenous dissenters, announced Zapatista 'Women's Revolutionary Law,' expelled *hacienda*-owning field overseers, and exchanged bullets with the Mexican army (Ramírez, Carlsen & Arias, 2008). The fighting lasted for a total of only 12 days, after which a ceasefire was negotiated.

Since that time, and despite an ongoing counter-insurgency being spearheaded by the Mexican Government and paramilitaries it finances, the Zapatistas have concentrated their efforts on establishing a peaceful existence that centers their Indigenous notion(s) of *sts'ikel vokol*. The polysemic term *sts'ikel vokol* (from Tsotsil, a Mayan language) roughly translates to 'resistance,' but when explained means 'withstanding suffering,' or more precisely, withstanding the suffering generated by the repressive products of capitalist social relations, state power, colonial hierarchies, racist and misogynistic mentalities, and xenophobia, to name a few. Broadly speaking, then, the Zapatista solution to the problems of alienation and dehumanization, exacerbated constituents of neoliberalism, has been autonomously constructing what they refer to as '*Un Mundo Donde Quepan Muchos Mundos*' ('a world where many worlds fit'). It is with a focus on the Zapatista creation of such a world that I address some of the key pillars of their resistance.

Building 'a world where many worlds fit'

Collective work, food sovereignty, and a moral economy

> *We agreed that if it wasn't possible to do it in this world, then we would make another world, a bigger, better one where all the possible worlds fit, for the ones that already exist, and the ones that we haven't yet imagined.*
>
> (EZLN, 2016b)

Imagination and critical thought are fundamental aspects of everyday life and daily work in Zapatista territory, meaning that neither envisioning new social relations, nor fostering political consciousness, function solely in the abstract. That is, the intellectual labor that goes into questioning the status quo, discussing ideas, seeking solutions, and learning new things is recognized as a necessary and material component of their struggle against exploitation, repression, and domination. Each are recognized as active, applied, and practical exercises of crafting a world/reality that mends the wounds (i.e. inequalities) inflicted by neoliberalism, as well as promotes a mutual recognition of dignity amongst people.

Part of building a 'world for many worlds' in the face of the 'capitalist hydra' (one of the metaphors the EZLN uses to describe neoliberalism) thus entails identifying threats to such an endeavor. The Zapatistas know their enemies, and they do not pull punches with them. They refer to the government of Mexico (i.e. consolidated power and the hierarchal state) as '*el mal goberino*' ('the bad/evil government'), and their analysis of capitalism is as follows:

> Because it not just in one place or in one way that capitalism oppresses. It oppresses you if you're a woman. It oppresses you if you're a white-collar worker. It oppresses if you're a blue-collar worker. It oppresses if you're a *campesino* (peasant). It oppresses if you if you're a young person. It oppresses you if you are a child. It oppresses you if you're a teacher. It oppresses you if you're a student. It oppresses you if you're an artist. It oppresses you if you think. It oppresses you if you are human, or plant, or water, or earth, or air, or animal.
>
> *(EZLN, 2015)*

An education promoter in Zapatista territory elaborated upon this critique to me by underscoring the links that free-market economics, the financialization of everyday life, and neoliberal social relations have with each other in the following statement:

> Ideas and work that produce profit for corporations and capitalists are elevated over those that contribute to community health and the overall well-being of our people, of all people . . . we are not going to live and work on these terms.
>
> *(Education promoter, 28 July 2016, Chiapas)*

Indeed, the Zapatistas took up arms against such terms, choosing instead to focus on Indigenous worldviews and the fruits of anti-capitalist collective labor over the ephemeral ego-boosts of individualism and fleeting comforts of consumerism. Not coincidentally, solidarity and mutual aid now pervade their communities, day-to-day exchanges, and social interactions. This is especially true regarding their production and distribution of food – a marked effort in food sovereignty that takes myriad forms. Some of these include seed saving, collectivizing harvests, refusing to use chemical products, maintaining Indigenous cultural ties with land and water, equitably distributing/sharing work, and even incorporating the tending of *milpas* (small fields of fertile land used in subsistence farming) into their autonomous education system.

Accordingly, food sovereignty for the Zapatistas, particularly when coupled with their perspectives on capitalism, means rejecting personal entitlements to wealth accumulation, eschewing state-legitimated notions of private property, and severing themselves from dependency upon corporate agro-business (Bobrow-Strain, 2007). More simply, it means that reciprocated respect, selflessness, and teamwork drive the Zapatista economy, rather than the exploitation, alienation, and advantage-taking of capitalist economies. In light of these descriptions, one might ask what this looks like in practice. In addressing this, the same Zapatista education promoter summed up their economy by noting that it is 'decentralized,' one in which 'everyone participates,' and is generated and modified by community assemblies through basic questions like 'Is everyone okay?' 'Is anyone going hungry?' 'Is the community healthy?' and 'Is the soil nourished?' to name a few. These were contrasted with the queries of 'How can I gain an advantage over others?' and 'What can I do to get more?' which were identified as fetishes and fixations that capitalists fret about. The economy constructed by the Zapatistas is thus one that works for the people, rather than vice versa. It foregrounds ethics, empathy, and the collective well-being, which was made clear for me when the education promoter finished by stating:

> We are not preoccupied with self-interest, individual gain, or power like those 'from above.' Our economy, or whatever you want to call it, asserts the value of life. It recognizes the dignity in each, no matter how *otroa* ('other,' meaning different) they might be.
>
> *(Education promoter, 17 March 2014, Chiapas)*

In material terms, the Zapatista food system provides an opportunity for labor to abandon capitalist markets and profit motives in order to position collective work and Indigenous notions of land/water/nature as essential in maintaining the cultural, spiritual, and environmental welfare of their bases of support (Lorenzano, 1998). This has come to fruition through their recuperation of colonially expropriated lands, which they reclaimed from wealthy *hacienda* owners during their 1994 uprising (Barmeyer, 2003). One way in which these sentiments take root and are made tangible is through the skills in organic agroecology the Zapatistas employ in moving towards food sovereignty. I experienced this at a rural community garden in a highland cloud forest of Chiapas where dozens of Zapatistas from the countryside – donning mud-splattered shoes and rubber boots while wielding worn, steel-headed hoes and tenured machetes – gathered in an open area surrounded by steep, rolling hills and low-hanging fog to plant vegetables. In fielding my many queries, an agro-ecology promoter explained:

> Collective work like this did not exist when the landowners were in control. We were servants. We were beaten, scolded, and alone. There was much suffering. Now we organize to grow and share vegetables. That is why we are all here (working together at the community garden): adults, children, and elders. Everyone can contribute something. Everyone has value.
>
> *(Agro-ecology promoter, 9 April 2014, Chiapas)*

Further illustrating this dynamic, a Zapatista *compa* (woman) later noted:

> We were not in control of our food, which meant they (landowning capitalists and the 'bad' government) were controlling us. Now, we have our own projects. We started to plant and sow and work the land collectively, *like before* [emphasis added]. You can see the results. We are planting beans and corn together, and eating radishes, cabbages, carrots, and cilantro. It is our work and we are happy. This is autonomy. You can see it in our garden.
>
> *(Compa, 15 August 2013, Chiapas)*

Due to their refusal to become complicit with entrepreneurial capitalism, the commodification of nature, and the privatization of land, the Zapatistas have built a sustainable food system that functions as a moral economy and renews their Indigenous practices – one that takes into consideration the health of both individuals and communities, as well as local ecologies, and one they are breathing life into with each new seed they sow.

Autonomous (place-based) education

> *To be Zapatista does not mean to hide one's face, but rather, to show one's heart.*
> (EZLN, 2016a)

Because tending to crops, children, food production/distribution, collective self-determination, and a life of rebellion are inherently learning experiences, the Zapatistas have constructed an independent education system that emerges from the bioregional assemblages, socio-political/historical contexts, and cultural-environmental settings they exist in. This is evident in the emplaced 'from below' focus they take in their approach to teaching and learning, as well as how they consider everyday life and their ecological surroundings a 'classroom.' Local knowledge of land and food systems are so central in their communities that the vast majority of the *promotores de educación* (education promoters) and *promotores de agro-ecología* (agro-ecology promoters) in each school often come from the same communities as their students.

The Zapatistas refer to teachers as 'education promoters,' as opposed to state-sanctioned 'experts,' to unsettle the rigid boundaries between 'those who know, and those who do not know.' This means children are not seen as static, empty vessels that need to be filled with information, but rather, are active agents of creativity, imagination, and knowledge in-and-of themselves, who are capable of learning and sharing knowledge with the community, as well as pursuing their own interests. The role of the education promoters is to share experience, provide context and information, offer guidance and direction, and foster a non-punitive environment as children follow their curiosities and ask questions. This awareness of the nuances of power in matters of taken-for-granted language, labels, and learning allows them to disrupt any individualistic claims to knowledge production that could potentially fragment their non-hierarchical system of education. It is also a step towards undermining the notion that knowledge can be privatized (mirroring their viewpoints on land and food), and subverting the vertical relationships that arise from the regimes of credentialization, 'excellence,' and award cultures that now govern many state institutions and corporate entities. These lessons are not only integrated into Zapatista schools, but also the food system, making for a more holistic learning experience in which critiques of power are ever-present and embedded in the daily routines of life.

To further effectively incorporate the practical application of knowledge in their curriculum, Zapatista students are frequently educated outside the classroom. This is so they can sharpen their planting and harvesting skills through the use of organic, sustainable, and agro-ecological farming techniques, as well as learn Indigenous and revolutionary history while being with the land. Consequently, 'going to school' for Zapatista children consists of engaging their bioregional and historical surroundings, and may very well involve gardening, tilling, composting, feeding animals, and performing a skit about the life of Emiliano Zapata – all activities that nurture both the fertility of their local soils, as well as their rebel spirits. Moreover, the Zapatistas have made the decision to eliminate the use of genetically modified organisms, chemical insecticides, herbicides, and pesticides in favor of utilizing biological deterrents and organic fertilizers (Vergara-Camus, 2007). This area of education stresses the importance of attaining the necessary applied skills to achieve food sovereignty for future generations, meaning their agro-ecological and education programs coincide with efforts they make in sustaining and revitalizing Indigenous knowledges (e.g. traditional ecological knowledge, companion planting, communal work, the celebration of Maya customs, etc.).

Land-based activities of this kind also end up providing children an incisive overview of how transgenic modifications and privatizations of seeds/plants/life are deemed to be overt threats to, and blatant attacks upon, their Indigenous ontologies because the Zapatistas are 'People of the Corn', a reality passed down from their Maya origin stories (Ross, 2006). Given their education system is independent from the state, and because it is rooted in defending, protecting, and preserving local Indigenous traditions, languages, and ancestral lands, the Zapatistas effectively practice decolonization in every aspect of their education, economy, and food system. What the Zapatistas reveal through their advances in sustainable farming and food sovereignty is that Indigenous autonomy, place-based education, and a moral economy can flourish outside of the neoliberal policies and corporate agro-industrial complexes that currently dominate the global food system. Consequently, what they have created is a world where anti-capitalist education and Indigenous worldviews not only fit, but thrive.

Women's Revolutionary Law and gender equity

> *. . . it was with the arrival of private property that men began to command.*
> (Guadelupe, Zapatista Education Promoter, ELZN, 2013, p. 8)

One of the most groundbreaking aspects of the Zapatista Insurgency has been the advances it has made in destabilizing patriarchal social relations, as well as exposing their links to the logics of capitalism and controlling land. In explaining how 'women's work' (i.e. household chores, child-rearing, domestic labor, etc.) became devalued because it is typically neither attached to a wage, nor thought to directly increase revenue streams, a Zapatista *compa* (woman)/education promoter states: 'The capitalists and "bad/evil government" ("*el mal gobierno*") had us believing the idea that women are not valuable, not capable – that women are not worth as much' (pers. comm., 21 April 2014). This dismissal of efforts that sustain communities/societies (i.e. socially reproductive work), tasks typically performed by women, was untenable for the Zapatista women . . . so they decided to organize against it. Hence, in 1993, just a few months before the word of the EZLN thundered across the globe, Indigenous women from the communities raised their voices and implemented what is known as 'Women's Revolutionary Law.'

Broadly speaking, Women's Revolutionary Law concretizes a woman's right to self-determination, bodily autonomy, and reproductive agency. More specifically, the laws mandate that women hold key positions in the guerrilla army (i.e. the EZLN), are equitably represented in the *Juntas de Buen Gobierno* ('Councils of Good Government'), take part in land recuperation (agro-ecological projects/work outside of domestic labor), are freely able to enter/exit relationships, can choose when and how many children they will have, can speak out/seek justice against domestic abuse, and have the freedom to develop their own alternative-economic cooperatives (Klein, 2015). The laws have subsequently reconstructed the quotidian rhythms of Zapatista communities, as it is now not uncommon to see women involved in all aspects of community life, in addition to seeing men participate in socially reproductive labor ('women's work'). Effectively, the Zapatista women have revived a world where women can exist without having to face condescension and shame simply because they are women.

Notably, when the revolutionary laws were being announced, many of the men were reluctant to accept and abide by them, but because resistance advances '*juntos y a la par*' ('together and side by side') in Zapatista territory, men eventually did consent to adopting Women's Revolutionary Law. This is due to a common recognition amongst Zapatistas that any struggle against colonialism and capitalism is also a struggle against patriarchy. Even given this progress, the Zapatistas remain humble in their reporting about the revolutionary laws, as there is admittedly 'still much work to do' with respect to equality and women's participation. Nevertheless, the steadfast determination of the Zapatista women often carries the day. And the tenacity they have regarding their own rights, which are acknowledged as contributing to the good of their communities, is reflected in a communiqué Subcomandante Marcos (now Galeano) released shortly after the 1994 uprising, in which he states: 'The first EZLN uprising occurred in March of 1993 and was led by the Zapatista women. There were no casualties – And they won' (Marcos, 1993, p. 1). This social transformation, while often written about in abstract and figurative terms, has largely been born out of the collective work and indefatigable iron will of the Zapatista women (Ramírez, Carlsen & Arias, 2008). It is also not without sacrifice and complexity.

Part of Women's Revolutionary Law includes the collective agreement to refrain from using alcohol and drugs. This major commitment was made not out of sanctimonious conceit or moral superiority, but because alcohol has historically been used as a weapon of colonization. It also has the tendency to, as one education promoter notes, 'put people to "sleep" or lead to abuse' (pers. comm., (7 March 2014). Since its inception, the decision to abstain from alcohol has resulted in less gender-based violence, less emotional abuse, less debt to landowners, and an overall improvement in the health and security of Zapatista communities, individuals, and even land. Because the Zapatistas also view their Indigenous culture as being evolving and fluid, they recognize that jettisoning the patriarchal social relations that intensified during colonialism, and are being exacerbated by global capitalism, do not in any way diminish their indigeneity. This dynamic outlook has even seen the Zapatistas queer their discourse, as for several years now they have been releasing communiqués in which they blend the masculine and feminine spellings of Spanish pronouns (e.g. *otroas* – 'others', *humanoas* – 'humans', *todoas* – 'everyone', *muchoas* – 'many', etc.) so as to be inclusive of everyone along differing gender and sexuality continuums (i.e. men, women, transgender people, queer folks, etc.). Their efforts in constructing 'a world where many worlds fits' thus applies to a wide array of people, and a plurality of varying social axes of identification.

Furthermore, Women's Revolutionary Law has merged with the way in which land and the local environment are viewed and tended to. As a result of upending rigid masculinist notions of what type of work women 'should do' and 'could not do', as well as obliterating regressive ideas that men are less capable of performing socially reproductive work and emotional labor, Zapatista communities now have women exercising greater decision-making power in developments pertaining to food cultivation and regional agro-ecology projects (Marcos, 2014). In attesting to the new reality the Zapatistas are constructing, Peter Rosset, a food sovereignty specialist with extensive experience in southern Mexico, indicates the impact of Women's Revolutionary Law by stating:

> Yesterday a Zapatista agro-ecology promoter was in my office and he was talking about how the young Indigenous women in Zapatista territory are different from before . . . he said they no longer look at the floor when you talk to them – they look you directly in the eye.
>
> *(Rosset, 2014)*

In moving towards gender equity, the Zapatistas have rapidly turned hundreds of years of gender-based oppression on its head in a span of just over three decades (Klein, 2015). Their convictions regarding the struggle of women is perhaps best captured in a quote often seen throughout their territories, which states: *Cuando Una Mujer Avanza, No Hay Hombre Que Retrocede* ('When a Woman Advances, No Man is Left Behind'). This conviction has seen Indigenous women in Zapatista communities transition from being one of the most marginalized, subjugated, and disregarded groups in the world – to becoming a beacon of what it means to engender compassionate resilience, dignified rage, and unyielding resolve.

Conclusion

> *Everyone fits within Zapatismo . . .*
> *There are no universal recipes, lines, strategies, tactics, laws, rules, or slogans.*
> *There is only a desire – to build a better world, that is, a new world.*
>
> (Navarro, 2004)

When viewed in its historical and contemporary geopolitical context, the Zapatista Insurgency has opened possibilities for a broad spectrum of emancipatory ways of re-organizing social relations, economies, education, governance, food systems, day-to-day activities, interpersonal interactions, and even thought. Given their resoluteness in foregrounding Indigenous worldviews, gender equity, mutual aid, and dignity, while concurrently rejecting, outright, the logics of neoliberalism and assertions of a patriarchal status quo, the Zapatistas can arguably be viewed as one of the most radical and progressive movements of decolonization, social justice, and hope in history.

What they prove through their practices of gender equity, autonomous education, and participatory democracy is that a recognition of Indigenous people's right to self-determination, in conjunction with anti-capitalist communal work and efforts towards food sovereignty, can certainly provide viable alternatives to, as well as withstand the suffering of, our current globalized corporate food regime. More tellingly, what they are demonstrating is that collective resistance and autonomy can create pathways out of structural violence. To end, I harken back to the Zapatista metaphor offered at the beginning of the chapter and suggest that constructing

Un Mundo Donde Quepan Muchos Mundo ('a world where many worlds fit') can, indeed, be a solution to the food insecurity, hunger, anxiety, and anguish induced by neoliberalism. And perhaps most encouragingly, what 'worlds' are imagined and eventually emerge – is up to us.

RECIPE: HOW 'TO REBEL AND STRUGGLE' (AS SHARED BY THE EZLN)

Ingredients

1 Neither leaders, Nor bosses,
2 Nor messiahs, Nor saviors,
3 One only needs a sense of shame,
4 A bit of dignity,
5 And a lot of organization.
6 As for the rest, it either serves the collective or it does not.

Source: Between Light and Shadow (EZLN Communiqué 2014): http://enlaceza patista.ezln.org.mx/2014/05/27/between-light-and-shadow/

This recipe is just that, a recipe. It is meant to be neither a prescription, nor doctrine. The implications of it, as with most recipes, is that it can be altered, added-to, and/or subtracted-from per one's needs, desires, tastes, contexts, situations, geographies, etc. . . . which provokes the question: What might your list of ingredients for revolution/social transformation be?

Questions

1 Capitalism can be compared to myriad different things, from a variety of perspectives (e.g. a virus, infection, hydra, monster, parasite, plague, answer, silver bullet, savior, etc.). What metaphor would you use to describe it? Given there is danger in reifying it in such a manner, who is actually responsible for it continuing to be our dominant system?

2 Much of what the Zapatistas have incorporated into their resistance is guided by what is known as a preferential option for the poor and vulnerable. Think of your local community; who would this apply to, and what might solidarity (which avoids turning into classist charity) with them look like?

3 Women's Revolutionary Law has transformed Zapatista territory in a variety of ways, with men in their communities (by and large) agreeing to incorporate the demands the women made. If you sat down and made a list of 'laws' regarding gender, sexuality, and bodily justice where you live, what might they be?

4   Think of the geography and place you currently live in – what are its history/ies, and how did you learn them?
5   Pretend you and your closest friends are Zapatistas – what are some of the collective things you would do to make your community a better place?

Acknowledgements

Throughout this chapter, I draw primarily from my experiences learning from the Zapatistas. Much of what I reflect upon throughout the essay emerges from listening to Zapatistas, not 'researching' them. Importantly, I neither speak for the Zapatistas, nor do my words do them justice. This piece is meant to raise awareness about what they offer in terms of alternatives. Any mistakes or errors are my own, and constructive clarifications are always welcome. Select content of this chapter originally appeared in *The Solutions Journal* Volume 7, Issue 4. Available from: https://thesolutionsjournal.com/article/food-sovereignty-in-rebellion-decolonization-autonomy-gender-equity-and-the-zapatista-solution/. I extend my gratitude to the Zapatista Army of National Liberation for the invitation to *La Escuelita*, as well as to the Coordinating Committee of the Zapatista Rebel Autonomous Education System of National Liberation (SERAZLN) for accepting me into their program. In addition, I offer my most sincere appreciation to *Bats'il K'op* and the Mexico Solidarity Network. I also extend thanks to The University of the West Indies (Trinidad and Tobago) Campus Research and Publication Fund for their support.

References

Barmeyer, N. (2003) The Guerrilla movement as a project: An assessment of community involvement in the EZLN. *Latin American Perspectives*. 30 (1), 122–138.

Bobrow-Strain, A. (2007) *Intimate Enemies: Landowners, Power, and Violence in Chiapas*. London, Duke University Press.

EZLN. (2005) *Sixth Declaration of the Lacandon Jungle*. Available from: http://enlacezapatista.ezln.org.mx/sdsl-en/ [Accessed: 17th November 2016].

EZLN. (2012) *The EZLN announces next steps*. Available from: http://enlacezapatista.ezln.org.mx/2013/01/02/ezln-announces-the-following-steps-communique-of-december-30-2012/ [Accessed: 19th November 2015].

EZLN. (2013) *Freedom According to the Zapatistas, Volume III: Participation of Women in the Autonomous Government*. Chiapas, Mexico, San Cristóbal de las Casas.

EZLN. (2015) *On the elections: ORGANIZE*. Available from: http://enlacezapatista.ezln.org.mx/2015/05/14/on-the-elections-organize/ [Accessed: 23rd February 2016].

EZLN. (2016a) *Open letter on the aggressions against the people's movement in San Cristóbal de las Casas, Chiapas*. Available from: http://enlacezapatista.ezln.org.mx/2016/07/23/open-letter-on-the-aggressions-against-the-peoples-movement-in-san-cristobal-de-las-casas-chiapas/ [Accessed: 11th August 2016].

EZLN. (2016b) The cat-dog and the apocalypse. Available from: http://enlacezapatista.ezln.org.mx/2017/02/22/the-cat-dog-and-the-apocalypse/ [Accessed: 11th March 2017].

Fanon, F. (1963) *The Wretched of the Earth*. New York, Grove Press.

Jordaan, J. A. (2012) *Foreign Direct Investment, Agglomeration and Externalities: Empirical Evidence From Mexican Manufacturing Industries*. England, Ashgate Publishing, Ltd.

Klein, H. (2015) *Compañeras: Zapatista Women's Stories*. New York, Seven Stories Press.

Lorenzano, L. (1998) Zapatismo: Recomposition of labour, radical democracy and revolutionary project. In: Holloway, J. & Pelaez, E. (eds.) *Zapatista!* London, Pluto Press, pp. 126–158.

Marcos, S. (1993) The first uprising. *La Jornada*. Available from: http://www.bibliotecas.tv/chiapas/ene94/26ene94.html [Accessed: 31st October 2016].

Marcos, S. (2005) *Conversations With Durito: Stories of the Zapatistas and Neoliberalism*. New York, Autonomedia.

Marcos, S. (2014) *The Zapatista women's revolutionary law as it is lived today*. Available from: www.opendemocracy.net/sylvia-marcos/zapatista-women%E2%80%99s-revolutionary-law-as-it-is-lived-today [Accessed: 17th July 2014].

Marcos, S. & de Leon, J. P. (2002) *Our Word Is Our Weapon: Selected Writings*. New York, Seven Stories Press.

Matsushita, M., Schoenbaum, T. J., Mavroidis, P. C. & Hahn, M. (2015) *The World Trade Organization: Law, Practice, and Policy*. Oxford, Oxford University Press.

Mohanty, C. T. (2013) Transnational feminist crossings: On neoliberalism and radical critique. *Signs*. 38 (4), 967–991.

Navarro, L. H. (2004) *Zapatismo Today: Five Views of the Bridge*. Americas Program, Interhemispheric Resource Center. Available from: https://www.organicconsumers.org/old_articles/chiapas/zapatismo.php [Accessed: December 2016].

Ramírez, G. M., Carlsen, L. & Arias, A. R. (2008) *The Fire and the Word: A History of the Zapatista Movement*. San Francisco, City Lights Publishers.

Ross, J. (2006) *¡Zapatistas!: Making Another World Possible: Chronicles of Resistance, 2000–2006*. New York, Nation Books.

Rosset, P. (2014) *Zapatista uprising 20 years later: How indigenous Mexicans stood up against NAFTA 'death sentence.'* Available from: www.democracynow.org/2014/1/3/zapatista_uprising_20_years_later_how [Accessed: 23rd January 2014].

Roy, A. (2003) *War Talk*. Cambridge, MA, South End Press.

Springer, S., Birch, K. & MacLeavy, J. (eds.) (2016) *Handbook of Neoliberalism*. New York, Routledge.

Vergara-Camus, L. (2007) The MST and the EZLN struggle for Land: New forms of peasant rebellions. *Journal of Agrarian Change*. 9 (3), 365–391.

Walia, H. (2010) Transient servitude: Migrant labor in Canada and the apartheid of citizenship. *Race & Class*. 52 (1), 71–84.

PART III

Challenging markets

9

KNOWING HOW TO BRING FOOD TO THE MARKET

Appreciating the contribution of intermediary traders to the future of food availability in Sub-Saharan Africa

Mirjam Schoonhoven-Speijer, Ellen Mangnus, and Sietze Vellema

Introduction

The agenda for global food security has often been driven by questions about how to increase production in agriculture. This chapter shifts attention from food production to the distribution and exchange of food (as defined by Ericksen, 2008; in Smit, 2016), and challenges two binary thought lines underlying intervention strategies and policies in the Sub-Saharan African context: formal-informal, and void-arrangement. Firstly, formal arrangements are favored over informal arrangements, as the latter might lead to high transaction costs. Secondly, institutional arrangements, functioning well in 'developed' economies, are preferred over so-called institutional voids or imperfect markets. It is assumed that these hamper market access for both producers and consumers. Intermediary traders are seen as both informal and the result of imperfect markets, and are therefore widely perceived to be a market channel to be avoided (Markelova et al., 2009). Two mainstream intervention models, proposed as an alternative to 'exploitative' intermediary traders, serve as reference point for our appreciative inquiry of intermediary traders: contracts between farmers and end-market buyers, and collective marketing by cooperatives.

Contracts can ensure companies obtain a consistent volume of raw materials or food products supplied by selected farmers in situations where it is presumed that there is no other way of accessing the market. Farmers are expected to benefit from a stable market outlet, higher or predictable prices, and opportunities to improve their farming practices and, subsequently, their production. Contracts often include services, such as extension and receiving planting material on credit, and formalization opens opportunities to access credit (Abebe et al., 2013). Collective marketing via cooperatives, on the other hand, is often based on the assumption that the only access to markets available to farmers is through exploitative intermediary traders, or middlemen, who have the power to unilaterally determine prices and make farmers dependent by providing credit. Bypassing intermediary traders through collective marketing grants farmers openings to obtain better margins and negotiate higher prices. In addition, the formal setup of cooperatives provides, similar to contract farming, access to market information, credit, extension services, and inputs (Fischer & Qaim, 2012; Markelova et al., 2009).

As a consequence of the formal-informal and void-arrangement binary thought lines, and related market models and interventions, activities of intermediary traders in the middle of the agri-food chain are considered to be lacking or exploitative, and therefore unnecessary. 'Elimination' of intermediary traders is hinted at, after which both producers and consumers will profit from a transformed market structure. However, both contract farming and collective marketing have downsides, while the sustained presence, predictable mode of operation, and reliable market outlet arranged by intermediary traders could importantly contribute to the food availability dimension of food security. The FAO (2008) considers food availability as one of the four dimensions of food security and defines it as the physical presence of food in the area of concern through all forms of domestic production, commercial imports and food aid. It is determined by production, trade, stocks, and transfers. Food availability thus includes production as well as distribution and exchange of food, and traders contribute to the latter. Vorley, del Pozo-Vergnes and Barnett (2012) argue that only a minority of farmers – i.e. capitalized, educated, commercial farmers – benefit from formal market linkages; for example, high entry barriers or strict quality and quantity requirements in contract farming potentially exclude groups of less-resourceful farmers. Moreover, there is a risk of getting 'locked' into a fixed-price contract (Abebe et al., 2013; Vorley et al., 2015). Cooperatives often suffer from delayed payments to farmers, mismanagement of funds, and free-riding and side-selling by cooperative members (Mude, 2007; Mujawamariya, D'Haese & Speelman, 2013). For many farmers, these barriers result in the need for intermediary traders to sell their produce. In addition, collective marketing managed by cooperatives as well as contract farming have less relevance for local food availability, as it mostly concerns high-value crops for export markets, such as coffee, tea, or cocoa (Reardon et al., 2009).

Food security in developing countries largely depends on availability of locally produced staple crops and market access for both producers and consumers shaped by intermediary traders. Research suggests that intermediary traders do not necessarily exploit farmers: margins for doorstep traders in maize markets in Eastern Africa are rather small, and competition for the purchase of produce limits opportunities for exploitation (Sitko & Jayne, 2014). Intermediary traders provide reliable and predictable market access at the farmer's doorstep or in their vicinity through dense networks of trade (Chamberlin & Jayne, 2013). Also, traders accept lower quality and smaller quantities of produce supplied by small-scale farmers, as opposed to the stringent quality and quantity requirements of formal market linkages (Milford, 2014; Mujawamariya, D'Haese & Speelman, 2013). And intermediary traders pay farmers cash on delivery and offer credit to small-scale farmers often excluded from formal financial institutions (Vorley, del Pozo-Vergnes & Barnett, 2012). Credit offered by intermediary traders might be interest-free or an intrinsic part of the negotiated terms of exchange, which differs from formal financial credit options, usually charging high interest rates (Bailey et al., 2016).

These concerns raise the question whether refashioning food markets on the basis of formalization and further integration, central to the above-mentioned binary thought lines, is an adequate response. It might risk undermining trading practices with proven capacities to organize market access for spatially distributed small-scale producers and arrange food availability for low-income consumers in rural and urban markets. To develop an alternative line of thinking, we use two case studies of intermediary traders with a stable and long-term presence in Uganda and Mali. We explore how practices and organizational setups of intermediary traders form an entry point for interventions targeting food security, rather than inducing entirely new and unproven organizational models into regional staple food markets. The case studies make use of Bailey et al. (2016) to explore how intermediary traders access and use assets (Chambers & Conway, 1992) relying on skills and capabilities (Sen, 1999) to organize trading and markets under harsh and unpredictable conditions. The contours of a solution aiming at food security are grounded in these skillful practices of intermediary traders using assets and demonstrating capabilities that are tailored to specific conditions in rural and urban food markets usually accessed by low-income consumers.

Organizing food availability in two rural Sub-Saharan African contexts: Uganda and Mali

Our research on trade practices and networks of intermediary traders in Uganda and Mali highlights two vital processes arranging linkages between farmers and markets: 1) managing a constant flow of produce from farmers to the market; and 2) managing a constant flow of ready cash from traders to the farmer. If a trader manages these two flows, a farmer is assured that produce is bought immediately, sometimes even collected from the farmer's home, and paid for with ready cash. These two flows structure the two case descriptions below.

The Ugandan case study is based on fieldwork done between November 2014 and April 2015. The methods used were interviews with key stakeholders in the oilseed sector; interviews among 15 traders in the town of Lira and nine of their 'agents' in a neighboring district, Apac; and participant observation of bulking practices (buying, storing, transporting, and selling).

The case study from Mali is based on the analysis of a network of cereal traders in N'golobougou carried out between November 2012 and January 2013. In-depth interviews were carried out with 24 traders and 37 of their collectors within the network. In addition, trading practices were documented and transporters and other service providers interviewed in smaller markets, and the big cereal market in Bamako was connected to the network of cereal traders.

Research areas

The first case study regards oilseeds (sunflower, sesame, and soya) trade in Northern Uganda. In this part of the country, oilseeds form an essential part of the diet, and they are also important cash crops for farmers. Ten years ago marked the end of a 20-year civil war between the Lord Resistance Army and the government. This peace agreement and changes in the international market triggered investments in the oilseed sector by major processing companies, non-governmental organizations (NGOs), and the government, leading to an increase in production and a stronger competition between traders for that produce (Schoonhoven-Speijer & Heemskerk, 2013). Managing efficient bulking practices by traders has therefore become more important. In addition to competition, and a society still recovering from the effects of civil war, traders in Northern Uganda face circumstances such as covering long distances over unpaved roads (up to 150 kilometers), and fluctuating produce flows due to climate change.

The second case concerns cereal (sorghum, maize, and millet) trade in South Mali, the most important cereal-producing zone of the country. For a long time, cereals mainly served as subsistence crops; however, in recent years, cereals have become an important source of cash revenue. Networks of traders emerged in the 1980s when Mali's cereal sector was liberalized. Due to increasing population, urbanization, and a growing middle class, the demand for cereals has grown and is now an important source of cash revenue for farmers and traders (Delarue et al., 2009; Dufumier, 2005).

Produce flows

Intermediary traders in Northern Uganda collect and aggregate oilseeds through an extended network of agents and transporters (see Figure 9.1). We studied oilseeds flows starting from one of the main trading hubs in Northern Uganda, Lira. Most of the intermediary traders there are located in one street, called 'produce lane'. We refer to them as produce lane traders. They buy produce mainly from so-called agents, smaller traders within the surrounding villages. On average, produce lane traders have been working with ten agents for about 15 years. Agents either buy directly from farmers, or from doorstep traders (small traders who buy directly from farmers, hence the term 'doorstep'). As there is fierce competition, it is important for traders not to *get stuck during the season*, i.e. not being able to buy, store, or transport produce.

Transporting produce starts with farmers who bring small amounts (up to one full bag weighing between 100 and 120 kilograms) by bicycles or motorcycles to the doorstep trader or agents. Larger amounts are collected by truck directly from the farm. The produce is then transported from the villages to the stores in Lira. Half of the produce lane traders invested in transport; they owned, on average, two or three trucks. As one trader told us, "if you have your own truck, you get something. You can go into the village, otherwise the costs of renting a vehicle are too much"

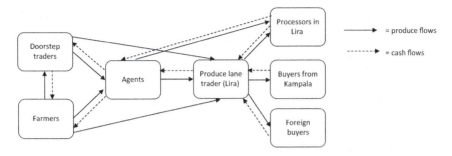

FIGURE 9.1 Produce and cash flows in the oilseed sector in Uganda

Source: M. Schoonhoven-Speijer

(female trader, Lira, Uganda, 20 February 2015). Owning a truck instead of renting means more flexibility. On the other hand, owning a truck implies high costs in terms of purchase and maintenance; not every trader could afford this. Produce lane traders maintain almost daily contact with their agents using cell phones, and buy produce two or three times a week. An important asset is a store; on average, traders owned two. Investing in a second store increases flexibility in managing produce flows and is used for stocking produce for a longer time as a way of risk management. Produce lane traders sell their oilseeds either to one of the many processors present in Lira or to buyers from Kampala, Sudan, and Kenya. The main season for buying produce is between November and February, depending on the timing of harvest.

In N'golobougou, Mali, trading is most intense from November to February, starting a month after the cereal harvest. During this period, small traders travel up to three times per week to the capital Bamako, either to bring cereals to their regular buyers in exchange for new pre-financing or to sell cereals directly at the Bamako market. Most small traders are based in N'golobougou or in its vicinities. They pre-finance so-called 'pisteurs', younger men, cousins, or sons with whom they have well-established relationships (see Figure 9.2), who collect cereals at the farm level. Pisteurs are not (yet) in the financial position to trade independently. All interviewed traders work with five pisteurs and for an average period of six to seven years. Pisteurs use several strategies for collecting at the farm level. Some visit different farms in the vicinity every week; others have a place at the market or along the road to the market where farmers can find them. Pisteurs are responsible for transport to the place of transaction. They use motors, carts, or minibuses. Some pisteurs live in areas that are not accessible during the rainy season, when they either stop trading temporarily or collect cereals by bike and store them at a friend's place in a neighboring village with better access.

An example of a quick adaptability to market supply and demand is that distribution of cereals works both ways. When prices in a village are higher than they are in Bamako, the chain of 'collecting and selling' reverses: traders bring cereals

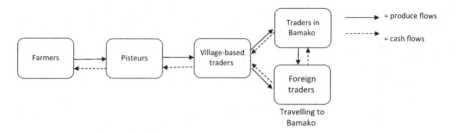

FIGURE 9.2 Produce and cash flows in the cereal sector in Mali

Source: E. Mangnus

from Bamako to sell in N'golobougou to their pisteurs, or to farmers. All traders own at least one store, a mud barn, in N'golobougou, and often a second one in a smaller trading hub. Less-affluent traders share storage. Cereals are usually only stored for a few days, until transport arrives to take the load to Bamako. Few traders have enough capital to store their purchase and speculate. Traders in N'golobougou mentioned that someone is regarded a 'real' trader when, after years of hard work, the trader is able to extend business to Bamako and own a store there. Of the 30 traders in the N'golobougou market, six had storage facilities in Bamako.

Cash flows

In Northern Uganda, produce lane traders in the network advance agents large amounts of money to buy oilseeds or other grains for them: from 1,500 to 7,500 euro each time. Agents use this money to buy produce. They might advance it to doorstep traders to buy produce for them, or give it to farmers as loans, which are paid back with produce. Relationships with agents also entail risks: in 2014, produce lane traders reported that an average of 2,500 euro was not paid back by their agents (in total). Traders need to be able to handle these losses in order to continue their businesses. Building trust is therefore essential for the trader–agent relationship. Agents are screened on their capacity to handle large amounts of money, for instance, by starting with small amounts, and recommendations from other traders or family. As one produce lane trader explained: "you have to do your best to choose good agents, which are those who have buildings and money" (male trader, Lira, Uganda, 10 April 2015). Agents are assessed on the cash and assets they currently own, as this gives an indication of the amount of money they are able to manage. In some cases, agents are family members, but more often not, because a family relationship might be difficult to manage professionally, as some traders explained. Traders also minimize risks by buying from the area where they originated from. Other ways of spreading risks are the multiple, formal and informal, sources of cash used: profits from last season; a bank loan at the beginning of the season; advance payments from big companies; income from their own farm; and borrowing small amounts from family and trusted traders on a weekly basis, for further smoothing of cash flows. Using these several sources is a way to keep up with the high frequency of buying and the 'rule' of paying farmers in cash. As one trader explained: "I sometimes get a loan, so that I have the money ready. [Because] farmers are always paid in cash" (male trader, Lira, Uganda, 4 December 2014).

Malian traders pre-finance pisteurs to collect cereals at farms. Traders are very selective in choosing pisteurs. They engage only with family members and friends they regard as capable. This 'regarding as capable' implies that the person was already engaged in other small trading practices, like selling cigarettes or breeding chickens. In case the trader does not know a pisteur beforehand, he would pre-finance only a small sum, between 15 to 38 euros. If the pisteur would be able to source a quantity that surpassed the value that was pre-financed, the trader was guaranteed that the pisteur was a 'trusted' person who could borrow money from his fellows. However, if it turned out that the person did not perform well, the trader would not continue working with him. For instance, one trader was asked by his sister to "keep her son busy". He pre-financed the boy with only a minimal amount, but as it turned out, "il n'est pas prudent (he is not careful)" (male trader, N'golobougou, Mali, 10 December 2012), and the pre-financing stopped. The frequency of the money transaction from trader to pisteur is higher than the frequency of cereal transactions. Many pisteurs receive pre-financing twice or even three times a week. The pisteur and the trader interviewed met at each other's houses, or at another market, or they arranged the transfer with acquaintances or their children. However, extra money was often needed. The majority of pisteurs (31 out of 37) borrowed money from relatives or other trusted villagers, such as store owners or livestock breeders. Traders mostly borrowed from other traders at the market. Also, two local store owners in N'golobougou were often approached for credit.

Analysis of trading practices

The case studies show that arranging food availability under unfavorable and changing conditions is far from easy. It entails acquiring assets; knowing how to organize produce and cash flows; building and maintaining complex relationships; and handling unanticipated problems in food markets, as well as nature. We explain the observed practices of intermediary traders in Uganda and Mali further by looking at assets and skills or capabilities used. Assets comprise the resources, or 'capital base' of a person, and can be subdivided in five types: physical, human, social, natural, and financial assets (Chambers & Conway, 1992). Physical assets refer to infrastructure and public goods; human assets include skills and knowledge; social assets reflect norms, networks, and relations that facilitate social organization and access to information; natural assets refer to the natural resource stock upon which production is based; and financial assets refer to actual or accessible income, savings, and credit (Ellis, 2000; in Bailey et al., 2016, p. 61). Skills and capabilities of traders refer to a person's opportunities and abilities to generate valuable outcomes, taking into account relevant personal characteristics and external factors (Sen, 1999). Table 9.1 summarizes which assets intertwined with skills are used in intermediary trade.

TABLE 9.1 An overview of assets and skills used in intermediary trade

Asset category[1]	Assets	Skills/capabilities
Physical *infrastructure, public goods*	Means of transport, storage space, bags, weighing scale, and other tools	Making decisions about how to select, acquire, and use physical assets and handle uncertainties related to investments made
Human *skills & knowledge*	Knowledge of markets, produce availability, (fluctuations in) prices, and competitors	(Learning how to) manoeuvre in markets through trial and error and learn from others in the network
Social *norms, networks, relations*	Relationships with farmers, agents and pisteurs, and buyers in a relatively stable trade network	Carefully selecting news members in the network and building relationships; using rules and routines underlying trade when resolving tensions or conflicts
Natural *resource stock*	Access to large production areas, in which farmers produce for two seasons and depend on rainfall; mostly unpaved roads	Attuning trade to fluctuations in demand and supply inherent to natural and physical conditions
Financial *actual or accessible income*	Available working capital as condition for deriving income from trading, possibly in combination with other economic activities	Constantly managing the financial conditions for trading, spreading risks, and monitoring financial viability of transactions with buyers and sellers

[1] Asset categories based on Bailey et al. (2016).

Physical assets, such as storage, transport, and bags, form the basis for starting a trade business. Traders gradually build their physical asset base, and they need the capability to carefully make investments in new assets if their profits allow, for example, acquiring multiple stores. Next to physical assets, *human assets*, such as finding locations to purchase produce, being informed about prices, and effectively dealing with market fluctuations, pave the way towards the 'art of trading'. This is learned in practice; new entrants take time to master the skills belonging to the role of trader and learn from more experienced traders.

Building relationships, agreeing on the distribution of responsibilities, and resolving tensions with a variety of actors within a network are skills entangled with *social assets:* durable relationships with actors functional to managing cash and produce flows. This also requires dedication and respect to the rules, norms, and routines merging in these networks, and to gradually take hierarchical steps in the network. Relationships with local collectors, pisteurs, and agents play a key role in accessing *natural assets*. Intermediary traders are only present in communities through their local collectors, which is a prerequisite for being informed on produce availability, and for arranging collection from isolated places and fast transmission of information regarding supply and demand in different markets. This way of distributing tasks requires specific skills and knowledge and is therefore only given to persons assumed capable to perform it. Lastly, the flows of produce from farmer to market could not be managed without the quick responsiveness regarding *financial assets* of intermediary traders. Traders spread their risks in the way they mobilize cash by using both formal and informal sources. This enables them to have money readily available for buying produce and paying agents or pisteurs. The high frequency of transactions ensures a continuous circulation of money in the network and the ability to buy any time from farmers who want to sell. Constant monitoring of the financial implication of a relationship or transactions is a skill central to intermediary trading.

Discussion: how to go beyond binary thinking by organizing trade schools

Our case studies are an appreciative inquiry of the practices of intermediary traders in Uganda and Mali, revealing their skillful work, the distribution of tasks among a variety of actors and geographical locations, and the constant management of relationships in stable networks reaching both small-scale farmers and low-income consumers. Our findings differ from the imposed formal organizational structures and rules associated with binary thought lines, as outlined in the introduction. The case studies suggest that it is not self-evident that such induced rules and arrangements become functional for ensuring food availability under the specific conditions in local and regional markets in rural Sub-Saharan Africa. Instead, the case studies highlight the complex whole of assets and capabilities needed for intermediary trade, and how these are slowly built over time. This proven capability of intermediary traders to make food available under specific conditions is therefore central to our proposed solution.

More specifically, we propose to explore the potential of **organizing a network of 'trade schools'** situated in the whimsical and harsh realities of local and regional food markets. This gives recognition to trade as a skillful and organized profession, and grants intermediary traders a position in strategies aiming at a public goal, namely access to sufficient and healthy food for all. It may also lead to innovations in the rules and arrangements in food markets, thereby enhancing mechanisms creating transparency and predictability. Below we elaborate four core elements of this proposal.

Mastering the art of trade

Organizing trade schools is strongly based on our observation that new members of trading networks gradually master 'the art of trade'. The schools should focus on learning from skillful practices of traders, which translates into building know-how about the use of assets, skills, and capabilities. It can start from basic logistics, such as transport and storage of produce, and work towards the integrative capacity to manage the multiple dimensions of trading, such as responding flexibly to changes in markets, adjusting to circumstances farmers are dealing with, and building relationships enabling access to working capital. It could even encourage specialization rooted in a division of tasks and responsibilities we observed in trading networks. A trade school can give space to 'older', more experienced traders to reflect on their practices: the assets, skills, and capabilities needed; and, for instance, what went wrong and why? In this way, the importance of 'learning trade in practice' is emphasized and made explicit. It thus gives younger, less experienced traders an opportunity to master trade.

Exchange of know-how

We envision that trade schools in different vicinities can be linked together in a network. This offers both beginning and established traders ample opportunities to obtain a detailed understanding of how traders operate under different circumstances, and to learn from them. The exchange of know-how between traders should always start from situated action – so to evade imposing pre-conceived organizational structures and rules that might not become functional within a specific setting. Exchange of know-how can also be done with external actors. A trade school could offer exchanges with, and trainings by, external experts on topics such as finance, international markets, quality standards, or other topics provided by the traders themselves. We emphasize that this is not only training, but an opportunity to exchange information between the two parties. Encouraging external finance agencies to connect with traders, for instance, might be an opportunity to re-think their finance models. They could benefit from the capacity of traders to provide farmers with ready cash, often arranged through a carefully managed network of agents.

A starting point for redesigning market institutions

A recognized network of trade schools emphasizes the importance of the work of traders for farmer's market access and food availability. This could be a starting point for encouraging traders to design and install organizational and regulatory measures for more transparent and reliable markets. For example, transparency about methods of weighing and quality checks influences reliability in buying. Or, access to market information at the marketplace would encourage farmers and traders to agree on realizing a certain degree of price predictability (Courtois & Subervie, 2014; Sitko & Jayne, 2014). Trade schools might also become hubs connecting skillful and capacitated traders to other modes of organizing the sourcing and trade of food. Traders could, for instance, be used as agents for companies, or as linkages between farmers and the cooperative, since they have the skills to bulk and transport produce. The network of trade schools can become a breeding ground for exploring innovative hybrid models arranging market access in dialogues between traders, cooperatives, and companies.

Coordination and partnering

Trade schools build on the observed capacity of trading networks to manage distributed tasks functional for trading and production. This resonates well with partnering processes making interdependencies work and resolving tensions as a condition for realizing food security. Working towards coordinated arrangements between traders, companies, and farmers may offer an attractive and reliable entry point for technical and financial service providers who may currently be hesitant to enter into the complex field of food and agriculture. The network of trade schools can connect a diverse portfolio of strategies working on organizing market access and arranging service provision. This may result in the emergence of novel rules and practices transforming the terms of inclusion of small-scale farmers, reshaping relations in markets, and constructing partnerships collaborating on food security.

Conclusion

To improve food security in developing countries, it is important to shift attention from improving food production to finding innovative ways of bringing food to the market. In this chapter, we challenged two binary thought lines (informal-formal and void-arrangement) underlying intervention strategies and policies arranging food availability in the Sub-Saharan African context. The consequences of these binary thought lines are reflected in intervention strategies of NGOs and policy-makers forging contracts between agricultural producers and buyers in end-use markets and in promoting collective marketing via cooperatives. Both see the efforts of intermediary traders to bring food to the market as unnecessary and possibly harmful to farmers. However, these binary thought lines and related intervention models may undermine food security, because in regional staple food markets, intermediary traders play a crucial role in facilitating food availability. Our case studies show that arranging food availability under unfavorable and fluctuating conditions is far from easy; it entails skills formation, acquiring and managing assets, and building and maintaining complex relationships. More appreciation for these aspects of trade in staple food crop markets led us to discuss novel ideas for interventions aiming at food security. We suggested the organization of a network of trade schools, which turns intermediary trade into an appreciated skillful profession, instead of 'eliminating' them from markets. A network of trade schools can be the starting point for learning, exchange, institutional innovations, and coordination and partnering processes that reinforce and enhance the contributions of traders to market access and food security.

Questions

1 What is the impact of eliminating intermediary traders on local food markets and food security?
2 What makes trading in food markets an attractive professional future for young people?
3 What conditions enable farmers and traders to collaborate in securing availability to food for consumers in rural and urban markets?

RECIPE: UGANDAN G-NUT AND SIM-SIM SAUCE (SERVES 4)

'G-nut' is short for groundnut, also called peanuts. 'Sim-sim' is the Luganda word for sesame seed.

Short description of the recipe: 'sim-sim paste' is a sauce made and consumed in Northern Uganda that is indispensable in the local kitchen. It can be eaten with basically all kinds of food regularly consumed: goat or beef, chicken, fish, rice, and beans. If you ask a Langi (a person from the Lango region in Northern Uganda) to bring one food item with them if they were to go abroad, they will likely mention sim-sim paste. It is therefore very much intertwined with local food consumption.

Ingredients

2 tablespoons vegetable oil
1 medium sized onion, diced
3 cloves of garlic, minced
1 tablespoon curry powder
1 teaspoon ground ginger
2 tomatoes, diced
1 cup smooth peanut butter (try to find a peanut butter in which the only ingredient is peanuts)
5 tablespoons tahini/sesame seed paste*
hot water, about 1–2 cups
salt to taste
cilantro, chopped (optional)

Directions

1   In a medium saucepan, sauté onions in vegetable oil until they are transparent. Add in minced garlic and sauté. Add in curry powder and ground ginger, stirring for just a moment before adding in diced tomatoes. Continue to cook until tomatoes become mushy.
2   Add in peanut butter, sesame seed paste, and 1 cup of hot water. Stir frequently as you continue to cook over medium heat and bring the mixture to a thick, bubbly boil. The mixture will continue to thicken as it is heated – keep stirring! Add additional hot water to make the sauce your desired consistency (some people prefer a thick paste-like sauce, while others prefer a more watery consistency. Salt to taste.
3   Garnish with chopped fresh cilantro, if desired. Serve over one of the following starchy foods: rice, potatoes (peeled and boiled), or sweet

potatoes (peeled and boiled). In Uganda, this is often served over steamed and mashed green bananas (matooke).

* tahini can be found in ethnic food stores and adds a rich flavor to the sauce. It can be omitted if you are unable to find it.

Recipe provided by Heather and Chris Lukolyo of ASSET

Source: https://diningforwomen.org/wp-content/uploads/2014/01/DFW_Nov2013_RecipesAndCuisine.pdf

Acknowledgements

We are grateful for the support received for the fieldwork in Uganda, financed by the Research Talent grant received from the Netherlands Organization for Scientific Research (NWO); and the fieldwork in Mali, financed by the Royal Tropical Institute (KIT).

References

Abebe, G. K., Bijman, J., Kemp, R., Omta, O. & Tsegaye, A. (2013) Contract farming configuration: Smallholders' preferences for contract design attributes. *Food Policy*. 40, 14–24.

Bailey, M., Bush, S., Oosterveer, P. & Larastiti, L. (2016) Fishers, fair trade, and finding middle ground. *Fisheries Research*. 182, 59–68.

Chamberlin, J. & Jayne, T. S. (2013) Unpacking the meaning of "market access": Evidence from rural Kenya. *World Development*. 41 (1), 245–264.

Chambers, R. & Conway, G. R. (1992) *Sustainable rural livelihoods: practical concepts for the 21st century*. IDS Discussion Paper No. 296. Sussex, Institute of Development Studies.

Courtois, P. & Subervie, J. (2014) Farmer bargaining power and market information services. *American Journal of Agricultural Economics*. 97 (3), 1–25.

Delarue, J., Mesplé-Somps, S., Naudet, J. D. & Robilliard, A. S. (2009) *Le paradoxe de Sikasso: coton et pauvreté au Mali*. DIAL Working Paper DT/2009-09. Paris, DIAL.

Dufumier, M. (2005) *Etude des systèmes agraires et typologie des systèmes de production agricole dans la région cotonnière du Mali*. Bamako, PASE/Institut National Agronomique Paris-Grignon (INAPG).

FAO. (2008) *An Introduction to the Basic Concepts of Food Security*. Rome, Italy, Food and Agriculture Organization (FAO).

Fischer, E. & Qaim, M. (2012) Linking smallholders to markets: Determinants and impacts of farmer collective action in Kenya. *World Development*. 40 (6), 1255–1268.

Markelova, H., Meinzen-Dick, R., Hellin, J. & Dohrn, S. (2009) Collective action for smallholder market access. *Food Policy*. 34 (1), 1–7.

Milford, A. B. (2014) Co-operative or coyote? Producers' choice between intermediary purchasers and Fairtrade and organic co-operatives in Chiapas. *Agriculture and Human Values*. 31 (4), 577–591.

Mude, A. G. (2007) Institutional incompatability and deregulation: Explaining the dismal performance of Kenya's coffee cooperatives. In: Barrett, C. B., Mude, A. G. & Omiti,

J. M. (eds.) *Decentralization and the Social Economics of Development: Lessons from Kenya*. Trowbridge, Cromwell Press, pp. 33–63.

Mujawamariya, G., D'Haese, M. & Speelman, S. (2013) Exploring double side-selling in cooperatives, case study of four coffee cooperatives in Rwanda. *Food Policy*. 39, 72–83.

Reardon, T., Barrett, C. B., Berdegué, J. A. & Swinnen, J. (2009) Agrifood industry transformation and small farmers in developing countries. *World Development*. 37 (11), 1717–1727.

Schoonhoven-Speijer, M. & Heemskerk, W. (2013) *The Ugandan oilseed sector*. KIT Case Study. Amsterdam, Royal Tropical Institute.

Sen, A. (1999) *Development as Freedom*. Oxford, Oxford University Press.

Sitko, N. J. & Jayne, T. S. (2014) Exploitative briefcase businessmen, parasites, and other myths and legends: Assembly traders and the performance of Maize markets in Eastern and Southern Africa. *World Development*. 54, 56–67.

Smit, W. (2016) Urban governance and urban food systems in Africa: Examining the linkages. *Cities*. 58, 80–86.

Vorley, B., del Pozo-Vergnes, E. & Barnett, A. (2012) *Small Producer Agency in the Globalized Market Small Producer Agency in the Globalized Market*. London, International Institute for Environment and Development (IEED).

Vorley, B., Lecoutere, E., Mubiru, S., Lunduka, R., Ubels, J., Beyssac, B. C. De & Ikaaba, D. (2015) *Growing Inclusion? Insights from Value Chain Development in Ugandan Oilseeds*. London, International Institute for Environment and Development (IEED).

10

CERTIFY SUSTAINABLE RETAILERS?

Simon R. Bush

Introduction: limits to certification

Aquaculture, the farming of fish and other aquatic organisms, has developed into one of the fastest growing sources of animal protein, and is important for international trade and domestic consumption alike (Belton & Thilsted, 2014; Troell et al., 2014). In the context of food security, these farmed fish not only provide protein, but also make a fundamental contribution to securing a range of essential micronutrients (Thilsted et al., 2016). Although increasingly varied in scale and intensity, for many of the species grown in tropical developing countries, aquaculture is still dependent in large part on small-holders, characterized by limited investment in assets, low operational costs, a large dependence on family labor, and a diversified portfolio of livelihood activities beyond fish farming (Edwards, 2013). As in other farming sectors, these small-holders are made economically vulnerable by their lack of investment capacity to expand production. But in addition, the vulnerability of small-holder aquaculture farmers is compounded by the high risk of shared poor water quality and the devastating effects of disease on their output.

Reducing the production risk across the industry is central to meeting wider ambitions of expanded global aquaculture production. One of the governance tools used to reduce risk is eco-certification, which sets voluntary auditable standards to improve ecological and social farming practices, and attach labels to products and enterprises that meet these standards (Hatanaka & Busch, 2008). It is assumed that certified products enable farmers to benefit from reduced production costs, as well as increased market access and higher market prices (Bronnmann & Asche, 2016; Wessells, 2002). The two most dominant aquaculture standards are the European-based Aquaculture Stewardship Council (ASC) standards and the US-based Global Aquaculture Alliance (GAA). While the number of certified farms has expanded at a phenomenal rate in recent years, this growth has been largely limited to larger-scale, vertically integrated firms (Jespersen et al., 2014; Trifković, 2014). Small-holders, who predominantly access Europe and US markets on the basis of short-term price contracts rather than long-term relational contracts, have proven less able to comply with these standards because of language, a lack of resources and poor literacy (Bush et al., 2013a).

Although voluntary in principle, these standards have become commonly linked to export market access. Since 2010, retailers in the US and EU, two of the largest seafood import markets in the world by value (FAO, 2016), have pledged to only sell certified products in response to non-governmental organization (NGO) campaigns directed at the unsustainability of both capture fisheries and aquaculture (Sampson et al., 2015; Bush et al., 2013a). The timeline for these pledges has been gradually delayed from 2012 to 2018 as the challenges of realizing 100% provision of certified fish has become apparent. The consequence is that for producers to maintain access to these markets, they have to comply with these eco-standards. In the short term, these changes directly affect their livelihoods and incomes through increased costs and efforts, while any benefits from sustainability remain a long-term and uncertain proposition.

The question of who should be held responsible for sustainable production has been widely debated. But when it comes to the use of eco-standards, or any other legal or market requirement, the burden of demonstrating improvements towards sustainability is narrowly assigned to producers. Indeed, this assumption is the very basis of voluntary eco-certification; farmers should upgrade their production practices and farm infrastructure to demonstrate compliance with standards before being rewarded through the market (see Cashore, Auld & Newsom, 2004, for a discussion on this key assumption). However, assuming farmers can simply respond to eco-standards as demanded by retailers does not take into consideration the highly differentiated capabilities of producers to respond. This is particularly important for aquaculture, which is ostensibly a developing-world activity, with over 85% of the volume of fish traded to Organization for Economic Co-operation and Development (OECD) countries stemming from developing countries (FAO, 2014). Shifting the burden of proof to producers in these developing countries does not consider the capacity of individual producers to demonstrate compliance with international standards, as well as the impact these standards have on them.

The assumption that producers have the capacity to respond to standards also overlooks key market dynamics, including how so-called 'lead firms' like retailers and food service companies coordinate global value chains and set contracts. Because of the strong levels of control that EU and US retailers and importers exercise in the seafood industry, they are more able to dictate the terms of trade to their suppliers. Not only do retailers demand sustainable seafood, they establish contracts in order to deliver high volumes with the lowest possible unit cost (Bjørndal et al., 2015; Fernández-Polanco & Llorente, 2015). It remains unclear whether any market premiums are observed for those products certified, and there is even less clarity as to whether these premiums are passed up the chain to producers (Ha et al., 2012; Marschke & Wilkings, 2014; Blomquist, Bartolino & Waldo, 2015). What instead appears to be happening is that the cost of certification is pushed back up the chain to producers, placing a disproportionate burden on small-holders who are less able to absorb these costs. In classical Marxist terms, this can undermine the value of production and therefore the viability of the producers upon whom these retailers rely for their supply of seafood. If certification is going to make a meaningful contribution to sustainability, it appears new models are necessary – models that change the ways in which buyers like retailers can promote more inclusive and effective modes of improvement.

Understanding value chain governance

To further explore the potential of alternative modes of eco-certification in the aquaculture sector, we now turn to global value chain (GVC) governance. In general terms, GVC governance refers to how firms cooperate to coordinate and impose product specifications or 'qualities' on the production and trade of a product through to the point of consumption (Bair, 2009; Gereffi, 2014). As variously argued (Ponte & Gibbon, 2005; Barrientos, Gereffi & Rossi, 2011; Bush et al., 2015), such analysis exposes how firms and their suppliers take into consideration new norms, values and practices, including those related to sustainability. In doing so, GVC analysis enables us to then understand how lead firms seek greater stability and higher quality of the products they buy by setting clear product specifications over suppliers.

One way these retailers set product specifications for their suppliers is through voluntary eco-standards, which in the case of aquaculture are designed to translate new norms around sustainability. These standards are an example of what Gibbon, Bair and Ponte (2008) call 'governance as normalization,' or the 're-alignment' of practice throughout a chain to mirror or materialize an introduced standard, code or norm. In the agri-food sector, which includes aquaculture, these standards primarily target the farm and processor level, with the assumption that standard compliance at this level enables firms to generate assurance and credibility on the open global market (Hatanaka, Bain & Busch, 2005). In turn, those complying with these standards are expected to benefit from balancing the risk and rewards of improved production practices, market access and even higher market prices.

Whether a lead firm chooses to employ voluntary eco-standards or not depends in large part on the level of control they (wish to) have over their suppliers. To understand this control or 'power' of some firms over others, Gereffi, Humphrey and Sturgeon (2005) developed the notion of governance as coordination, which explains the ways in which control is leveraged by the transmission of product specification (such as eco-standards) along the chain given the capacity of suppliers to meet these specifications. They identify a spectrum of five value-chain configurations, which move from low levels of so-called 'market' coordination, to high levels of so-called 'captive' coordination, and end in complete control over production through vertical integration (Gereffi, Humphrey & Sturgeon, 2005). Moving along this spectrum, the degree of control and power over suppliers increases.

Governance as 'normalization', or setting and transferring norms to others in the value chain, can influence coordination in a number of ways. If more complex information can be incorporated in voluntary eco-standards, then retailers and food service companies may be able to maintain control over suppliers at a distance without having to directly invest in internal surveillance and control (Ponte, 2009). However, for sustainability standards, this creates a potential paradox. The sustainability norms embodied in these standards will force suppliers to develop new capabilities to improve the performance of production (Nadvi, 2014; Gereffi, Humphrey & Sturgeon, 2005). But the high level of capabilities required will mean that retailers who aim to sell only certified products will likely exclude a large proportion of their suppliers from the market. In doing so, retailers may limit their own supply of product and limit any gains in sustainable production. Faced with this paradox, it appears a more inclusive certification model is needed.

Rewarding 'developmental' chain coordination

Developing a more inclusive improvement agenda for aquaculture certification requires a 'double shift'. First is a shift away from certification's focus on the farm scale and farmers as a target of regulation, to instead focus on the actors who play an active role in setting and demanding normative claims like sustainability. Second is a shift away from the lead firm as coordinator, to the lead firm as *partner* for improvement. If both of these shifts can be realized, then more inclusive forms of sustainability improvements may be possible through eco-certification.

Moving beyond environmental or social standards at the farm level would then move to assessing the performance of buyers in supporting farmers to improve their production practices. This is a clear break from current observations that retailers use standards to outsource the cost and risk for dealing with complex normative issues like sustainability by pushing compliance and assessment back up value chains to their suppliers (Riisgaard et al., 2010). Making retailers the target of standards and certification would instead require them to internalize production risk, because their performance would be the subject of assessment. More specifically, they would be assessed on their support to suppliers to demonstrate improvements in production, whether that be a set of normative voluntary standards or basic legal compliance. In turn, these retailers would be rewarded by a certificate and/or eco-label for 'inclusive sustainability'.

While such an approach would be a radical shift in how certification is applied in the aquaculture and wider seafood industry, the idea is not altogether new. In their study of Ikea, the lifestyle and furnishings multi-national corporation based in Sweden, Ivarsson and Alvstam (2010) observe what they refer to as the 'developmental' mode of chain coordination. They distinguish this form of coordination from other forms, such as arms-length market relations with suppliers or 'capturing' suppliers through long-term binding contracts. They argue that the buying relationship Ikea has with their suppliers is developmental for two reasons. First, it is based on the provision of technological and organizational assistance, co-inno-vation, human capacity building, and financial and administrative advice, all aimed at helping suppliers meet their stringent product specifications. Second, Ikea does not capture these suppliers through exclusivity clauses in their contracts, but instead allows them to use the support they receive to expand their client base. The philos-ophy is that an open form of support increases the pre-competitive quality of their sector overall. What this means is that buyers work with producers, seeing them as a fundamental part of their business rather than simply suppliers of products.

Retailers are already partially engaging in developmental modes of coordina-tion over currently 'un-certifiable' fish farmers through 'aquaculture improvement projects' (AIPs). Either coordinated directly by retailers or with the support of NGOs or consultants, AIPs support producers to move towards certification by, for example, directly financing improved farm practices, providing support for train-ing on stocking, and pharmaceutical use, or paying for consultants to assist with the paperwork required to demonstrate improvement (SFP, 2016). In coordination terms, there are two general categories of these improvement projects (Tolentino-Zondervan et al., 2016). First, top-down projects promote improvement by linking market access and higher prices with standard compliance. Second, bottom-up projects develop a wide range of farmer and government capabilities with the hope that buyers will recognize and reward any improvements with market access. In both cases, it is hoped that these improvements will ultimately be supported with secure market access as buyers meet demand for sustainable aquaculture production.

But unlike farm-level certification, which provides market recognition through an eco-labelled product, retailers engaging in these developmental-like forms of coordination receive very little recognition for the support they provide. This is because current certification schemes are based on the binary logic of compli-ance/non-compliance, which is in turn based on a static moment of auditing and certification. They do not, by design, take into consideration the capabilities of the producers being assessed, or the level of support that is given by other chain actors such as retailers. In other words, they are limited in making sustainability claims around their support because there remains contested interpretations of what makes a credible and effective aquaculture improvement project (Sampson et al., 2015). Retailers therefore run the risk of not being able to make claims in the market around the support they are providing because there is no inde-pendent third party substantiating their supposed support. It is exactly here that retail-level certification would fill this gap by providing a system of verification, market recognition, and ultimately greater incentives for further investment in small-holder support.

The impact of retail-level certification may also foster the kind of inclusive sustainability improvement that is currently lacking in the industry in two distinct ways. First, voluntary certification is most commonly taken up by producers who already exhibit a degree of compliance, or are willing and capable of applying

(Tlusty, 2012). By inadvertently cherry-picking better performers, the degree of overall improvement across the industry remains limited. Recognizing and promoting continuous improvement towards sustainability would increase the involvement of less well-performing producers who cannot currently comply with high-level ASC or GAA standards. Such an inclusive approach is of key importance, because it is with these aquaculture producers that the greatest overall sustainability gains are still to be made. Making retailers responsible for demonstrating a developmental mode of sustainability support could also lead to considerable gains because the cost (and therefore the choice) to improve is no longer dispersed across literally millions of producers.

Second, shifting the cost of certification down the value chain would also put pressure on retailers and suppliers to search for innovative and more efficient forms of organizing aquaculture sustainability. One outcome would be the need for greater efficiencies for retailers to deliver support to individual producers beyond the farm through, for example, cooperative forms of management. Cooperative management of aquaculture has been met with mixed success, largely because of poor internal capacity, weak state support, and the complexity of environmental and health issues such as water quality and disease (Ha, Bush & van Dijk, 2013). A developmental approach with buyer investment may prove more successful than current cooperative approaches because it would link the level and quality of producer support to the reputation and market demand of buyers. Because buyers would still be driven by environmental outcomes, the cooperatives they support may also engage in ecosystem or area-based forms of management (Macfadyen et al., 2016), and in doing so, link farm-level practices to issues like water quality that extend well beyond the boundaries of a single farm (Soto, Aguilar-Manjarrez & Hishamunda, 2008).

The 'developmental' coordination of suppliers could also lead to improved risk management in the industry. By moving certification beyond the farm level and creating incentives for support from buyers in export markets, opportunities for insurance and new forms of financing may also emerge. Such opportunities would be transformative in the seafood sector in developing countries, given the high degree of production risk experienced by producers and the associated lack of formal insurance and finance opportunities (WorldFish, 2011). The outcome would be two-fold: producers would benefit from receiving the necessary capacity to reduce production risk and sustainably intensify production, while buyers would benefit from a more stable supply of sustainably produced fish.

New or existing certification schemes?

Would such a system need new certification schemes beyond the ASC and GAA? Not necessarily. The goal of these certification schemes is to assure buyers that the products they are purchasing have been responsibly produced. While this goal would remain the same, a new standard would be required that focuses on verifying the developmental credentials of buyers. To this end, both ASC and GAA could incorporate a new 'developmental' or 'inclusive improvement' standard to their certification. GAA already offers a reporting-based Best Aquaculture Practices (BAP) standard that is modular to the extent that different 'sub-standards' are applied across four processes in the chain – processing plants, farms, feed mills and hatcheries – with the certification of each process (in the order presented here) rewarded with an additional star rating (GAA, n.d.). Moving to a retail-level certification may result in the addition of a standard 'star'. ASC, on the other hand, is a metric-based farm-level standard. For them, it may be that a new standard, auditing approach and label would be required. If neither ASC nor GAA would be interested in adapting the scope of their existing certification, a standard or accreditation could be developed.

The scope of a developmental standard could reflect the need to support the capabilities of producers or communities of producers to continually improve their production rather than setting a single and 'fictitious' level or goal of sustainability (Micheli et al., 2014; Tlusty & Thorsen, 2016). In practical terms, such a standard could follow Ivarsson and Alvstam (2010) and focus on new process-oriented categories, such as the provision of technological and organizational assistance, co-innovation, human capacity building, and/or financial and administrative advice. Alternatively, the standard could focus on supporting the broader capabilities of producer communities by investing in social and human capital. Doing so, they argue, would require assessing support for education, socioeconomic development, fair conditions of employment and diversification of livelihoods in cases of overexploitation. Bringing in these wider categories for an industry like aquaculture may appear to be moving beyond the scope responsibility of any buyer, but it is not without precedent. As notions of 'extended responsibility' of the retail sector grows (Bush et al., 2015), especially in the context of sourcing from developing countries, such activities may become the norm, especially if EU and US firms see such activities as a means to an end: that of securing a 'sustainable' product.

Finally, the emergence of a developmental standard would not make farm-level standards irrelevant. Aquaculture sub-sectors that are able to absorb and cope with the requirements of certification could still opt for one of the existing global standards. But for producers unable to cope, engaging with retailers that offer developmental support could be a means to create long-term market relations and/or develop their capabilities to engage directly with the existing global standards. By providing alternatives, such producers will, at the very least, have more and different incentives for improvement than is currently the case.

Concluding remarks

A retail-led 'developmental' model for aquaculture sustainability would inevitably create new kinds of dependencies between buyers and producers. And there is no guarantee that buyer certification will improve conditions for developing-world producers to be incorporated into global seafood value chains. But by giving market recognition for 'developmental' modes of chain coordination, we can ensure that the responsibility for sustainable aquaculture is not placed on those with the least capacity for independent improvement. Instead of retailers undermining the capacity of farmers to respond to sustainability demands, responsibility will be placed at the feet of retailers (and other buyers) who do not replace the end consumer but do orchestrate global demand for fish products. Such an approach would also reinvigorate market-based approaches to sustainability governance. If retailers and other buyers are being recognized for the support they provide rather than the individual products on their shelves, then the race to be the greenest grocer on the high street may yet still drive substantial sustainability improvements in aquaculture and other sectors.

RECIPE: CANH CHUA CÁ TRA (SWEET AND SOUR PANGASIUS FISH SOUP)

Ingredients

7 cups water
3 tablespoons tamarind paste
2 tablespoons (preferably palm) sugar
2 large tomatoes, sliced and diced
1 celery stick, chopped into bite-size pieces
1 tablespoon (Vietnamese) fish sauce (*Nước mắm*)
300 g Vietnamese pangasius (*cá tra*, a kind of catfish) cutlets (not fillets!), which
    you'll have to search for at a Vietnamese or Asian specialty supermarket
100 g Asian bean sprouts
1 teaspoon finely chopped red chilli, sweet basil and fresh coriander

Preparation

1   Put the tamarind paste in cold water to dilute and strain.
2   Throw the tamarind paste into a pot with the water and add the sugar, tomatoes, celery and fish sauce. Let simmer for about 15 minutes.
3   Add the pangasius cutlets, bean sprouts and chillies, and simmer for a further 3 minutes.
4   Serve in individual soup bowls and garnish with plenty of mint, sweet basil or coriander.
5   Serve with a side dish of Vietnamese fish sauce.

(Adapted from www.food.com)

Critical questions

1   Why would (or wouldn't) a retailer agree to be certified against a developmental standard?
2   Does a developmental standard overcome the constraints that developing-world or small-holder producers face when selling to export markets?
3   What might the impact of a development standard be for local and global food security?
4   Are market-based governance approaches, like voluntary eco-certification, the only way to promote inclusive modes of sustainability improvement? Can you think of others?

Acknowledgements

This chapter contributes to research under the Netherlands Organisation for Scientific Research (NWO) funded 'Supermarket Supported Area-based Management and Certification of Aquaculture in Southeast Asia' (SUPERSEAS) project (grant number W08.250.205).

References

Bair, J. (2009) Global commodity chains: Genealogy and review. In: Bair, J. (ed.) *Frontiers of Commodity Chain Research*. Stanford, Stanford University Press, pp. 1–34.

Barrientos, S., Gereffi, G. & Rossi, A. (2011) Economic and social upgrading in global production networks: A new paradigm for a changing world. *International Labour Review*. 150 (3–4), 319–340. Available from: doi: 10.1111/j.1564-913X.2011.00119.x [Accessed: 1st March 2017].

Belton, B. & Thilsted, S. H. (2014) Fisheries in transition: Food and nutrition security implications for the global South. *Global Food Security*. 3 (1), 59–66.

Bjørndal, T., Child, A., Lem, A. & Dey, M. M. (2015) Value chain dynamics and the small-scale sector: A summary of findings and policy recommendations for fisheries and aquaculture trade. *Aquaculture Economics & Management*. 19 (1), 148–173. Available from: doi: 10.1080/13657305.2015.994241 [Accessed: 1st March 2017].

Blomquist, J., Bartolino, V. & Waldo, S. (2015) Price premiums for providing eco-labelled seafood: Evidence from MSC-certified cod in Sweden. *Journal of Agricultural Economics*. 66 (3), 690–704. Available from: doi: 10.1111/1477-9552.12106 [Accessed: 1st March 2017].

Bronnmann, J. & Asche, F. (2016) The value of product attributes, brands and private labels: An analysis of frozen seafood in Germany. *Journal of Agricultural Economics*. 67 (1), 231–244. Available from: doi: 10.1111/1477-9552.12138 [Accessed: 1st March 2017].

Bush, S. R., Belton, B., Hall, D., Vandergeest, P., Murray, F. J., Ponte, S., Oosterveer, P., Islam, M. S., Mol, A. P. J., Hatanaka, M., Kruijssen, F., Ha, T.T.T., Little, D. C. & Kusumawati, R. (2013a) Certify sustainable aquaculture? *Science*. 341 (6150), 1067–1068. Available from: doi: 10.1126/science.1237314 [Accessed: 1st March 2017].

Bush, S. R., Oosterveer, P., Bailey, M. & Mol., A. P. J. (2015) Sustainability governance of chains and networks: A review and future outlook. *Journal of Cleaner Production*. 107, 8–19. Available from: doi: 10.1016/j.jclepro.2014.10.019 [Accessed: 1st March 2017].

Cashore, B., Auld, G. & Newsom, D. (2004) *Governing Through Markets: Forest Certification and the Emergence of Non-State Authority*. New Haven and London, Yale University Press.

Edwards, P. (2013) Review of small-scale aquaculture: Definitions, characterization, numbers. In Bondad-Reantaso, M. G. & Subasinghe, R. P. (eds.) *Enhancing the Contribution of Small-Scale Aquaculture to Food Security, Poverty Alleviation and Socio-Economic Development: FAO Fisheries and Aquaculture Proceedings 31, 21–24th April 2010, Hanoi, Viet Nam*. Rome, Food and Agriculture Organization of the United Nations, pp. 37–61.

FAO. (2014) *The State of World Fisheries and Aquaculture: Opportunities and Challenges*. Rome, Food and Agriculture Organization of the United Nations.

FAO. (2016) *The State of the World's Fisheries and Aquaculture: Contributing to Food Security and Nutrition for All*. Rome, Food and Agriculture Organization of the United Nations.

Fernández-Polanco, J. & Llorente, I. (2015) Price transmission in the Spanish fresh wild fish market. *Aquaculture Economics & Management*. 19 (1), 104–124. Available from: doi: 10.1080/13657305.2015.994238 [Accessed: 1st March 2017].

Gereffi, G. (2014) Global value chains in a post-Washington consensus world. *Review of International Political Economy*. 21 (1), 9–37. Available from: doi: 10.1080/09692290.2012.756414 [Accessed: 1st March 2017].

Gereffi, G., Humphrey, J. & Sturgeon, T. (2005) The governance of global value chains: An analytic framework. *Review of International Political Economy*. 12 (1), 78–104. Available from: doi: 10.1080/09692290500049805 [Accessed: 1st March 2017].

Gibbon, P., Bair, J. & Ponte, S. (2008) Governing global value chains: An introduction. *Economy and Society*. 37 (3), 315–338. Available from: doi: 10.1080/03085140802172656 [Accessed: 1st March 2017].

Global Aquaculture Alliance (GAA). (n. d.) *Multi-star integrity*. Available from: http://bap.gaalliance.org/program-integrity/multi-star-integrity/ [Accessed: 1st March 2017].

Ha, T. T. T., Bush, S. R, Mol, A. P. J. & van Dijk, H. (2012) Organic coasts? Regulatory challenges of certifying integrated shrimp – mangrove production systems in Vietnam. *Journal of Rural Studies*. 28 (4), 631–639. Available from: doi: 10.1016/j.jrurstud.2012.07.001 [Accessed: 1st March 2017].

Ha, T. T. T., Bush, S. R. & van Dijk, H. (2013) The cluster panacea? Questioning the role of cooperative shrimp aquaculture in Vietnam. *Aquaculture*. 388–391, 89–98.

Hatanaka, M., Bain, C. & Busch, L. (2005) Third-party certification in the global agrifood system. *Food Policy*. 30 (3), 354–369. Available from: doi: 10.1016/j.foodpol.2005.05.006 [Accessed: 1st March 2017].

Hatanaka, M. & Busch, L. (2008) Third-party certification in the global agrifood system: An objective or socially mediated governance mechanism? *Sociologia Ruralis*. 48 (1), 73–91.

Ivarsson, I. & Alvstam, C. G. (2010) Supplier upgrading in the home-furnishing value chain: An empirical study of IKEA's sourcing in China and South East Asia. *World Development*. 38 (11), 1575–1587. Available from: doi: 10.1016/j.worlddev.2010.04.007 [Accessed: 1st March 2017].

Jespersen, K. S., Kelling, I., Ponte, S. & Kruijssen, F. (2014) What shapes food value chains? Lessons from aquaculture in Asia. *Food Policy*. 49 (1), 228–240. Available from: doi: 10.1016/j.foodpol.2014.08.004 [Accessed: 1st March 2017].

Macfadyen, S., Tylianakis, J. M., Letourneau, D. K., Benton, T. G., Tittonell, P., Perring, M. P., Gómez-creutzberg, C., Báldi, A., Holland, J. M., Broadhurst, L., Okabe, K., Renwick, A. R., Gemmill-Herren, B. & Smith, H. G. (2016) The role of food retailers in improving resilience in global food supply. *Global Food Security*. 7, 1–8. Available from: doi: 10.1016/j. gfs.2016.01.001 [Accessed: 1st March 2017].

Marschke, M. & Wilkings, A. (2014) Is certification a viable option for small producer fish farmers in the global south? Insights from Vietnam. *Marine Policy*. 50 (A), 197–206. Available from: doi: 10.1016/j.marpol.2014.06.010 [Accessed: 1st March 2017].

Micheli, F., De Leo, D., Shester, G. G., Martone, R. G., Lluch-Cota, S. E., Butner, C., Crowder, L. B., Fujita, R., Gelcich, S., Jain, M., Lester, S. E., McCay, Pelc, R. & Sáenz-Arroyo, A. (2014) A system-wide approach to supporting improvements in seafood production practices and outcomes. *Frontiers in Ecology and the Environment*. 12 (5), 297–305. Available from: doi: 10.1890/110257 [Accessed: 1st March 2017].

Nadvi, K. 2014. "Rising powers" and labour and environmental standards. *Oxford Development Studies*. 42 (2), 137–150. Available from: doi: 10.1080/13600818.2014.909400 [Accessed: 1st March 2017].

Ponte, S. (2009) Governing through quality: Conventions and supply relations in the value chain for South African Wine. *Sociologia Ruralis*. 49 (3), 236–257. Available from: doi: 10.1111/j.1467-9523.2009.00484.x [Accessed 1st March 2017].

Ponte, S. & Gibbon, P. (2005) Quality standards, conventions and the governance of global value chains. *Economy and Society*. 34 (1), 1–31. Available from: doi: 10.1080/0308514042000329315 [Accessed: 1st March 2017].

Riisgaard, L., Bolwig, S., Ponte, S., Du Toit, A., Halberg, N. & Matose, F. (2010) Integrating poverty and environmental concerns into value-chain analysis: A strategic framework and practical guide. *Development Policy Review*. 28 (2), 195–216.

Sampson, G. S., Sanchirico, J. N., Roheim, C. A., Bush, S. R., Taylor, J. E., Allison, E. H., Anderson, J. L., Ban, N. C., Fujita, R., Jupiter, S. & Wilson, J. R. (2015) Secure sustainable seafood from developing countries. *Science*. 348 (6234), 504–506.

SFP. (2016) *Ca Mau Shrimp aquaculture improvement project*. Available from: www.sustainable fish.org/aquaculture-improvement/ca-mau-shrimp-aip (Login required).

Soto, D., Aguilar-Manjarrez, J. & Hishamunda, N. (eds.) (2008) Building an Ecosystem Approach to Aquaculture. *FAO Fisheries and Aquaculture Proceedings, 7–11th May, 2007, Palma de Mallorca, Spain*. Rome, Food and Agriculture Organization of the United Nations.

Thilsted, S. H., Thorne-lyman, A., Webb, P., Rose Bogard, J., Subasinghe, R., Phillips, M. J. & Allison, E. H. (2016) Sustaining healthy diets: The role of capture fisheries and aquaculture for improving nutrition in the post-2015 era. *Food Policy*. 61, 126–131. Available from: doi: 10.1016/j.foodpol.2016.02.005 [Accessed: 1st March 2017].

Tlusty, M. F. (2012) Environmental improvement of seafood through certification and ecolabelling: Theory and analysis. *Fish and Fisheries*. 13 (1), 1–13. Available from: doi: 10.1111/j.1467-2979.2011.00404.x [Accessed: 1st March 2017].

Tlusty, M. F. & Thorsen, Ø. (2016) Claiming seafood is 'sustainable' risks limiting improvements. *Fish and Fisheries*. July. Available from: doi: 10.1111/faf.12170 [Accessed: 1st March 2017].

Tolentino-Zondervan, F., Berentsen, P., Bush, S. R., Digal, L. & Lansink, A. O. (2016) Fisher-level decision making to participate in Fisheries Improvement Projects (FIPs) for yellowfin tuna in the Philippines. *PloS One*. 11 (10), 1–22. Available from: doi: 10.1371/journal. pone.0163537 [Accessed: 1st March 2017].

Trifković, N. (2014) Certified standards and vertical coordination in aquaculture: The case of pangasius from Vietnam. *Aquaculture*. 433, 235–246. Available from: doi: 10.1016/j. aquaculture.2014.06.010 [Accessed: 1st March 2017].

Troell, M., Naylor, R. L., Metian, M., Beveridge, M., Tyedmers, P. H., Folke, C., Arrow, K. J., Barrett, S., Crépin, A., Ehrlich, P. R., Gren, A., Kautsky, N., Levin, S. A., Nyborg, K., Österblom, H., Polasky, S., Scheffer, M., Walker, B. H., Xepapadeas, T. & de Zeeuw, A. (2014) Does aquaculture add resilience to the global food system? *PNAS*. 111 (37), 13257–13263. Available from: doi: 10.1073/pnas.1404067111 [Accessed: 1st March 2017].

Wessells, C. R. (2002) The economics of information: Markets for seafood attributes. *Marine Resource Economics*. 17 (2), 153–162.

WorldFish. (2011) *Financing smallholder aquaculture enterprises*. WorldFish. Policy Brief 2011-07.

11

THE SOLUTION CANNOT BE CONVENTIONALIZED

Protecting the alterity of fairer and more sustainable food networks

Raquel Ajates Gonzalez

Introduction

We are not short of evidence on the impacts of the industrial food system on both the environment and public health: from a spiraling obesity epidemic claiming more obese people than underweight globally (NCD-RisC, 2016), to a decreased diversity of diets and cultivated crops (Lang & Heasman, 2015). Reduced biodiversity of breeds, plant varieties and wildlife, stagnated yields, increased pests and damaged soil fertility is the price we pay for industrial farming to be able to offer large retailers a year-round supply of consistent produce, standardizing purchasing and consumption patterns (Burlingame & Dernini, 2010). This standardization is the cause and the result of reduced diversity in all its manifestations in food and farming (diversity of growers, varieties, market channels, etc.), and presents a serious risk to food security (Thrupp, 2000). In more affluent countries, labor in the food system (in farming, processing, retailing and catering) is predicted to face shortages as this work is not adequately recognized or fairly paid. In the UK, for example, this is reflected in unbalanced financial flows, with farming accounting for only eight per cent of the total gross value added of the agri-food sector (DEFRA, 2012).

These problems are symptoms of a dysfunctional system. It can be argued that one of the biggest challenges facing the food system is the continuous co-optation of potential solutions by the dominant regime. This process perpetuates current dynamics and suffocates more balanced alternatives. Alternative Food Networks (AFNs) emerge with the aim to tackle the imbalances discussed above. When the strategies of AFNs are co-opted by the industrial food system, their transformative power is reduced or neutralized. One example of this trend is the organic movement that first started as a grassroots initiative and gradually became absorbed by large retailers as a mere additional product line (Buck, Getz & Guthman, 1997). While the reduced use of chemical pesticides is still a win, the fact that many organic products are now grown in monocultures, often miles away from their place of consumption, is a loss that the organic movement is having to negotiate (Jaffee, 2010). Fair trade certification has had a similar development (Goodman, 2010), with a new label for products including "unfairly traded" ingredients attracting criticisms (Taylor, 2005; BTC, 2014).

In this sense, the signifiers become uncoupled from the signified. Fragmentation of what it means to be organic or fair-traded or cooperatively produced has facilitated the take-up of the most market-friendly dimensions by the very actors and modes of production they originally aimed to resist and transform (Goodman, DuPuis & Goodman, 2011; Griffiths, 2012). This process shifts focus towards improving dominant systems and away from addressing the root problems. This institutionalization of a standards-based and measurable approach to organic farming, fair trade or agricultural cooperativism is encouraged by policies that require groups of farmers to conform to certain criteria to be eligible for certain certifications or subsidies. In this sense, there is a rupture from the original visions of transformations as these movements are diluted by substituting their process-based approaches to standards-based ones of "allowable inputs", or in the case of agricultural cooperatives, "allowable cooperative principles or practices". Current literature (both from academia and civil society) is also discussing the danger of co-optation in the realm of agroecology, an approach to farming based on three interconnected pillars: a science, a set of growing practices and a socio-political movement (Levidow et al., 2014).

The "conventionalization thesis" has been put forward to explain how oppositional solutions able to catalyze transformation and social justice end up becoming institutionalized by codified regulatory bodies that adapt them into the logic of markets and consumer choice (Goodman, DuPuis & Goodman, 2011). This chapter proposes a set of strategies for resisting the uptake of alternatives to the dominant industrial and large-scale food production and retailing units to prevent them from becoming "conventionalized" and absorbed by the same system they are trying to convert. Conventionalization means quantity, standardization and price becoming the benchmark, favoring large monocultures and penalizing diverse production. Profit is prioritized over diversity, quickly moving from "value for money" to "values for money" (Lang, 2010).

But can the conventionalization thesis ever be overcome? If so, how? From a selection of solution-based grassroots projects in Spain and the UK, this chapter discusses four interlinked strategies of bottom-up cooperative endeavors that aim to effect long-lasting and transformational change by creating alternatives that are harder to be appropriated by large, powerful players. These projects suggest grassroots innovation is limitless and constantly bubbling up new initiatives, while becoming more savvy and aware of the danger of being co-opted.

While etymologically the word radical sometimes has a positive meaning, as in getting to the roots of problems rather than just focusing on symptoms (radix being the Latin word for root), being labelled as "radical" often comes with negative connotations, such as being too drastic or unreasonable. AFNs are often associated with the more negative sense of the word. This labeling can increase the "otherness" of these initiatives and reduce their impact by presenting them as too removed from reality or "normal" consumers. I argue that labels such as radical and extreme are more adequate to define the dominant agrifood regime, a regime that is radical in its management of natural (including human) and financial resources as well as in its concentration of power and ruthless expansion (Friedmann, 2005; Lang & Heasman, 2015).

I argue that a long-term solution to the risk of being co-opted involves a combination of strategies that resist conventionalization. This chapter presents a layered framework of four interwoven strategies that stand out from the cases analyzed: rediscovering new allies, fostering diversity, rethinking access to resources while redefining success and democratizing knowledge production. The four strategies come together as a solution to address two key challenges to social justice and sustainability in food systems: lack of diversity in the conventional food system and risk of co-optation of alternative and fairer practices.

The conceptual assumption underlying these strategies refers to three cores of diversity (quantitative and qualitative diversity) in the food system: nature, producers and consumers. The relationship amongst the four resistance strategies and the three cores of diversity generation is represented by the double hourglass in Figure 11.1. As the necks in the hourglass illustrate, the cores of diversity generation in the food system are separated by a handful of powerful companies, e.g. agribusinesses developing a small range of varieties for production separate the diversity found in nature from millions of farmers worldwide. Large processors and retailers separate producers from over seven billion consumers (today's world population). All of these actors (humans and natural ecosystems on which we rely to survive and produce food) interact and react in a contested food policy terrain that in turn is shaped by the wider socio-economic context in which food systems exist (Lang, Barling & Caraher, 2009). The strategies discussed below aim to alter the current dynamics between actors and widen power bottlenecks.

It is important to mention at this point that the food system is not linear, but circular (although not a neat closed system, but a messy, complex one). Waste and environmental impacts in every link of the chain take place, affecting the capacity of biodiversity to reproduce itself, and in turn, reducing the food system's ability to sustainable reproduce as well. Therefore, this model does not advocate a simplistic linear

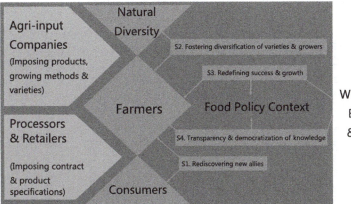

FIGURE 11.1 Double hourglass: strategies to tackle power imbalances in the food system

Source: R. Ajates Gonzalez

TABLE 11.1 Cooperative initiatives exploring new practices to protect their alterity

Cooperative name	Location	Produce/Services	Notes
Esnetik	Basque Country, Spain	Dairy products	MSC of sheep shepherds, workers, organizations and buying groups.
Cooperativa Abastecimiento Catalana of the Cooperativa Integral Catalana (CIC)	Catalonia, Spain	Vegetables (for growers' self-consumption) Different food items	CIC is an MSC creating a cooperative network to cover education, health, housing, transport and energy needs of members.
Actyva	Extremadura, Spain	Fruit, vegetables, wool, bread, etc.	Actyva is an MSC bringing together communication and marketing professionals with ecological farmers to help them market their products more efficiently.
La Verde	Cadiz, Spain	Vegetables for direct selling and self-consumption	Workers' cooperative that was set up by a group of agricultural workers in 1986.
OrganicLea	London, UK	Vegetables and some fruit	Workers' cooperative following permaculture practices and a sociocratic model.
Manchester Veg People	Manchester, UK	Vegetables (now also sell some fruit – sometimes imported – through their vegbox scheme)	MSC of growers, workers and buyers from restaurants, cafes and the University of Manchester who are growing, trading and educating about local organic food.
Moss Brook Growers	Manchester, UK	Vegetables	Workers' cooperative. Members of Manchester Veg People. The land owner is Unicorn, a workers' cooperative organic food store.
Biodynamic Land Trust	UK	Land investments	Its purpose is to secure land for biodynamic farming, gardening and food growing in the long term through partnerships, community involvement and shares.
Ecological Land Cooperative	England	Ethical investment company (Farmland)	MSC set up to address the lack of affordable sites for ecological land-based livelihoods in England. Their solution and core business is the creation of small clusters of three or more affordable residential smallholdings.

Source: R. Ajates Gonzalez

vision of the food system that assumes infinite resources at one end and a limitless capacity to absorb waste at the other. Figure 11.1 is just zooming in and providing a closer look at the unequal power relations these multi-stakeholder cooperative initiatives are trying to tackle through the different strategies discussed in this chapter. A list of the case studies and their locations can be found in Table 11.1.

Rediscovering new allies

For decades, large retailers have presented themselves as the indispensable middle link helping producers market their products and looking after the interests of consumers by offering cheap and "convenient" food. This discourse claims growers and consumers' interests cannot ever be reconciled. Under what conditions can consumers and farmers become allies rather than opponents? Multi-stakeholder cooperatives (MSCs) are emerging as one possible solution. As opposed to conventional agricultural cooperatives formed by farmer members only, MSCs offer membership to consumers, buyers and worker members (Gray, 2014). MSCs normally have weighted voting for each group of members to ensure growers can maintain a voice and decision-making power even when consumer members outgrow them. In the UK, MSCs even have a new set of cooperative rules approved in 2009 called the Somerset Rules (Somerset Cooperative Services, 2009). As a worker and consumer member from a dairy MSC in the Basque Country called Esnetik told me, joining an MSC offers a welcomed opportunity to individuals wanting to develop agency and participate in agrarian projects while still maintaining their identity as consumers.

In the UK, Manchester Veg People (MVP) is another MSC bringing together growers, coordinators and buyers from restaurants, cafes and Manchester University. MVP is the only provider of food in Manchester that is both local and organically grown (Manchester Veg People, 2014; Ajates Gonzalez, 2017). MVP is working with schools to adjust their menus so that they can incorporate seasonal food cultivated by MVP growers. By tapping into public procurement, MVP aims to reach people who might not otherwise eat MVP vegetables, creating more demand for fairer and more sustainable food while democratizing access to local organic food. In London, OrganicLea, a workers' farming cooperative very close to its consumers, has liaised with Waltham Forest Council to access and lease land for food production "in the city, for the city" (OrganicLea, 2014). These collaborations reclaim the right to have enabling local authorities supporting local communities (Böhm, Pervez Bharucha & Pretty, 2014), transforming local governments from enemies posing obstacles into allies, while connecting bottom-up initiatives with top-down resources.

Additionally, MSCs target collective rather than individual consumption for bigger impact, serving groups with a minimum number of households, neighbors associations, non-governmental organizations (NGOs), workplaces, etc. This approach contrasts with the focus on individualization promoted by big food brands and retailers. It also encourages long-term relations that foster new sustainable habits of food provision and consumption (Brunori, Rossi & Guidi, 2012).

As explained in the introduction, most farmers and consumers are separated by a narrow stronghold of power dominated by large processors and retailers. Local governments are also normally seen as distant actors and a problem rather than as potential enablers. However, when this distance is overcome, mutual points of interests can be found, and alliances forged. Co-opting these new alliances is hard for large actors as they lack the flexibility to adapt to micro-local dynamics; big retailers thrive by separating, rather than bringing together, farmers and producers.

Fostering diversification instead of specialization

Diversity as a solution becomes key at all levels: from the plot to the global (Morgan & Sonnino, 2010). On the farm, agroecological approaches that try to mimic cycles found in nature help growers move from monoculture to polycultures that offer more varied produce and lowers the need for artificial inputs, reducing dependency on the agri-industrial conglomerate (Actyva, 2014). By sharing land, new workers' cooperatives in farming such as OrganicLea and Moss Brook Growers (members of MVP) are able to attract growers from different backgrounds, meaning that not only crops, but also producers, are diverse (Moss Brook Growers, 2014). Some MSCs, such as Esnetik, are keen to move away from specialization and are happy to support new shepherds to install themselves with a small herd and a multi-crop plot mainly for self-consumption. This allows them to reduce the start-up investment required for standard large herds and fosters the diversity of foods they are producing.

Diversification is present not only within these cooperatives' farm systems, but also in their social systems. By including workers and consumers in the cooperative organization, MSCs offer several avenues through which different actors are able to share and negotiate their concerns or objectives, whatever they are: environmental, political, gender or health-related (Ajates Gonzalez, 2017). Diverse members bring their own networks and struggles with them, which takes them from local to global food – such as La Via Campesina, an international movement of peasants, agricultural workers and landless people (La Via Campesina, 2011). Some are also developing "local to local" partnerships with the aim of bringing together like-minded initiatives in different countries, trading in their own terms and without losing the trust characteristic of face-to-face exchanges (Baggini, 2014). Esnetik also organizes "street protest markets", a critical version of standard farmers' markets where members sell products and talk to the public about food issues.

Importantly, these global networks are going beyond food into other aspects of life. The Cooperativa Integral Catalana offers not only food, but also health, education and finance solutions to their members (Cooperativa Integral Catalana, 2014). Catasol, in northwest Spain, is also aiming to cover a wide range of needs for its members (see Tienda Catasol, 2017). Other MSCs, such as Esnetik, have a close involvement with REAS (the Spanish branch of the Social Solidarity Economy

Network) to work for a new society that takes into account the social and ethical dimension in all its economic activities (RIPESS, 2015). It was interesting to learn that REAS has six principles that, along with feminist and food sovereignty ones, are more central and core to the raison d'etre of Esnetik than the International Cooperative Alliance cooperative principles in themselves (REAS, 2011).

Diversification for Actyva means bringing together people from different professions: media, marketing, farming, etc. under the same cooperative umbrella, with the aim of supporting small farmers with extensive farming methods but no marketing skills to market their products more effectively. At the same time, they are creating employment in a very rural area of Spain that has the highest rate of undeclared or shadow economy in the country at 31.1 per cent (6.5 percentage points higher than the national average) with over 30 per cent unemployment (GESTHA, 2014).

Referring back to the double hourglass concept, this second strategy aims to emphasize the diversity that can be found in nature, farmers and consumers: e.g. by trying new varieties instead of the mass-produced ones, and by offering new products through new channels instead of through supermarkets. This strategy is hard to conventionalize as it goes against the standardization characteristic of the industrial food system: reducing costs and risks while maximizing profit.

Accessing resources while redefining success and growth

Another strategy to avoid conventionalization involves accessing finances to be able to help new growers with fewer resources. Some models, such as workers' cooperatives, are centuries old, but are being reintroduced into farming, which is quite rare as most cooperatives in agriculture nowadays are for supply, processing and marketing services that do not require farmer members to share land or work together on a daily basis. Evidence suggest members of large supply and marketing cooperatives embedded in industrial food operations are likely to behave more like detached customers rather than owners of their cooperatives (Nilsson, Svendsen & Svendsen, 2012). Furthermore, for people who are keen to make a living as food producers but do not come from a farming family, workers' cooperatives can be a tool to access land and resources, thus facilitating access and diversity of growers from different backgrounds.

One of these initiatives is the Ecological Land Cooperative (ELC), an MSC offering positive investment opportunities to members who can buy shares in organic farms that are then offered to new tenant farmers (Ecological Land Cooperative, 2015). ELC's solution and core business is the creation of small clusters of three or more affordable residential smallholdings. Growers are given permission to build their own sustainable home. Another organization is the Biodynamic Land Trust (BLT). Similarly to ELC, BLT works to take back land from intensive farming methods, put it into trust, retaining the freehold in order to protect it for agricultural and ecological use, and keep it affordable in perpetuity (Biodynamic Land

Trust, n.d.). The BLT follows a tripartite model of the economy based on public, private and community ownership that is also being adopted by some community farms (Large, 2010). BLT is also supporting a seed cooperative project (Biodynamic Land Trust, n.d.). In Spain, many cooperatives are also rethinking the wider economic system they exist in and fostering the use of alternative and social currencies (Cooperativa Integral Catalana, 2015).

While large players in the conventional food systems are constantly chasing new markets, tight profit margins and short-term returns for their shareholders, a new trend for decent livelihoods based on non-profit farming is slowly emerging (Carvel, 2010). This quote from an OrganicLea member offers an insight into the vision for a non-for-profit food system:

> So when we say we are non-for-profit we don't mean we are against fair livelihoods, it means we are against the extraction of profit from other people's labor, so after paying livelihoods, we re-invest any surplus into the organization or into similar organizations and that for us it is a bigger social movement I suppose, a bigger drive to try and create a more equal society and farmers and growers should be able to make a dignified livelihood from their labor.
>
> *(OrganicLea worker, 2014, London)*

When this research was taking place, Esnetik members' objective was in fact to de-grow to a sustainable size they could maintain while growing more collective demand for their produce. This process involved not only redefining success, but also moving from vertical to horizontal growth, an approach also shared by MVP members – who, like Esnetik, see their success as the proliferation of sister cooperatives in other cities.

On the other hand, strategies for growth to reach more consumers and create more impact are also considered, but not at any price. Closely linked to their systemic thinking and allies beyond food, new models to overcome logistics barriers and achieve economies of scale are being developed. Collaborations with other ethical initiatives producing and trading non-food products to share transport costs or with driver cooperatives in the framework of the solidarity economy are in the making.

This and the previous strategy highlight how long-term solutions must acknowledge and tackle intersectionalities, e.g. gender issues, economic background, etc. (Roth, 2013). The work on redefining success and growth links back to the wider socio-economic context (outer circle in the double hourglass Figure 11.1), e.g. having de-growth as a strategy or trying to tackle current barriers to land ownership.

Transparency and democratization of knowledge production

From the pursuit of diversification emerges an ambition for the democratization of knowledge production. The starting premise is that diverse agroecological approaches bring abundance and increase resilience in the realm of crops, animals and people, while valuing different types of knowledge – both scientific and farmers' knowledge (Levidow et al., 2014). Peer-to-peer learning in MSCs strengthens growers' networks, both in food relocalization initiatives (Fonte, 2008) but also in online communities. These networks function to share seed varieties and practices (Seed Cooperative, 2016). The FarmHack community shares peer-to-peer designs of new tools and machinery (FarmHack, n.d.). Participatory research projects help give value to farmers' knowledge (Center for Agroecology, Water & Resilience, n.d.) and can have a long-term impact (Scialabba, Grandi & Henatsch, 2003; Da Via, 2012; Wakeford et al., 2017).

An example of this long-lasting impact is the case of a participatory research project with Spanish workers' cooperative La Verde, often quoted because it has been operating since it was set up in Cadiz in 1986 by agricultural workers with the aim to overcome their previous precarious labor situation. With the help of the Institute of Sociology and Farming Studies at the University of Cordoba, the Council of the Assembly of Andalusia and the Syndicate of Farm Workers of Andalusia, a research project called "Study of the potential use of local varieties of horticultural crops for organic agriculture" was initiated in 1988. Since then, they have had an ongoing involvement in saving and recovering traditional seed varieties. Their impact has been multilevel: locally, by recuperating forgotten varieties and re-starting an interest in the subject; nationally and internationally, as they host one of the largest organic seed banks in the European Union and have become the main organic seed supplier in Spain. La Verde has received recognition from the UN's Food and Agriculture Organization (FAO) for its work on alternative breeding and participatory research (Scialabba, Grandi & Henatsch, 2003). Their work on local, regional and national seed networks has not stopped (Red Andaluza de Semillas, 2010).

Transparency is also a key mechanism to protect the alterity of these initiatives; the cooperatives discussed are open for visits, a practice that serves both to educate members and to reinforce relationships of trust that do not require labels. Another solution inherently based on transparency is Esnetik's double labeling (see Image 11.2). All dairy products sold by this cooperative carry a label with a breakdown of the agreed price paid to the shepherds, and the percentage that goes to processing, packaging and marketing. Large retailers would not be able to absorb this practice, becoming a strategy for resistance that Esnetik's members are very aware of:

> When I arrived it was already in place and it was one of the things that attracted me to participate in the project. [. . .] Often from the agro-industrial model, many of the initiatives or the language end up being absorbed as their own, they commercialize their own organic lines even if they come from monocultures or far away places from the place of consumption [. . .]. The local part has also been integrated in the discourse of many big retailers, even if it also comes from big producers, from monocultures, intensive methods, no fair pay to local producers. [. . .] So then we thought that what

FIGURE 11.2 Transparency: Esnetik's double labeling

Photo credit: R. Ajates Gonzalez

characterizes big retailers is the impoverishment of the peasantry, the more you deliver, the more indebted you become, tightening prices all the time even more and the other conditions in the contract, so they are not going to be able to copy this [. . .] And when the commercialization goes over 20%, then they are never going to be able to do double labelling.

(Esnetik member, 2014, Spain)

This final strategy goes beyond challenging dominant practices in food systems and refers to efforts addressed at the transformation towards new ways of producing and sharing knowledge that supermarkets cannot capitalize on.

Conclusion

This chapter has presented a layered framework of four interconnected strategies used by MSCs: rediscovering new allies, fostering diversity, rethinking access to resources while redefining success and democratizing knowledge production. These four strategies come together to form a solution to improve food systems by reducing the risk of co-optation and increasing multilevel diversity (of growers, varieties, market channels, etc.). This solution is rooted in, and depends on, developing practices that are more difficult to conventionalize. The strategies discussed avoid co-optation by making it more difficult for large retailers and processors to co-opt certain practices: by increasing autonomy of growers, maintaining traditional production methods and varieties that cannot be mass-produced and industrialized; and by having a clear political and transformative vision.

MSCs offer inclusive umbrellas where struggles, but also skills, energies and hopes, converge. The connection of strategies discussed allows intersectionalities often neglected in AFN discourses to arise, providing a space for debate and the generation of potential ways forward. Aspects such as the gender and age of farmers, land ownership, disparities in income and decision-making power are often ignored or dismissed by conventionalized and standardized food production and retailing models that reward homogeneity of growers and produce that fit strict logistic and power dynamics. Multi-stakeholder food networks, in contrast, acknowledge these issues and tackle them through their practices, treating them as interconnected rather than independent cradles of both inequality and resilient diversity.

Multiple knowledges and peer-based knowledge production offer opportunities to overcome asymmetrical social power structures. Creative forms of governance and exchange give people a new identity as members of connected networks and an avenue for collective action, beyond typical classifications that label them as consumers or growers. Based on the importance of processes, not labels or certifications, the risk of replication becomes minimized as these modes of production and exchange are harder to copy by large players.

Inspired by food systems thinking that goes beyond reductionist and mechanistic models, these initiatives emerge from the awareness of being small pieces of the bigger jigsaw puzzle that food is (livelihoods, taste, tradition, etc.); the starting point is to question whose voices are missing in the current system. The systemic approach of these strategies is characterized by their strong local character combined with a deep awareness of and participation in global struggles. A bold next step for these MSCs, who already include in their management boards representatives of farmers, workers and consumers/buyers, could be the addition of a representative for the environment and for future generations in their boards to ensure all key short and long term interests are taken into account.

The food system needs systemic change. There is a growing humble awareness amongst grassroots innovators that no one thinker or group is going to single-handedly achieve a fair and food-secure future. The solution lies in the hands of many allies across and beyond food movements coming together under a solidarity economy model able to create solid alternatives for regenerative ways of eating and living that cannot and should not be conventionalized.

RECIPE: POLITICAL MAFTOUL (GIANT COUSCOUS) WARM SALAD WITH ROASTED VEGETABLES

I wanted to share this recipe because, through its ingredients, this dish can trigger a thousand reflections and conversations about the interwoven complexities and joys soaked in every meal we eat: tradition, trade, gender, climate, geo-politics, land, certifications and farming methods, amongst many others.

All foods have a political dimension. This could be about the government subsidies promoting the cultivation of a particular ingredient, the conditions of the agricultural workers who harvested another or if the eaters are local people or distant and better-off far-away consumers, etc. Probably no other food gets as political as the organic and fair-traded Palestinian maftoul, or giant couscous, used in this recipe. This particular maftoul is commercialized in the UK by Zaytoun, the company that launched the world's first fair trade olive oil in 2009 and that aims to create and develop a UK market for artisanal Palestinian produce. Zaytoun aims to support farming communities in Palestinian territories through a sustainable initiative that works through trade and not aid. Organic and fair trade farming in the West Bank coupled with finding a niche market with politically-minded consumers in the UK is a solution that enables them to reproduce political and social resistance. The packaging and labeling are also done in Palestine to create additional employment opportunities.

The whole-wheat grain is boiled, sun-dried, cracked and then hand-rolled in ground organic whole-wheat flour. It is then steamed and sun-dried by women-owned cooperatives. Maftoul is traditionally made for special occasions.

I like recipes I can adapt using whatever ingredients I have at home. This reduces waste and increases creativity and confidence as a cook. I have tried to introduce as much flexibility as possible in the list of ingredients and instructions so that you can make it your own.

Ingredients

Zaytoun maftoul giant couscous (250g serves 4, calculate accordingly)
Vegetables – Select whatever vegetables you have at home, or if you are buying, buy whatever is seasonal, but avoid potatoes as the couscous will give you enough carbohydrates. Explore your local options for supporting different purchasing channels such as food assembly groups, allotment surplus, etc. Keep them varied for a more nutritional and colourful dish.
Dressing – You can simply add extra virgin olive oil or prepare the following dressing:

- honey (try to buy local as evidence suggests it is good to protect you from hay fever; also buy honey from natural beekeepers who do not feed the bees sugar and only collect a proportion of the honey produced by the hive and leave enough for the bees to feed on and survive over winter)
- extra virgin olive oil
- vinegar
- pepper
- salt

Cooking

This dish has three cooking stages:

1 Roasted vegetables

Turn on the oven to 180 degrees C. To make the most of the energy used to heat the oven up, try to fit in a baking session, e.g. baking oats and seeds for 10 minutes while the oven is heating up will give you the basis base for a tasty and healthy homemade muesli.

In the meantime, wash, peel (if needed) and chop the vegetables, e.g. onions, carrots, garlic (use garlic unpeeled and note it needs less roasting time), beetroot (roast in a separate small dish or it will taint all your vegetables a pink-reddish color), parsnips, cauliflower, mushrooms (also need less roasting time), etc. For green leafy vegetables, either roast for less time or steam and add at the end.

Drizzle olive oil and add a pinch of salt and pepper over the vegetables; put them in the oven and roast until you can put a knife through them easily.

2 Maftoul

While the vegetables are roasting, rinse the maftoul, then bring it to a boil in 400ml of water or stock. Simmer for around 12–15 minutes until the liquid is absorbed. The grains will change from white to a golden color.

3 Dressing

While the maftoul is simmering, whisk together the honey, oil, vinegar, pepper and salt in a separate bowl to form a smooth dressing.

Toss all ingredients together in a bowl, add dressing to taste and serve warm. After eating, if there is anything left, you can enjoy it for lunch the following day; top it up with some salad leaves and tomatoes, cucumber or whatever salad-prone ingredient you have available. Love food hate waste!

Critical questions

1   To what extent are the interests and objectives of consumers and producers irreconcilable?
2   If most people are unable to grow everything they eat, what ways of trading can foster multi-dimensional food system sustainability?
3   Can more sustainable methods of food growing and provisioning ever become a serious and widespread alternative without overcoming labor and logistics issues?

4 To what extent can linking up with other transport, retail and processing cooperatives or social enterprises sharing the same values and vision be part of a solution to those logistic issues?

5 How can international solidarity economy networks and principles take Alternative Food Networks (AFNs) to the next stage, where they start becoming the norm and not the alternative?

Acknowledgements

I would like to thank all my case studies, especially those whose members are giving up easy comforts to work towards more just and sustainable food systems.

References

Actyva. (2014) *Somos granjeros y urbanitas en transición*. Available from: www.bbbfarming.net/somos [Accessed: 4th March 2017].

Ajates Gonzalez, R. (2017) Going back to go forwards? From multi-stakeholder cooperatives to open cooperatives in food and farming. *Journal of Rural Studies*. Available from: doi: 10.1016/j.jrurstud.2017.02.018

Baggini, J. (2014) *The Virtues of the Table: How to Eat and Think*. London, Granta Books.

Biodynamic Land Trust. (n.d.) *Securing and protecting land*. Available frmo: www.biodynamic landtrust.org.uk [Accessed: 4th March 2017].

Böhm, S., Pervez Bharucha, Z. & Pretty, J. (eds.) (2014) *Ecocultures: Blueprints for Sustainable Communities*. Oxon, Routledge.

Brunori, G., Rossi, A. & Guidi, F. (2012) On the new social relations around and beyond food. Analysing consumers' role and action in Gruppi di Acquisto Solidale (Solidarity Purchasing Groups). *Sociologia Ruralis*. 52 (1), 1–30.

BTC. (2014) *New fair trade labels attract criticisms*. Available from: www.befair.be/en/content/new-fairtrade-labels-attract-criticism [Accessed: 4th March 2017].

Buck, D., Getz, C. & Guthman, J. (1997) From farm to table: The organic vegetable commodity chain of northern California. *Sociologia Ruralis*. 37 (1), 3–20.

Burlingame, B. & Dernini, S. (eds.) (2010) *Sustainable Diets and Biodiversity: Directions and Solutions for Policy, Research and Action*. Rome, Italy, Food and Agriculture Organization of the United Nations.

Carvel, J. (3 February 2010) Residents join forces to feed themselves. *The Guardian*. Available from: www.theguardian.com/society/2010/feb/03/martin-communal-food [Accessed: 5th March 2017].

Center for Agroecology, Water & Resilience. (n.d.) *Research group: Community self organization for resilience*. Available from: www.coventry.ac.uk/research/areas-of-research/agroe cology-water- resilience/community-self-organization-for-resilience/ [Accessed: 4th March 2017].

Cooperativa Integral Catalana. (2014) *Cooperative public system*. Available from: http://co operativa.cat/en/cooperative-public-system/ [Accessed: 4th March 2017].

Cooperativa Integral Catalana. (2015) *Social currency*. Available from: http://cooperativa.cat/en/economic-system/social-currency-2/ [Accessed: 4th March 2017].

Da Via, E. (2012) Seed diversity, farmers' rights, and the politics of repeasantization. *International Journal of Sociology of Agriculture and Food*. 19 (2), 229–242.

Department for Environment, Food and Rural Affairs (DEFRA). (2012) *Food statistics pocket book 2012*. Available from: http://webarchive.nationalarchives.gov.uk/20130123162956/ http://www.defra.gov.uk/statistics/files/defra-stats-foodfarm-food-pocketbook-2012-130104.pdf [Accessed: 4th March 2017].

Ecological Land Cooperative. (2015) *Investing*. Available from: http://ecologicalland.coop/investing [Accessed: 4th March 2017].

Esnetik. (n.d.) *¿Qué es Esnetik?* Available from: www.esnetik.com/?page_id=14 [Accessed: 4th March 2017].

FarmHack. (n.d.) *Tools*. Available from: http://farmhack.org/tools [Accessed: 4th March 2017].

Fonte, M. (2008) Knowledge, food and place. A way of producing, a way of knowing. *Sociologia Ruralis*. 48 (3), 200–222.

Friedmann, H. (2005) From colonialism to green capitalism: Social movements and emergence of food regimes. *Research in Rural Sociology and Development*. 11, 227.

GESTHA. (2014) *La economía sumergida pasa factura*. Available from: http://www.gestha.es/archivos/actualidad/2014/2014-01-29_InformePrensa_EconomiaSumergida.pdf [Accessed: 8th November 2016].

Goodman, D., DuPuis, E. M. & Goodman, M. K. (2011) *Alternative Food Networks: Knowledge, Practice, and Politics*. Oxon, Routledge.

Goodman, M. K. (2010) The mirror of consumption: Celebritization, developmental consumption and the shifting cultural politics of fair trade. *Geoforum*. 41 (1), 104–116.

Gray, T. (2014) Historical tensions, institutionalization, and the need for multistakeholder cooperatives. *Journal of Agriculture, Food Systems, and Community Development*. 4 (3), 23–28.

Griffiths, P. (2012) Ethical objections to fairtrade. *Journal of Business Ethics*. 105 (3), 357–373.

Jaffee, D. (2010) Fair trade standards, corporate participation, and social movement responses in the United States. *Journal of Business Ethics*. 92 (2), 267–285.

La Via Campesina. (2011) *What is La Via Campesina?* Available from: https://viacampesina.org/en/index.php/organisation-mainmenu-44/what-is-la-via-campesina-mainmenu-45 [Accessed: 5th March 2017].

Lang, T. (2010) From 'value-for-money' to 'values-for-money'? Ethical food and policy in Europe. *Environment and Planning A*. 42 (8), 1814–1832.

Lang, T., Barling, D. & Caraher, M. (2009) *Food Policy: Integrating Health, Environment and Society*. Oxford, Oxford University Press.

Lang, T. & Heasman, M. (2015) *Food Wars: The Global Battle for Mouths, Minds and Markets*. Oxon, Routledge.

Large, M. (2010) *Common Wealth: For a Free, Equal, Mutual and Sustainable Society*. Gloucestershire, Hawthorn Press.

Levidow, L., Pimbert, M., Stassart, P. M. & Vanloqueren, G. (2014) Agroecology in Europe: Conforming or transforming the dominant agro-food regime. *Agroecology and Sustainable Food Systems*. 38 (10), 1127–1155.

Manchester Veg People. (2014) *Manchester veg people*. Available from: http://vegpeople.org.uk/about [Accessed: 5th March 2017].

Morgan, K. & Sonnino, R. (2010) The urban foodscape: World cities and the new food equation. *Cambridge Journal of Regions, Economy and Society*. 3 (2), 209–224.

Moss Brook Growers. (2014) *Who we are*. Available from: www.mossbrookgrowers.co.uk/?page_id=2 [Accessed: 5th March 2017].

NCD Risk Factor Collaboration (NCD-RisC). (2016) Trends in adult body-mass index in 200 countries from 1975 to 2014: A pooled analysis of 1698 population-based measurement studies with 19.2 million participants. *The Lancet*. 387 (10026), 1377–1396.

Nilsson, J., Svendsen, G. L. & Svendsen, G. T. (2012) Are large and complex agricultural cooperatives losing their social capital? *Agribusiness*. 28 (2), 187–204.

OrganicLea. (2014) *Our history*. Available from: www.organiclea.org.uk/about/history/ [Accessed: 5th March 2017].

REAS. (2011) *Carta de Principios de la Economia Solidaria*. Available from: www.economia solidaria.org/carta.php [Accessed: 5th March 2017].

Red Andaluza de Semillas. (2010) *La Verde, S.C.A.* Available from: www.redandaluzade semillas.org/centro-de-recursos/alianzas-y-convenios/la-verde-s-c-a/ [Accessed: 5th March 2017].

RIPESS. (2015) *Intercontinental network for the promotion of social solidarity economy*. Available from: www.ripess.org/about-us/?lang=en [Accessed: 5th March 2017].

Roth, J. (2013) *Entangled inequalities as intersectionalities: Towards an epistemic sensibilization*. Research Network on Interdependent Inequalities in Latin America. Working Paper Series No. 43.

Scialabba, N. E. H., Grandi, C. & Henatsch, C. (2003) *Organic agriculture and genetic resources for food and agriculture*. Food and Agriculture Organization of the United Nations (FAO). Biodiversity and the ecosystem approach in agriculture, forestry and fisheries.

Seed Cooperative. (2016) *About*. Available from: www.seedcooperative.org.uk/index.html [Accessed: 5th March 2017].

Somerset Cooperative Services. (2009) *The Somerset rules – register an IPS multistakeholder co-op*. Available from: www.somerset.coop/somersetrules [Accessed: 5th March 2017].

Taylor, P. L. (2005) In the market but not of it: Fair trade coffee and forest stewardship council certification as market-based social change. *World Development*. 33 (1), 129–147.

Thrupp, L. A. (2000) Linking agricultural biodiversity and food security: The valuable role of agrobiodiversity for sustainable agriculture. *International Affairs*. 76 (2), 283–297.

Tienda Catasol (2017). *Facebok page*. Available from: www.facebook.com/Catasol.S.Coop. astur [Accessed 27th March 2017].

Wakeford, T., Chang, M. and Anderson, C. (2017) *Action Research for Food Systems Transformation*. Centre for Agroecology, Water and Resilience: Coventry University.

PART IV

Designing sustainable food futures

12

CULTURED MEAT, BETTER THAN BEANS?

Cor van der Weele

Introduction: from pulses to cultured meat

That global levels of meat production and consumption are untenable no longer needs extensive introduction, and it is equally clear that those global levels continue to increase. Let me therefore start with only a brief history of major problems that have successively appeared on the public agenda, in order to comment on what paying attention to them has and has not accomplished so far.

The growth of meat consumption and production after the Second World War, first in Western countries and later in many other countries, came with intensification and industrialization. Ruth Harrison attacked this trend in 1964 in her book *Animal Machines*. She protested "the new factory farming industry" in which animal lives revolve around profit. The book was hugely successful in drawing attention to animal welfare and setting in motion still-flowing rivers of information, education, research, policy and action. But it was not successful in putting an end to industrial production; today, intensive animal farming is spreading around the world.

In 2006, *Livestock's Long Shadow* addressed environmental issues (Steinfeld et al., 2006). This report by the Food and Agriculture Organization (FAO) calculated that livestock production takes up 70% of all agricultural land, directly or indirectly (through feed crops), produces 18% of global greenhouse gas emissions, uses and pollutes huge amounts of water and plays the leading role in the destruction of biodiversity. It also projected roughly a doubling of meat production globally for 2050. This report, too, was greatly successful in extending the problem agenda, encouraging discussion and more research, but not successful, so far, in putting an end to the global growth of meat production and consumption.

In 2015, a third problem appeared on the agenda. The World Health Organization called attention to the health risks of eating too much meat – primarily red and processed meat – as wealthy humans now do (Bouvard et al., 2015). And again, this led to much discussion.

Proposals for more responsible diets preceded this problem accumulation. As early as 1971, Frances Moore Lappé wrote *Diet for a Small Planet* (Moore Lappé, 1971). She argued that the losses involved in turning plant protein into animal protein are outrageous given that half of humanity is starving. The book did not just list this and other problems of meat – it also focussed on a simple and readily available alternative: pulses, in combination with grain, were offered as the ideal solution. In order to facilitate the dietary move, Lappé provided many recipes.

The book became a bestseller and was translated into many languages, but here was another successful book that did not reverse trends: not only did meat consumption continue to go up, pulse consumption continued, and continues, to decrease throughout the world. In Spain, to take one example, pulse consumption at present is estimated to be about a quarter of what it was in the early 1960s (around 16 kilos per person per year then, around 4 kilos now), while meat consumption tripled and is considered to be 'very high' in comparison with the traditional Mediterranean standard (Varela-Moreiras et al., 2010). The authors argue that due to these changes, the Spanish diet can no longer be characterized as a traditional, healthy Mediterranean diet.

Though figures differ greatly (Schneider, 2002), the dominant global trends are clear. In the Netherlands, meat consumption grew from about 35 kilos per person in 1950 to more than 80 kilos in 2010, while pulse consumption, never very high, is now only about 1 kilo per person per year. In China, meat consumption has risen very quickly, from 14 kilos per person per year in 1970 to levels that now approach that of Western countries, while pulse consumption went down and is now comparable to the Netherlands (Alexandratos & Bruinsma, 2012).

From various perspectives, pulses seem to be ideal meat alternatives. They contain large amounts of protein, typically well over 20%, and are very high in fibre. Although amino-acid composition of the proteins needs complementation, this can easily be provided by grains. Pulses are good for the soil because their roots live in symbiosis with nitrogen-fixing bacteria; through this cooperation, they not only make their own nitrogen, they also reduce the need for fertilizers of other crops that are grown in rotation. Their consumption, however, rather seems to move in accordance with their reputation as 'meat for the poor': as the world grows richer, pulses are replaced by the real thing. By now, pulses could be characterized as underutilized or even neglected crops (Majumdar, 2011). The United Nations designated 2016 as the International Year of the Pulses in order to call the world's attention to the benefits of pulses. Is this going to reverse trends?

We are 'meathooked', according to the title of Marta Zaraska's book (Zaraska, 2016), which explores the backgrounds of meat consumption. Zaraska starts with the story of her mother, who decided to become a vegetarian and two weeks later was back on meat. When she was asked about it sometime later, she just shrugged and said "I like meat, I eat it, end of story" (Zaraska, 2016, p. 1). Chapter after chapter, the book describes the various mechanisms that keep us hooked – that meat satisfies our 'protein hunger' and is extremely tasty, that it symbolizes power and welfare, that changing cherished habits is hard, that the meat industry works hard to keep or make us satisfied meat eaters, and that more generally, there are great economic interests at stake. Despite the urgent reasons for meat reduction, "the problem is that people around the planet are not particularly willing to do so. They don't want lentils; they want steaks" (Zaraska, 2016, p. 185). Zaraska therefore thinks that before the world is ready for really getting off the hook, which will require awareness of the many meanings of meat, hope is mainly directed at the search for 'the perfect meat replacement'.

The idea that we are meathooked aligns with the observation that in Western countries, where information about the problems of meat consumption is well-communicated, people have hardly been doing better than to stabilize their meat consumption. Meat is so attractive that peas, lentils and beans as hopeful alternatives have been replaced by the idea that alternatives need to mimic meat. At first, such meat-imitating alternatives were plant-based, and they resembled meat in form (e.g. the form of a burger) but hardly in taste or structure. But these, too, did not really fly, and the diagnosis was that they simply did not mimic meat well enough (Hoek, 2010; Hoek et al., 2011).

Based on the assumption that only alternatives that perfectly resemble meat will be able to compete with meat, cultured meat appears as the ideal solution. The goal of cultured meat was, and is, to grow animal muscle tissue starting from animal (stem) cells, outside an animal body. What to call this meat alternative – *in vitro* meat, cultured meat, clean meat, or simply "meat' – remains unsettled. Whatever the outcome of this battle for framing, it is often emphasized that this potential alternative will not just resemble meat; it will *be* meat, that just happens to be produced in a different (more sustainable, more animal-friendly) way.

This chapter looks at the ways in which cultured meat can be a potential food solution. I will first give a brief overview of the young history of research on cultured meat, and also discuss the changing position with regard to other alternatives that are also becoming more successful in mimicking meat. The next question is what can and cannot be learned from responses to the idea of cultured meat. For example: (how) can such a technological fix ever lead to moral and political change? I will discuss how the mere idea of cultured meat triggers latent ambivalences on meat and opens up new search spaces. Finally, I will wonder about the prospects of cultured meat in a changing planetary diet. Apart from simple options – complete failure, perfect solution – there are also more complex scenarios for the role of cultured meat, for example, as a stage in a wider transition.

Cultured meat and beyond, a brief history

Winston Churchill was a visionary thinker. Already in 1932, he wrote about the idea of cultured meat in his essay *Fifty Years Hence* (Churchill, 1932), saying that it is in fact an "absurdity" to grow a whole chicken in order to eat only the breast or the wing; better to grow these parts "separately, under a suitable medium".[1] Several decades later, the Dutch businessman Willem van Eelen arrived at the same idea from a different background, namely an incessant brooding of food production after experiences of severe hunger in Asian internment camps during the Second World War.

The notion lingered on with hardly anyone paying attention. As long as meat was not seen as a problem by most people, no solutions were needed, let alone weird solutions. Willem van Eelen, meanwhile, kept cherishing the idea, and in 1998 he acquired a patent on a production method, even though this method could not yet be put to practice. At the same time, in the USA, NASA funded attempts by Morris Benjaminson to culture goldfish muscle tissue, guided by the idea that such a technology might serve useful goals on space flights. Though that project was stopped after a while, the problems of meat had become more conspicuous by then, and while existing alternatives remained marginal, the idea of *in vitro* meat began to attract attention. An artist and a student were influential in spreading this idea. The bio-artist was Oron Catts, who specializes in working with living tissue. In his 2003 project *Disembodied Cuisine*, he managed to culture cells from a frog and presented them as tiny frog steaks during a dinner performed at a museum in Nantes, France (Catts & Zurr, 2007). The frog that acted as cell donor was present at the performance. The student was Jason Matheny, who was appalled by intensive chicken raising. He read about Benjaminson's work, became dedicated to the idea that this promised to be a more responsible way of producing meat (Pincock, 2007), and founded the lobby organization New Harvest. When he was invited to the Netherlands in 2004, van Eelen and Matheny met with each other and the Dutch government, which led to a four-year research project at three Dutch universities.

Hope for *in vitro* meat had different motivations (Van der Weele & Driessen, 2013). Most researchers saw it primarily as a way to keep meat available in affordable and sustainable ways. Others saw it as the best hope for animals. In 2008, a first ethical evaluation concluded that because of its promise of reducing the need for animals to suffer for our meat eating, *in vitro* meat might not just be a good idea but "something we might be morally required to support" (Hopkins & Dacey, 2008, p. 595). In the same year, the animal organization PETA (People for the Ethical Treatment of Animals) offered a one million dollar prize to whomever would be able to make *in vitro* chicken meat and sell it commercially by 2012. But hope had to be delayed. Nobody claimed the PETA prize. The Dutch research project yielded four PhD theses with fundamental insights, yet cultured meat as a product was not in sight. There was only modest follow-up money available from the Dutch government, and that was meant in part for studying moral and societal aspects – this was the start of my own research (see the Acknowledgements). Overall, money was hard to come by. In 2011, the *in vitro* meat research community, gathering in Gothenburg, estimated that only a handful of people worldwide were working on *in vitro* meat. The meeting also thought that '*cultured*' meat might sound less scientific and more attractive than *in vitro* meat.

It had become clear that there were serious challenges to overcome. Stem cells of cows and pigs were not well enough understood; the growth medium would have to get rid of animal ingredients; how to make tissue larger than small fibers was an open question, and so was the quest for up-scaling. But from 2011 onward, a new and bolder second wave emerged, which also led to a diversification of approaches. An extremely hopeful tentative Life Cycle Analysis (LCA) was published in 2011 that foresaw, among other things, a 99% reduction in land requirement for cultured meat compared to beef (Tuomisto & Teixeira de Mattos, 2011). In the same year, Mark Post announced that he had agreed with an American private funder to make a hamburger that would be imperfect in many ways, but good enough to serve as a proof-of-principle, and thus would attract more attention and research money. Also in 2011, Gabor and Andras Forgacs founded the company Modern Meadow – helped by private money, too – to make cultured leather as well as meat by using 3-D printing instead of tissue engineering. Another 2011 initiative illustrated again how cultured meat also triggered the imagination of bio-artists and designers: Koert van Mensvoort at Eindhoven University in the Netherlands made his design students use their imagination on cultured meat: what might it look like, apart from a hamburger?

Modern Meadow presented the first small piece of leather in 2012. Mark Post presented his hamburger in 2013. Koert van Mensvoort's students' designs led to the publication of the *In Vitro Meat Cookbook* in 2014 (van Mensvoort & Grievink, 2014). Today, Modern Meadow's website confirms the importance of a mix of disciplines: it is presented as a company of "designers, scientists and engineers".

For Modern Meadow, meat was not the only or even the primary goal: leather had priority. This is indicative of a widening process in which boundaries are blurring, not only between meat and other animal products, but also between animal-based research and plant-based research. New generations of plant-based meat alternatives increasingly resemble meat; Impossible Foods (USA) as well as the Vegetarian Butcher (The Netherlands), for example, offer plant-based products they claim to be indistinguishable from meat. Other companies have developed plant-based egg products, bio-engineered milk, et cetera. Start-up companies are conspicuous at the forefront of research – as *Bloomberg News* announced in 2013: "Silicon Valley embraces innovation in sustainable foods" (Fehrenbacher, 2013), while do-it-yourself scientists also have started to experiment with making cultured meat. In 2015, New Harvest shifted from promoting cultured meat to promoting cellular agriculture, which encompasses a wider range of new technologies (including synthetic biology) and a wider range of products; the aim is a 'post-animal bio-economy' (see http://www.new-harvest.org/about, accessed on 1 June 2017).

Cultured meat thus no longer seems to be in a separate category; it has become part of a larger field of engineered agricultural products. Despite the variety of approaches, the overall goal is to make replacements of animal-based products that cannot be distinguished from them. Is technological innovation on its way to disrupt factory farming, or even agriculture more generally?

Opening up ambivalent silence

Narrowing down again to cultured meat: the question whether it might replace animal products requires that it is (widely) welcomed as a food product. Until there are real products, only responses to the idea can be studied. When I started to study such responses in 2010, the expectation in the air was that cultured meat, or *in vitro* meat as it was then called, would lead to extensive 'yuck' feelings. But when I talked to people and audiences, *yuck* seemed to be the first response of just a modest minority of people, in the Netherlands at least. Besides, first responses quickly gave rise to more complex considerations. This dynamic makes sense, since it takes some time to think and feel through such a novel idea, to explore uneasiness and associations, to learn more, to imagine possible consequences. We therefore preferred to explore responses not through initial responses or surveys, but through group discussions. We did this in two rounds.

In the first round, we held two workshops about possible futures of cultured meat, partly with the help of the designs made by Koert van Mensvoort's students, which were meant to create an imaginative atmosphere. Both workshops generated mixed and uneasy thoughts and feelings, not only about cultured meat, but at least as much about 'normal' meat. The remark that cultured meat is unnatural, for example, backfired: yes, but how natural is our present way of making meat? For many participants, the idea of cultured meat immediately triggered their unhappiness with factory farming. In one of the two workshops, an idea emerged that warmed people to cultured meat as a possible solution: to make it in small local factories, from cells (small biopsies) taken from happy pigs in urban farms or backyards. The idea, which we named *the pig in the backyard* scenario, was experienced as almost too good to be true, as it combined the benefits of meat eating with happy animals and the option of intimate relations with them: a great example of local/urban food production. Hesitations that cultured meat may be too technological, unnatural or alienating seemed to evaporate with this scenario; it was experienced as a remedy against our alienation from food (Van der Weele & Driessen, 2013).

In the second round, we held a series of follow-up focus groups among meat-eating people of various ages and backgrounds. We introduced the basics of cultured meat in the most minimal way, without any reasons or goals, inviting first responses and questions. After that, we introduced various scenarios, using again different visualizations to make the idea more concrete and to encourage the imagination. The general atmosphere that emerged in the focus groups was a kind of hesitant sympathy, which (again) largely emerged from widespread negative feelings towards factory farming. Apart from that, the central findings in that second round revolved around an unanticipated difference between young and older participants. We had expected that the young (and the urban) would be more open to the idea of cultured meat than older and rural people, but we found no evidence for that. Instead, the young and the old differed in how they approached cultured meat. The trend among younger people was to appreciate the technological novelty and to wonder "Would I eat it?" The answer tended to be "yes, (but only) if it is exactly like meat" (i.e. a hamburger): their present personal preferences were leading. Older people, on the other hand, tended to relativize their own food preferences and looked at the new food from a somewhat larger distance, realizing how much their diet had already changed during their lifetimes. They made historical comparisons

("Margarine was also very strange at first") to explore chances of societal acceptance for cultured meat, or they discussed the prospects for societal transition ("McDonalds should do this"). Their discussion also developed into reflections on how meat consumption and production have changed over the years ("we eat too much of it nowadays", "the quality is not what it used to be"). For them, the idea of cultured meat thus figured as an invitation to discuss wider problems of meat and pathways of change. Insofar as they spoke about their own behaviour, they did not seem to see themselves as moral pioneers. Rather, older people were inclined to explore whether cultured meat might be a source of a collective road to societal change, comparable to earlier food changes, and whether it might thus be a source of collective moral hope (Van der Weele & Driessen, 2014a).

Under the surface of routine behaviour, meat has become an ambivalent food for many people, beloved and rooted in tradition on the one hand, and associated with moral problems on the other hand. While these problems raise concern, they also threaten to disturb the option to eat meat with a clear conscience. People respond differently to this uncomfortable position. Facing the ambivalence is one option, trying to evade it is another.

In a qualitative study about the kind of information that people were interested in about food, avoidance of meat issues through 'strategic ignorance' conspicuously surfaced through remarks such as "If you want to eat meat, you should not know too much about it" or "If I paid attention to every factory farmed chicken, shopping would be much more expensive" (Van der Weele, 2013b). A quantitative parallel study found that about 30% of respondents recognized this strategy from their own behaviour (Onwezen et al., 2013). Together, the studies suggested that strategic ignorance is a routine way of dealing with ambivalences concerning meat, and that for most people, the strategy may not be completely conscious in everyday life, but neither is it hard to access.

Strategic ignorance is easily confused with indifference, because it comes with the same (meat-eating) behavior. Yet they are different; indifferent people have no reason to avoid information, while ambivalent people, are in need for means to restore their peace of mind. Evading the issue is one option (Onwezen & van der Weele, 2016; Van der Weele, 2013a; Van der Weele & Driessen, 2014b). In our focus groups, cultured meat, with its philosophy of eating meat without hurting animals, opened a door to a psychological space in which such tensions can be acknowledged and explored. Thereby, cultured meat also relativizes the dichotomy between technological fixes and moral/political change. Though at first sight cultured meat looks like a technological fix that addresses people just as consumers, depoliticizing them and/or making them morally lazy, it is also "world disclosing" (Driessen & Korthals, 2012), exposing the tensions and ambivalences in the present situation and revealing new directions for potential solutions. The proposal of cultured meat does not immediately change meat consumption, but it does change the moral and cultural landscape in which our thoughts and decisions about meat, or protein consumption, take place. 'Normal' meat becomes less normal. The editorial comment in *The New York Times* (6 August 2013) on Mark Post's cultured hamburger of

2013 illustrates this effect: "How absurd is it to imagine all our meat one day being produced by a similar process? Not much more absurd than it is to imagine all our meat continuing to be produced as it is now".

Interactions with other developments unavoidably influence the direction of this process. The *pig in the backyard* scenario illustrates that the idea of cultured meat can be combined simultaneously with the idea of old traditions of keeping pigs and with new trends of urban farming, even though, at first sight, they seem to point in very different directions. Such interactive tinkering may typically take place in the boundary areas of science, art and participative exploration, and make us rethink meat, our relations with animals and our moral identities with regard to meat.

With pulses?

Cultured meat may thus open up new spaces of exploration and moral identity. But imagine if it were real. What kind of solution would it be? Meat production would then still be industrial and involve technology, yet it would also be very different from what it is now. Would it solve the problems listed at the start of the chapter concerning animal lives, sustainability, health and the availability of food?

First, what would it mean for animals and for our relations with them? If it can be grown on a vegetarian medium and if that yields really good products, cultured meat might put an end to the need for animal lives to be spent in situations that are reigned by the need for efficient and profitable production. While efficiency and profit would not disappear, animals would no longer pay the price. What this would mean, in turn, depends on how cultured meat is combined with other developments and ideas. Some see horror on the horizon. According to Simon Fairlie (Fairlie, 2010, p. 229), for example, with cultured meat we travel a road on which the "convergence of interests between factory farming, veganism and genetic engineering" may result in a transhumanist world full of cyborgs and chimeras, in which we will no longer be in contact with real animals. A very different possible consequence would be that the end of factory farming leaves and creates room for a limited but significant amount of animal-friendly farming. When we imagine this in terms of our weekly food, we might eat real meat on Saturdays, for example, from pigs we can relate to, who live in barns and meadows instead of being invisible in huge plants. During their lives, some of these pigs' cells are being used for making cultured meat, so that we can imagine eating cultured meat balls on Wednesdays.

Second, how sustainable will it be? The first speculative LCA spoke of huge gains, not so much of energy but of greenhouse gas emissions, land and water use (Tuomisto & Teixeira de Mattos, 2011). Later LCAs point out that energy and resource use might in fact be weak points for cultured meat (Mattick et al., 2015; Smetana et al., 2015). How problematic this is really going to be will depend on developments in (the price of) sustainable energy and on the success of making cheap and animal-free culture media, for example, on the basis of algae. Generally speaking, all forms of processing and transformation come with losses of energy and resources, so in terms of sustainability, all meat alternatives that require elaborate processing, even when they are plant-based, will lose out to pulses, which require no more extended processing than cooking. So maybe if we eat plant-based burgers on Tuesdays, we may turn to pulses on Thursdays, and again to pulses, or to nuts, cultured cheese or cultured fish – made from cells of (whole/real) fish in the pond nearby – on Fridays?

That's not all there is to sustainability. For example, if – again an if – cultured meat can, in the future, grow on algae, its production might free large amounts of land: a chance for rewilding, for growing more grain and pulses, for creating greener cities? Potentially at least, it would be very good news for wild animals, as well as for human food security.

Third, what will it mean for health? On the one hand, cultured meat can in principle be engineered to be especially healthy, so that it might e.g. contain very little fat or be enriched with specific nutrients. It might also be relatively easy to check cultured meat for infections. On the other hand, Western diets are low in fibre. Meat contains no fibre, which is why (partial) replacement of meat with plant-based food is good for us. As cultured meat consists of animal tissue, it is not going to help in this respect. Since the Western diet contains too much protein anyway, simply leaving out meat and replacing it by nothing, or by vegetables, is also a healthy option. Maybe for Mondays?

Another open question: what would cultured meat mean for farmers and agriculture? The intended idea is clearly to disrupt intensive farming. This potential intensifies when we think of the wider field of research and development that aims for the alternatives for animal products. The extent to which traditional products and technological alternatives will be able to exist alongside each other no doubt varies. Concerning meat, it does not look very likely that the availability of meat alternatives, plant-based and animal-based, will soon end the demand for 'real' meat. In fact, producers of extensively produced quality meat might greatly profit.

All the while, the assumption that guides and justifies the search for the perfect meat imitation is that humanity is and will remain meathooked. Can we also imagine that this changes, considerably? For example, how unthinkable is it that the reputation of pulses changes from 'meat for the poor' to 'meat for the rich'?

Let me end with an imaginary scenario, based on real developments. It has become clear in recent years not only that our bodies host billions of microbes, but also that we depend on these guests: a disturbed microbiome disturbs our health. Through the gut microbiome, several groups of medicines turn out to have negative side effects, and so has the current Western diet; clear correlations have been emerging, for example, between the low amounts of fibre in our diets and reduced health. Since the gut has a nerve system of its own that is in direct 'dialogue' with the brain, it need not surprise that mental health is implicated as well. Much research is currently directed at unravelling these relations. Now suppose that somewhere in the coming years, new evidence about the relation between high-meat/low-fibre diets and susceptibility to depression becomes the focus of intensive media attention. And imagine some other developments more or less simultaneously: an animal flu virus emerges that is deadly for animals as well as humans, nitrogen pollution leads to an environmental crisis, the rise of the ocean level is speeding up and a newly bred kidney bean is introduced that has a cooking time of only 15 minutes instead of a few hours.

This scenario leads to my proposal for a recipe for Sundays. The recipe assumes the existence of a 'pig in the backyard', some of whose cells are cultured into minced meat in the local meat factory.

RECIPE: CHILI CON CARNE CULTIVADA

Go to the local store and buy 200 grams of minced cultured meat, a small can of cultured sour cream and a pound of the new short-cooking breed of kidney beans. Find a recipe for chili con carne and make sure you have all the other ingredients at hand.

Questions

1   How compatible is cultured meat with food sovereignty?
2   What would it take to make pulses widely and globally popular as a main source of protein?
3   Might resemblance to meat become a weakness for a meat alternative?
4   How plausible is it that cultured meat leads to moral change?
5   How (un)attractive is cultured meat if it is made by huge companies?

Acknowledgements

This chapter draws on research in the context of an interdisciplinary project: "Cultured meat as a co-construction of science, ethics and social science" (2010–2014). The project was a follow-up of the first Dutch *in vitro* meat research programme (2005–2009). Both projects were subsidized by the Dutch government and led by Henk Haagsman of Utrecht University. Many thanks to the ministry and to my co-researchers, and special thanks to Clemens Driessen, with whom I conducted workshops and focus groups.

Note

1 Available from: http://rolandanderson.se/Winston_Churchill/Fifty_Years_Hence.php

References

Alexandratos, N. & Bruinsma, J. (2012) *World agriculture towards 2030/2050: The 2012 revision.* ESA Working paper.

Bouvard, V., Loomis, D., Guyton, K. Z., Grosse, Y., Ghissassi, F. E., Benbrahim-Tallaa, L., Guha, N., Mattock, H. & Straif, K. (2015) Carcinogenicity of consumption of red and processed meat. *The Lancet Oncology.* 16 (16), 1599–1600.

Catts, O. & Zurr, I. (2007) Semi-living art. In: Kac, E. (ed.) *Signs of Life: Bio Art and Beyond.* Cambridge, MIT Press, pp. 231–247.

Churchill, W. (1932) *Thoughts and Adventures.* New York, C. Scribner's Sons.

Driessen, C. & Korthals, M. (2012) Pig towers and *in vitro* meat: Disclosing moral worlds by design. *Social Studies of Science.* 42 (6), 797–820.

Fairlie, S. (2010) *Meat: A Benign Extravagance.* Chelsea, VT, Chelsea Green Publishing.

Fehrenbacher, K. (2013) Silicon Valley embraces innovation in sustainable foods. *Bloomberg News,* 21st February. Available from: https://www.bloomberg.com/news/articles/2013-02-21/silicon-valley-embraces-innovation-in-sustainable-foods

Harrison, R. (1964) *Animal Machines.* London, Vincent Stuart Publishing.

Hoek, A. C. (2010) *Will novel protein foods beat meat? Consumer acceptance of meat substitutes – a multidisciplinary research approach.* Submitted doctoral thesis, Wageningen University.

Hoek, A. C., Luning, P. A., Weijzen, P., Engels, W., Kok, F. J. & de Graaf, C. (2011) Replacement of meat by meat substitutes: A survey on person-and product-related factors in consumer acceptance. *Appetite.* 56 (3), 662–673.

Hopkins, P. D. & Dacey, A. (2008) Vegetarian meat: Could technology save animals and satisfy meat eaters? *Journal of Agricultural & Environmental Ethics.* 21 (6), 579–596.

Majumdar, D. K. (2011) *Pulse Crop Production: Principles and Technologies.* Delhi, India, PHI Learning Pvt. Ltd.

Mattick, C. S., Landis, A. E., Allenby, B. R. & Genovese, N. J. (2015) Anticipatory life cycle analysis of *in vitro* biomass cultivation for cultured meat production in the United States. *Environmental Science & Technology.* 49 (19), 11941–11949.

Moore Lappé, F. (1971) *Diet for a Small Planet.* New York, Ballantine Books.

Onwezen, M. C., Snoek, H., Reinders, M. & Voordouw, J. (2013) *De Agrofoodmonitor: maatschappelijke waardering van de Agro & Food sector.* Wageningen, The Netherlands, LEI Wageningen UR.

Onwezen, M. C. & van der Weele, C. N. (2016) When indifference is ambivalence: Strategic ignorance about meat consumption. *Food Quality and Preference.* 52, 96–105.

Pincock, S. (2007) 'Meat, in vitro?' *The Scientist.* Available from www.the-scientist.com/?articles.view/articleNo/25358/title/Meat – in-vitro-/ [Accessed: 22nd February 2017].

Schneider, A. V. (2002) Overview of the market and consumption of pulses in Europe. *British Journal of Nutrition.* 88 (S3), 243–250.

Smetana, S., Mathys, A., Knoch, A. & Heinz, V. (2015) Meat alternatives: Life cycle assessment of most known meat substitutes. *The International Journal of Life Cycle Assessment.* 20 (9), 1254–1267.

Steinfeld, H., Gerber, P., Wassenaar, T., Castel, V., Rosales, M. & de Haan, C. (2006) *Livestock's Long Shadow: Environmental Issues and Options.* Rome, FAO. Available from www.fao.org/docrep/010/a0701e/a0701e00.HTM [Accessed: 21st February 2017].

Tuomisto, H. L. & Teixeira de Mattos, M. J. (2011) Environmental impacts of cultured meat production. *Environmental Science & Technology.* 45 (14), 6117–6123.

Van der Weele, C. (2013a) Meat and the benefits of ambivalence. In: Röcklinsberg, H. & Sandin, P. (eds.) *The Ethics of Consumption: The Citizen, the Market and the Law.* New York, Springer, pp. 290–295.

Van der Weele, C. (2013b) *Willen weten: wel/niet, vlees/kweekvlees.* Wageningen, The Netherlands, Wageningen Universiteit.

Van der Weele, C. & Driessen, C. (2013) Emerging profiles for cultured meat; ethics through and as design. *Animals.* 3 (3), 647–662.

Van der Weele, C. & Driessen, C. (2014a) *Burgers over kweekvlees: Ambivalentie onder het ooper-vlak.* Wageningen, The Netherlands, Wageningen UR.

Van der Weele, C. & Driessen, C. (2014b) *In vitro* meat, animal liberation? In: Van Mensvoort, K. & Grievink, H. J. (eds.) *The In Vitro Meat Cookbook.* Amsterdam, BIS Publishers, pp. 76–88.

van Mensvoort, K. & Grievink, H.-J. (2014) *The In Vitro Meat Cookbook.* Amsterdam, Bis Publishers.

Varela-Moreiras, G., Avila, J., Cuadrado, C., Del Pozo, S., Ruiz, E. & Moreiras, O. (2010) Evaluation of food consumption and dietary patterns in Spain by the food consumption survey: Updated information. *European Journal of Clinical Nutrition.* 64, S37–S43.

Zaraska, M. (2016) *Meathooked: The History and Science of Our 2.5-Million-Year Obsession With Meat.* New York, Basic Books.

13

SOIL CURRENCY

Exploring a more equitable, sustainable, and participatory economic system

Randall Coleman

Introduction

Imagine a world where every household ensures their organic waste goes to urban gardeners and farmers in exchange for currency or points. Once they have accumulated enough points, they can then "buy" produce from the farmer. This is a mutually beneficial relationship. The farmer needs inputs to create valuable compost for his/her operations, and the eater has free access to healthy local produce. In addition, nearby restaurants and cafes can participate by providing food waste for farmers, buying ingredients for their menus, and selling salads and sandwiches to participating households, all with an alternative currency based on soil.

We have all heard the expression "cheaper than dirt." But many experts would disagree that dirt is in fact cheap. Rather, soil is a vital resource that, as estimated by the UN's Food and Agriculture Organization (FAO), globally contributes about USD $16.5 trillion in ecosystem services annually (FAO, 2011a). In fact, the FAO named 2015 the International Year of the Soils as a tribute to the importance of soil to food systems.

Worryingly, arable soil (the ability to cultivate crops) is depleting at a rapid rate, around 24 billion tons each year, due to erosion (UNCCD, 2014). This rate of erosion is 10 to 100 times greater than the rate at which soil is being replenished (Cameron et al., 2015), with the major contributing factors being urban development, desertification, and industrial agriculture. The use of chemicals, intensive machinery, and monoculture are increasing productivity in the short term but leading to fallow soil and desertification over the long term (UNCCD, 2014). Some of the most widely discussed solutions to these problems include polyculture, reforestation, and climate-smart agricultural practices. But what if the reason we do not see soil being replenished is because we are not properly valuing it? Some practitioners, artists, and scholars are exploring the idea of soil as a *currency*. Because we can create certain types of topsoil, and because we already have ways of valuing it, the question can be asked: can we create an economic system that is based on that value?

Renowned artist Claire Pentecost played with this idea in her international exhibit at the art festival dOCUMENTA(13) (see Figure 13.1) (Pentecost, n.d.). There she made "coins" and "ingots" out of compost (soil-erg) and placed them on top of gold-plated tables to illustrate the fact that compost currency is more valuable than gold. In addition, there were drawings of many of the micro-organisms found in healthy soil with descriptions of the life-supporting services they provide to both plants and humans. There is intrinsic value in soil, and Ms. Pentecost used coins and ingots as a metaphor to demonstrate their value.

Like others, I believe the value of soil can be "monetized" and used in the real world, not just as a metaphor. Soil currency provides answers to several problems. Firstly, by putting a value on soil, the inputs that make soil become assets that are valued too. Secondly, it can democratize access to fruits and vegetables in low-income and marginalized communities. Thirdly, it can help to reduce methane emissions. In addition to these three main outcomes, valuing soil can help to create more soil, thus addressing the challenge of net soil loss. In what follows, I introduce the idea and practice of more widely known alternative currencies, before going on to discuss how a soil currency could function and what the benefits could be.

FIGURE 13.1 Soil-erg exhibit at dOCUMENTA(13), Kassel, Germany

Photo credit: R. Coleman

Alternative currency

In essence, soil currency creates an alternative market with an alternative currency based on a natural resource. As all natural resources diminish over time, their economic value (as well as other uses for humans) is likely to increase as well. The idea is to calculate, educate, and promote the value of soil so that people will participate in alternative markets where a fiat currency is not needed to make an economic transaction (e.g. soil assets for food). The inspiration for soil currency emerges from our understanding of ecosystem services and the concept of alternative currencies. We need to understand these two concepts in order to be able to bring the solution of soil currency to fruition. An alternative currency is a currency that is used separately from the national or fiat currency of a country. There are many reasons why people use alternative currencies, but in this chapter, I focus on the similarities between soil currency and two examples: the Bristol Pound and Bitcoin.

The Bristol Pound may be the world's most successful and sustainable alternative currency. Started in 2012, the currency has issued £B 1 million in total with a circulation of £B 700,000 in 2015 (Hickey, 2015). Over 800 businesses in the city of Bristol accept the currency. As the name suggests, the Bristol Pound is an alternative to the British Pound. The Bristol Pound is a particular type of alternative currency; it is complementary and strictly local. It is complementary because the value of the Bristol Pound is par with the value of the British Pound. So the two currencies always have a 1:1 exchange rate. It is strictly local, which means the currency is only accepted by businesses in Bristol and the surrounding area. You cannot buy a Beatles shirt with Bristol Pounds in Liverpool. Sorry, Paul McCartney!

You can spend your Bristol Pounds online or through your mobile phone using a very simple SMS text message payment system. This digital component is a smart (and relatively cheap) way to exchange goods and services and could be part of any soil currency system, as it is in the Bronx with Hello Compost. Interestingly, though, the Bristol Pound is also printed and can be exchanged for British Pounds. The Founder of the Bristol Pound, Ciaran Mundy, explained to me that this tactile experience of touching paper money is thought to be part of the reason why the currency is so successful in Bristol (Mundy, 2015). Printing money also generates revenue for the community interest company when previous editions are sunset and no longer accepted by Bristol businesses. Could the pioneers of soil currency work with artists as the Bristol Pound has done to create something tactile, exciting, and inspiring? Since many people are not comfortable using mobile phones, this tactile option may be essential to reach certain demographics.

The Bristol Pound's local orientation seeks to strengthen community resilience, and one reason why people participate in local currencies is because they increase the multiplier effect of the local economy. By restricting the use of Bristol Pounds to Bristol, the system guarantees that the money is re-circulated only in the local economy. In a similar vein, the scale of soil currencies would likely need to remain small, because composting on a large scale would require a lot of space, and space is at a premium in cities. By keeping the system small and hyper-local, we increase the multiplier effect of locally grown and sourced food for local people.

Bitcoin may be an even more well-known and groundbreaking example of an alternative currency. Bitcoin is a worldwide peer-to-peer network for online transactions with no centralized authority such as a bank. To obtain bitcoins, you can purchase them with any fiat currency or obtain them through a process called mining, which involves users verifying transactions by running a series of calculations on their computer. These transactions are grouped into what are called block chains, and a user receives bitcoins proportional to the amount of computing power they offer to validate this block of transactions. Once confirmed, these block chains are permanently added to a public ledger of every Bitcoin transaction distributed across any machine in the world that is connected to the Bitcoin network. This keeps this open-source software transparent and auditable in case of fraud or other malicious behavior.

As this currency is open-source and completely decentralized, Bitcoin has been used as an investment, to send money to other users, to purchase tacos from a food truck, or to even buy illicit substances or weapons. Given the lack of centralized authority and the infinite uses and applications of Bitcoins, the value of the currency is extremely volatile. At one point, Bitcoins went from USD $266, down to $76, back up to $160, all within six hours (Bitcoin Simplified, n.d.). The instability and lack of regulation makes Bitcoin risky and unattractive to most people.

But notice the differences between Bitcoin and the Bristol Pound. Bitcoin derives its value completely apart from the value of any national currency. This is exponentially more disruptive to the dominant capitalist market, because it challenges the traditional role of the state as the only institution which can create currency. If anyone with a computer and time can earn Bitcoins, it creates a vastly more decentralized and participatory economic system. Both Bitcoins and soil currency derive their value from the intrinsic work being done. The more work you do, the more currency you earn. At the same time, there are physical limits to both soil currency and bitcoins, making both markets complementary to the fact that we live on a finite planet.

From waste to assets

Before exploring the benefits of soil currency, it should be noted that the waste in question is waste that cannot or will not be consumed as food again. Examples include egg shells, coffee grounds, used paper towels, and kitchen scraps. This waste is not the same as food losses (i.e. food lost at the level of the farm). Food losses are a different, yet as important, issue facing humanity. We know that households and industry are wasting perfectly good food at the same time that millions of people are experiencing hunger and malnutrition (Gustavsson et al., 2011).

The goal of soil currency is to incentivize people to compost who ordinarily would not and to encourage people to eat more fresh fruits and vegetables. The way to achieve that goal is by changing people's understanding of food waste so that they don't see it as waste to begin with. Soil currency demonstrates that this "waste" has value and therefore should not be called waste at all. These "soil assets" are what is used to build the natural capital in the soil so that we can receive helpful services, such as growing food. However, this could introduce an unintended incentive of throwing out edible food or not finishing what one has in the fridge in order to acquire soil currency. There are components to this system that will help to check this moral hazard: when someone engages in risky or unwanted behavior and is protected from the consequences.

As it is presented here, soil currency can *only* buy more fresh produce, so the participant does not gain anything by throwing out edible food. Different growing seasons for different crops will limit participants' ability to game the system. The farmers on site could reject any soil assets that are still edible and uneaten. One part of this system could be to provide participants with bins designed for the right amount of browns and greens, further encouraging the right kind of collection for soil development.

Following the examples of the Bristol Pound and Bitcoin, soil currency needs an exchange rate. In this case, the exchange rate is between soil assets and food. We need to answer the question, "how much food is produced from how much waste?" Because we know the amount or volume of soil needed to grow various crops, we can estimate how much waste is needed to produce that amount of soil. To do that, we need the exchange rate between the volume of decomposing waste to the volume of finished soil. According to Breitenbeck and Schellinger's (2004) research, on average, waste reduces in volume by about 40% when composting. So to produce 1 cubic (cu) foot of soil, you need approximately 1.6 cu feet of waste. So, for example, if you need 1 cu foot of soil to grow 1 head of lettuce, then the exchange rate is 1.6 cu feet of waste for 1 head of lettuce or 1 unit of soil currency. Furthermore, you need about 3.5 cu feet of waste for 2 cu feet of soil to grow watermelon, or 6.5 cu feet of waste for 4 cu feet of soil to grow summer squash. See Table 13.1 for some examples.

TABLE 13.1 Waste to soil currency exchange rate

Waste to Soil Currency Exchange Rate: 1.6:1			
Amount of waste needed (ft^3)	*Crop*	*Amount of soil needed for crop (ft^3)*	*Unit of soil currency*
0.4	Basil	0.25	0.25
1.6	Head of lettuce	1	1
1.6	Kale	1	1
3.5	Watermelon	2	2
3.7	Broccoli	2.25	2.25
6.5	Summer squash	4	4

These were calculated using Bartholomew's (2005) square foot gardening techniques and an assumption of 1 foot of soil for depth.

Source: R. Coleman

Using this exchange rate, a farmer can plan how much soil he/she will need to grow for the participating households throughout the season, as well as how much waste he/she needs. In order to determine how much waste and food participants can produce, a waste audit would need to take place before the start of the project for each household. This will give the project leads a basic estimate of how much soil, space, and compost capacity is needed, and whether the garden or farm can accommodate. If more waste is provided than food is available, participants will stop composting because they will feel it is not worth the time. On the other hand, if not enough waste is produced, then that reduces the total amount of food being grown or distributed. Getting the right balance is of utmost importance.

When talking about waste or soil assets, it is not only the amount or quantity that matters, but also the type of waste. For instance, to create quality compost, you need both materials high in nitrogen (greens) and materials high in carbon (browns). Materials high in nitrogen are kitchen scraps, fresh grass clippings, and manure. Materials high in carbon are paper products, dried leaves, and wood chips. Both are required but the volumes for each differ, thus adding important qualitative information to the waste-food calculation. This might sound complicated, but there is no need for participants to become experts in composting. Different sized bins can be distributed to allow for the right amount of brown assets and green assets, usually 2:1 by volume.

This proposal admittedly raises a number of challenges. What is clear is that for this to work, there needs to be active participation and cooperation between waste producers and farmers. Let's say the compost site is low on browns or micronutrients like calcium. The project leads can send out a notice to participants that they will get twice the amount of soil currency if they bring cardboard boxes, egg shells, or shrimp tails. Incentives and keeping open lines of communication as circumstances change will help to ensure all stakeholders receive what they need, and is evidence for an adaptive and flexible soil currency program. Furthermore, perhaps sweat equity can be rewarded with soil currency. If labor on the farm is low in a given week or month, people can be rewarded by giving them soil currency for turning the compost heap. These are just a few examples, but the participants of such a scheme should be open and adaptable as things change.

Potential benefits

The first benefit is that soil currency raises awareness of the importance of soil by placing an economic value on it – something everyone can relate to. This economic incentive will not only contribute more to improved soils, but should increase the amount of fresh produce a household consumes because the kitchen scraps are now reframed as assets. If households are buying more produce because it equals "free food," we might be able to assume these households are eating healthier, whole fruits and vegetables. This is an area that needs further study, but if true, even in some cases, could be a groundbreaking solution that would encourage healthy eating habits.

Using soil as a currency could be an economic system best suited for low-income and marginalized communities, where the need for affordable and healthy food is great (Chinni, 2011). Often, people in low-income communities do not have access to healthy food either because it is too far away (in so-called "food deserts") or it is too expensive. Soil currency could help people get access to healthy food, without spending any legal tender to get it. This benefit is critical for community and household resilience as food prices are predicted to become more volatile as time goes on (FAO, 2011b).

Soil currency can also decrease the amount of methane, a greenhouse gas (GHG), emitted into the atmosphere. When organic waste is sent to a landfill, it decomposes anaerobically (without oxygen), which produces methane. If that same waste is put toward a compost pile that is being turned, the waste decomposes aerobically (with oxygen) and therefore produces carbon dioxide, a GHG 25 times less potent than methane (UNFCCC, 2014). Landfills and methane are significant contributors to emissions and climate change in the United States (USEPA, n.d.) as well as throughout the world. If enough soil is produced, we may see an offset of the CO_2 created because the soil (with the help of plants) will sequester carbon from the atmosphere.

Finally, soil currency directly addresses the issue of declining arable soil by incentivizing ordinary citizens to make more of it (albeit in much smaller quantities than is needed). This not only raises awareness around declining arable soil, but instills a practical hands-on approach to the problem. It should be noted that compost is but one of many types of soil, most of which take millennia to form, so this concept will not replenish all soil types. However, finished compost (mixed with soil or by itself) is a very good choice for growing food and is considered one of the most important necessities for sustainable agriculture (Cogger, 2005). Furthermore, when using space-efficient vertical gardens and composters – for example, like those designed and built by the non-profit Can YA Love (CYL) – one maximizes the limited amount of space for food and compost production as well. This is critical in an urban setting where there is not much space for composting or agriculture.

Challenges ahead

Many ecologists and some economists declare that the global population cannot continue to grow without acknowledging the planet's physical limitations. Soil currency could be a practical tool to help us transition to a new economic model. The potential benefits of an alternative market based on soil are numerous. But some critical questions need to be answered in order to scale this up and across different communities and contexts.

One key issue to be addressed is how to assign the correct value to soil. The question is difficult to answer from a technical perspective, as well as a practical one. To help answer it, we turn to the concept of ecosystem services. Soil provides many services for our planet, but these services can be hard to valuate. The quality and value of those services depends on the stock of natural capital a plot of soil has. Natural capital consists of "stocks of natural assets (e.g. soils, forests, water bodies) that yield a flow of valuable ecosystem goods or services into the future" (Costanza & Daly, 1992, p. 38). For example, the amount of soil biota or micro-organisms in the soil are natural capital, whereas the bounty of nutritious food we get from the soil is an ecosystem service, known as a provisioning service. What makes quantifying services derived from soil so difficult is the complex web of structural, chemical, and biological assets that make each plot of soil unique from another. In the discussion above, I only included the volumes of waste and soil in the exchange rate calculation. The quality and diversity of natural assets found in the finished soil is assumed because the farmer or gardener involved should know what is needed to create quality compost. Common natural assets found in compost include plenty of micro-organisms, plenty of space for oxygen and water, and enough carbon and nitrogen for plants. These assets are also not included in the exchange rate because they are very difficult to quantify.

It is difficult to comprehensively quantify soil because of the many services it provides. In fact, soil contributes to all four main categories of ecosystem services: 1) provisioning, 2) regulating, 3) cultural, and 4) supporting (MEA, 2005). Soil provides food and material to build structures; it regulates the climate through cycling carbon and water; it is used for cultural ceremonies like burying the deceased; and it supports other life, such as plants and animals. There have been attempts to quantify these different components from various disciplines, but we still lack a comprehensive picture. Furthermore, the next step after quantifying the services is to place a monetary value on said services, another difficult proposition (Dominati, Patterson & Mackay, 2010). Sandhu et al. (2008) and Porter et al. (2009) both used a methodology where they identified one ecosystem service of soil and the underlying process behind that service by measuring one indicator of that process. For example, measuring the quantity of earthworms (indicator) in soil will dictate how the soil is formed (process), which in turn tells us how well that soil will be at cycling water (service). They then calculated an economic valuation based on that indicator. However, this is only based on one indicator, again making a holistic valuation of all the services soil extremely complex.

In this chapter, I focused solely on the provisioning service of supplying food but still discovered questions about practical considerations – questions like, what factors about the waste do we include in the valuation? I have included the volume of waste as an important factor, the composition (browns and greens), and what trace elements or minerals may be present based on the composition. Do we include the local price of crops in the valuation of soil currency? This would unnecessarily complicate matters. I used 1 cubic foot of soil as my base denomination for 1 soil currency. Not including actual monetary prices in the valuation better encompasses the essence of soil currency, because it is then an alternative currency completely separate from the adjacent monetary market. The two main strengths of soil currency are that it is hyper-local, and it is separate from the dominant capitalist market. There are many other practical and logistical questions researchers and practitioners will want answered but that will depend on the context of the particular market in question. I hope I have provided some provisional answers.

Is this all pie in the sky?

In many ways, it *is* just an idea at this point, but there are groups who are trying to make this a reality, like Hello Compost in the Bronx, NYC (Keller, 2013). Hello Compost is a "home composting service" that collects soil assets from residents in specially designed pouches and delivers those assets to a nearby urban farm called Project EATS. Participating residents receive "credits" for the assets they produce via a mobile app, where they can track their progress and redeem their credits for food grown at a Project EATS site. The urban farm can use the compost it has made or sell it to make some income. The Hello Compost operation is still in the early stages and has yet to include nearby businesses that serve food, as described earlier. However, after one year in operation, this project has contributed to making soil currency a reality for working-class residents of the Bronx.

The question still remains: can the value of soil be enough for people to change their behavior? This key question has not been answered because soil currency has not existed nor been implemented (until very recently). Perhaps the value of growing a crop is not enough to persuade people to make compost out of their waste? But maybe, adding the value of carbon storage, water retention, and other ecosystem services soil provides, could push the value high enough to make this idea worthwhile? As briefly mentioned, there is still much work to do in quantifying and valuing these other services and translating that value to a currency framework. What if there is demand for the compost produced? Could it be sold in other markets, thus adding more value and more incentive? Other studies have already shown that improvements in soil health (increased humus content) directly correlate to increased economic value for farmers (Sait, 2013). This information is being used to persuade farmers to go organic. This same beneficial relationship can be used to persuade households and urban gardeners to compost.

If we can place an accurate and high enough value on soil, it may change people's behavior to waste less, create quality topsoil, increase community well-being through access to healthy and affordable food, and mitigate methane emissions. Soil currency will not be a panacea, but it could be another tool in our arsenal to move ourselves to a more food-secure future.

RECIPE: MEL'S SOIL MIX

1/3 vermiculite
1/3 peat moss or coconut coir
1/3 finished blended compost

A lot of people think you need topsoil to grow food, but Mel Bartholomew's recipe (2005) proves that you don't. The author of the popular book *Square Foot Gardening* uses the above mix to achieve his plentiful bounty, and

I have found good results from it too. This mix probably works best in a relatively small and contained growing area, like raised beds or pots.

Key things to consider

1   You have to have good compost in order to grow a variety of crops with this mix. A compost derived from only horse manure or only one source won't have a broad enough variety of nutrients for all crops.
2   I prefer coconut coir because it is less exploitative than uprooting moss from a fragile ecosystem.
3   Depending on what crops you grow, you may want perlite instead of vermiculite to help drain excess water fast.

Critical questions

1   What should the correct monetary value of soil be in order to change behavior?
2   What factors or methods should be included when valuing soil?
3   What is the appropriate scale for soil currency?
4   How do we determine the appropriate scale?
5   Should we place value on natural resources like soil?
6   What risks do we face when we monetize nature's services?

References

Bartholomew, M. (2005) *Square Foot Gardening: A New Way to Garden in Less Space With Less Work*. Emmaus, Rodale Press.

Bitcoin Simplified. (n.d.) *History*. Available at: http://bitcoinsimplified.org/learn-more/history/ [Accessed: 3rd March 2017].

Breitenbeck, G. & Schellinger, D. (2004) Calculating the reduction in material mass and volume during composting. *Compost Science & Utilization*. 12 (4), 365–371.

Cameron, D., Osborne, C., Horton, P. & Sinclair, M. (2015) *A Sustainable Model for Intensive Agriculture*. Sheffield, UK, University of Sheffield, Grantham Centre for Sustainable Futures.

Chinni, D. (2011) The socio-economic significance of food seserts. Available from: www.pbs.org/newshour/rundown/the-socio-economic-significance-of-food-deserts/ [Accessed: 4th March 2017].

Cogger, C. (2005) Potential compost benefits for restoration of soils disturbed by urban development. *Compost Science & Utilization*. 13 (4), 243–251.

Costanza, R. & Daly, H. E. (1992) Natural capital and sustainable development. *Conservation Biology*. 6 (1), 37–46.

Dominati, E., Patterson, M. & Mackay, A. (2010) A framework for classifying and quantifying the natural capital and ecosystem services of soils. *Ecological Economics*. 69 (9), 1858–1868.

Food and Agricultural Organization of the United Nations (FAO) (2011a) *The State of the World's Land and Water Resources for Food and Agriculture: Managing Systems at Risk*. Rome, Italy, Food and Agricultural Organization of the United Nations.

Food and Agricultural Organization of the United Nations (FAO). (2011b) *The State of Food Insecurity in the World: How Does International Price Volatility Affect Domestic Economics and Food Security?* Rome, Italy, Food and Agricultural Organization of the United Nations.

Gustavsson, J., Cederberg, C., Sonesson, U., van Otterdijk, R. & Meybeck, A. (2011) *Global Food Losses and Food Waste: Extent, Causes and Prevention.* Rome, Italy, Food and Agricultural Organization of the United Nations.

Hickey, S. (2015) The innovators: The bristol pound is giving sterling a run for its money. *The Guardian*, 7th June. Available from: www.theguardian.com/business/2015/jun/07/the-innovators-the-bristol-pound-is-giving-sterling-a-run-for-its-money [Accessed: 4th March 2017].

Keller, L. (2013) Hello Compost: Trading Food Waste for Local Healthy Food. *Good*, 5th October. Available from: www.good.is/articles/hello-compost-trading-food-waste-for-local-healthy-food

MEA. (2005) *Millenium Ecosystem Assessment: Ecosystems and Human Well-Being: Synthesis.* Washington DC, Island Press.

Mundy, C. Interviewed by: Coleman, R., 8th July 2015.

Pentecost, C. (n.d.) *soil-erg.* Claire Pentecost. Weblog. Available: www.publicamateur.org/?p=85 [Accessed 4th March 2017].

Porter, J., Costanza, R, Sandhu, H. S., Sigsgaard, L. & Wratten, S. D. (2009) The value of producing food, energy, and ecosystem services within an agro-ecosystem. *Ambio.* 38 (4), 186–193.

Project EATS (n.d.) *About the mission.* Available from: http://projecteats.org/about-us/ [Accessed: 4th March 2017].

Sait, G. (2013) *Humus saves the world.* Available from: http://blog.nutri-tech.com.au/humus-saves-the-world/ [Accessed: 4th March 2017].

Sandhu, H. S., Wratten, S. D., Cullen, R. & Case, B. (2008) The future of farming: The value of ecosystem services in conventional and organic arable land. *Ecological Economics.* 64 (4), 835–848.

United Nations Framework Convention on Climate Change (UNFCCC) (2014) *Global warming potentials.* Available from: http://unfccc.int/ghg_data/items/3825.php [Accessed: 4th March 2017].

United States Environmental Protection Agency (USEPA) (n.d.) *Overview of greenhouse gases: Methane emissions.* Available from: http://www3.epa.gov/climatechange/ghgemissions/gases/ch4.html [Accessed: 4th March 2017].

United Nations Convention to Combat Desertification (UNCCD). (2014) *Land Degradation Neutrality: Resilience at Local, National and Regional Levels.* Paris, United Nations Convention to Combat Desertification (UNCCD).

14

FROM PIRATE ISLANDS TO COMMUNITIES OF HOPE

Reflections on the circular economy of food systems

Stefano Pascucci and Jessica Duncan

Introduction

Mounting evidence on the negative impacts of conventional agriculture illustrates the need to re-think how we grow, process, sell, eat and dispose of food. Today, agriculture is the leading driver of deforestation and forest degradation globally, a process that accounts for 17% of global carbon emissions. Furthermore, 19–29% of global greenhouse gas emissions are directly attributed to agriculture (Vermeulen, Campbell & Ingram, 2012). Given this, business as usual is not an option (McIntyre et al., 2009).

Conventional production is defined by large-scale, highly industrialized agriculture that is further marked by six dimensions: centralization, dependence, competition, domination of nature, specialization and exploitation (Beus & Dunlap, 1990). It is clear that conventionally-designed food systems have provided unprecedented growth in agricultural productivity, advanced an abundance of technologies and infrastructure dedicated to food production and distribution, and in so doing have generated wealth and generous returns on investments for several food system actors. However, despite its promise, the current model of conventional agriculture, and related markets and distribution mechanisms, have proven unable to feed the world in a safe, sustainable and just way (FAO, IFAD & WFP, 2015). One key reason is that conventional food systems are designed in a linear way. In conventional linearly-designed food systems, natural resources are extracted, made into products (food, feed or fibre), consumed and disposed of, generating waste, detrimental emissions and pollution (Braungart, McDonough & Bollinger, 2007). It is for this reason we argue that linearly-designed food systems have heavily contributed to the 21st century food crisis. While linearly-designed food systems can be highly resource efficient, the drive to standardize and simplify leads to over-reliance on a few productive varieties and an over-dependency on external inputs, including biological materials. These systems are supported by a set of technological and institutional assumptions, principles and practices which result in the creation of waste and reduction of diversity. Linear food systems are also designed to be highly specialized, for example to separate production from distribution, in turn disconnecting use of materials from the places they have been produced and distributed.

Within the constraints of a linear approach to food production, distribution and consumption, there have been several attempts to tackle key challenges and limitations (Braungart & McDonough, 2002). For example, environmental degradation and climate change connected to conventional food activities have been addressed through assessment of the impacts of those activities through approaches like Life Cycle Assessment (LCA), the carbon footprint and eco-efficiency (Verfaillie & Bidwell, 2000; Braungart, McDonough & Bollinger, 2007). These approaches are all, in one way or another, concerned with using less resources and producing less emissions. These approaches attempt to minimize the speed, toxicity and volume of material flows, but fail to challenge, let alone re-imagine, the linear approach and disposal of materials at the end of the life cycle (Ghisellini, Cialani & Ulgiati, 2016). To better understand what we mean, let us consider in more detail the example of eco-efficiency. From an economic point of view, eco-efficiency can result in a short-term cost reduction as a result of using fewer materials. However, in the long(er) term, eco-efficiency implies socio-economic growth at the expense of the environment (Braungart, McDonough & Bollinger, 2007). Indeed, a key limitation of eco-efficient approaches to enhanced sustainability is that (harmful) waste and negative impacts on the environment remain an outcome of the production process (Braungart, McDonough & Bollinger, 2007).

Reflecting on these approaches brings us to the conclusion that moving away from conventional linearly-designed food systems requires more than adaptation: it necessitates re-imagining and re-designing conventional food systems. But how do we design our way out of this system that has a destructive impact on health and ecosystems (Lang, 2003; Stuckler & Nestle, 2012; Booth & Coveney, 2015)? The problem we focus on in this chapter thus lies less in the industrial nature of conventional food systems, and more in the way that they have been designed.

To address the limitations of linearly-designed food systems, we draw inspiration from the cyclical metabolisms of circular economy (Ellen McArthur Foundation, 2013). In what follows, we introduce the guiding principles of circular economy and discuss how they can help in re-imagining conventional food systems. We then present different cases of circular food systems and a typology to support classification and analysis. We base the typology on two key features emerging from the analysis of the cases, namely whether they operate in isolation (e.g. alone) or in collaboration with others, and whether they are inspired by and foster technological or social innovations. We then analyse the main tensions, ambiguities and potentials emerging in the different discourses around circular food systems. In the concluding section, we identify key points for discussion and highlight topics for future research.

The guiding principles of circular economy for sustainable food systems

In circularly designed food systems, the aim is to counter the "taken, used and disposed of" tradition of conventional food production by designing approaches where natural resources can be used, reused and/or safely returned back to the eco-system (Oliver et al., 2015). More broadly, circular economy (CE) envisions food systems intentionally re-designed around a set of principles: (i) *closing loops* of nutri-ents and fostering *regenerative* approaches; (ii) *sharing* and *optimizing* use of resources; (iii) *innovating* by *dematerializing* and exploring the potentials of *new technology*, for example to transport materials and design products; and (iv) *celebrating diversity* (Ellen MacArthur Foundation & McKinsey Center for Business and Environment, 2015). The approach draws on, and fits within, localized systems and mimics natural systems (Ellen McArthur Foundation, 2013; Ghisellini, Cialani & Ulgiati, 2016).

Closing loops and using regenerative approaches

The first principle, *closing loops and using regenerative approaches*, is perhaps the most known and compelling principle of circular economy design. As such, much more information and reflection is available about this principle compared to the other three. Closing loops and using regenerative approaches is about re-using, re-cycling and taking back materials, as well as about making use of renewable energy sources. Following this principle, production, distribution and consumption processes should be designed around the use of renewable energy and recovering materials, taking into account the properties of ecosystems. The aim is to design processes capable of returning biological nutrients safely back into natural cycles: a regenerative food system able to produce and distribute food while avoiding the use of fossil fuels.

Following this principle, food systems need to be designed eco-effectively so that the use of hazardous and toxic materials is eliminated. In this way, the growing or development of the food product would contribute to design metabolisms, promoting a positive synergistic relationship between ecological and social systems, and economic growth (Tukker, 2013; van Weelden, Mugge & Bakker, 2015; Smol et al., 2015). By contrast, one of the main challenges facing linear food systems is the use of key ele-ments, such as phosphorus, nitrogen and water, as non-renewable resources. While in principle these resources are all renewable, the rate at which they are used in conven-tional, industrialised food production is such that they need to be extracted or mined from the earth in their fossil form. In a regenerative food system, the design includes strategies to recover nutrients such as phosphorus, nitrogen or water, and include agri-cultural practices that avoid the use of fossil nutrients, as in the case of organic agri-culture and permaculture. For example, one strategy could be to extract phosphorus, nitrogen and water from urine and manure. This strategy is most likely to be seen in the designs of food systems in urban environments (Kalmykova et al., 2012).

The circular economy aims to inspire a transition towards a post-carbon/ post-fossil-fuel society, and it demands a re-think of the way we associate energy production and consumption to food. In fulfilling the renewable energy principle, farmers and food processors are stimulated to design more integrated systems to produce and exchange energy, to innovate and adopt new technologies, and to source energy locally. In this respect, a regenerative food system combines strategies to recover valuable materials and nutrients with the use of renewable energy (Braungart & McDonough, 2002; Ellen MacArthur Foundation & McKinsey Center for Business and Environment, 2015).

Closing loops and regenerating also means re-using materials. Inspired by industrial ecology, in a circular economy, food products are designed to be used and consumed such that their biological and technical (non-biological) components (i.e. packaging) are not mixed. This results in a waste product that cannot easily be returned to the system, leading some to label such materials as "monstrous hybrids" (Braungart & McDonough, 2002). A typical example of a monstrous hybrid would be packaging where cellulose and aluminium are mixed together in a way that they cannot be disassembled or easily re-used, such as in the most commonly used containers for milk and other drinks. This example illustrates the need to design food products and manage materials in ways that facilitate easy separation and re-use. Issues related to how residual outputs (i.e. packaging or wastewater) will be used by another actor/participant in the cycle after usage/consumption must also be incorporated in the design of the product. In this way, within CE, it is not only products that are being designed, but also "streams" of nutrients. In practice, this means that the design of a food product will include the use of biodegradable or compostable packaging, or any packaging which can be upcycled as a technical nutrient in a given metabolism (e.g. paper, glass, plastics).

Sharing and optimizing

The second principle of circular economy is *sharing and optimizing*, which relates to the tension between streamlining and seeking efficiency on the one hand, and collaborating, networking and sharing key resources on the other hand. In linearly-designed food systems, this tension is reflected in a trade-off between resource efficiency and resilience. While resilience can be achieved by interconnection and diversification of food systems, such that perturbations can be absorbed by and dealt with by the different components in the system, efficiency is oriented to streamline production processes and celebrate standardization in isolation. Diversified systems are more likely to be resilient and adaptive, but are not always efficient in the short-term. Vice versa, highly specialized systems may gain efficiency in terms of resource use in the short-term, but because they rely on resource-intense and standardized processes and are over-dependent on external inputs, they may lose the ability to adapt to change, thus being non-resilient in the long run.

A food system designed around sharing resources can reconcile the tension between efficiency and resilience through adaptive optimization processes. This requires a systems-led design and flexibility in terms of technology, practices and capabilities used. At the farm level, sharing and optimizing stimulate the adoption of technology towards, for example, a more deliberate use of fertilizers and water (e.g. precision farming), the use of crop rotation, reduced tillage (or eliminate it), and the adoption of permaculture and/or agro-ecological practices. Sharing and optimizing along the supply chain can prolong the life span of key materials by, for example, re-using and upcycling packaging. At the level of distribution, this principle also deals with eliminating food waste, for example, by improving the use of big data and information technology (IT)-based platforms to better organize operations and inventories in the retailing space. At the level of consumption, reducing food waste means engaging with changing food habits, challenging and redesigning models of consumption, fighting malnutrition and re-planning food landscapes.

Dematerializing and using new technology

The third principle of the circular economy is *dematerialization and using new technology*. With respect to food, a focus on dematerialization can include reducing the use of materials that go into packaging, as packaging is a resource-intense component of current food systems. The design and implementation of alternative systems to deliver food products to consumers, as well as inputs along the food supply chains, for example, through the enhanced use of virtual and Information and Communication Technology (ICT)-based platforms, can be seen as a way of combining the two ideas that make up this third principle. Virtual value chains and online shopping are examples of practices moving us towards the combination of new technologies and dematerialized delivery systems. At the farm level, precision agriculture practices, as well as use of, IT and big data, are considered to be technologies capable of supporting resource efficiency and recovery in food production processes (Ellen MacArthur Foundation & McKinsey Center for Business and Environment, 2015).

Celebrating diversity

The final principle is *celebrating diversity*. Celebrating diversity is meant to trigger a re-think of the way we approach food. Indeed, a CE approach is not just about a more integrated way to design (food) waste or resource recovery, or a new tool for corporate social responsibility. It is also about inviting actors involved in the food system to think about local communities, justice and power imbalances, as well as to collaboratively design rules and decision-making mechanisms. To a certain extent, the call to celebrate diversity is meant to encourage people to think about how to foster collaborative interactions. This is arguably the most under-recognized and in turn under-developed principle, or at least the most difficult to quantify. It is perhaps for this reason that less information and examples are available for this principle.

Taken together, the four principles of CE should be seen as guidelines emerging from a community of practitioners and scholars engaged at various levels in changing and transforming the current linear industrial system. Moreover, it should be noted that the very concept of circular economy and its meanings, principles and applications are far from being unified. Similar to the UN Global Compact, or the Organization for Economic Cooperation and Development's (OECD) Guidelines for Multinational Enterprises, CE is unfolding as a principle-oriented initiative reflecting broadly defined norms for corporate behaviour without any monitoring, standards or certification initiatives, including verification and auditing mechanisms (Bernstein & Cashore, 2007; Rasche, Waddock & McIntosh, 2013). In practice, CE has assumed a multi-actor, cross-sectoral and platform-oriented configuration, but unlike other principle-based initiatives (e.g. UN Global Compact), CE is not emerging from, or captured by, one specific platform or organization. As such, CE has become a diversified domain in which cases of circular industrial systems have been implemented and developed by different actors, in different contexts and scales.

A variety of circular food systems

Having reviewed the four key principles of circular economy, in this section we present, and briefly discuss, how these principles have been translated into practices to re-design food products. To help us make sense of existing cases, we propose a typology for classifying CE-inspired food initiatives. We then reflect on consequences of these designs at a systems level. We derive information from cases and initiatives related to the food sector. Although the motivations, structures and sustainability of these initiatives are diverse, reflecting the heterogeneity of actors and contexts, they all contribute directly or indirectly to promote and spread out principles of circular economy.

Our research has uncovered a growing number of examples where the principles of CE are being taken up in the redesign of various parts of the food system. We identified two key trends that relate to (i) innovation perspectives, and (ii) level of implementation. Reflecting on the first trend, we note that different initiatives have used some of the principles of circular economy as a way to provoke change. In other words, the CE principles have been used as means to an end. Here we see a strong strategic focus on using CE to gain competitive advantages by innovating products, processes and business models (Ellen MacArthur Foundation & McKinsey Center for Business and Environment, 2015). Particularly, several food companies have applied CE principles to develop new products and business models to better comply with the environmental burdens or constraints related to their activities, and to expand their license to operate when it comes to combining corporate social responsibility and new products, processes or technologies (Ellen MacArthur Foundation & McKinsey Center for Business and Environment, 2015). In our view, there are thus two dominant perspectives which make up the technological innovation dimension of CE for food: (i) circular economy as a pathway to technological development applied to food products and processes, or (ii) circular economy as a pathway to social innovation. These two dimensions make up a key part of the typology.

We also note that CE initiatives have been developed at very different levels and scales, ranging from projects developed in isolation to those developed through collaboration, setting the second dichotomy of our typology. Isolated initiatives refer mainly to projects initiated and developed in corporate and private actor spaces. These initiatives are particularly observed in food companies that are developing new business models along different stages of the food supply chain in line with CE principles. Fewer projects appear to have been developed outside the corporate space, in what we label a collaborative space (although we recognize that many such initiatives exist but that they may not explicitly subscribe to the CE principles). The examples that we do have of collaborative initiatives are mainly connected to regenerative farming practices (e.g. permaculture) or reduction and recovery of food waste.

The two dimensions of CE initiatives described above (i.e. innovation and implementation) can help us to define a typology in which four main categories of cases can be identified (see Table 14.1):

(i)   Islands of Pirates,
(ii) Spiders in the Web,
(iii) Towns of Renaissance, and
(iv) Communities of Hope.

The typology is relevant from an academic and practitioner perspective. First, it highlights the diversity of frames and applications of CE principles, and confirms the heterogeneity behind the motivations and the practical implications related to the uptake of CE principles in the design food systems. Taken together, the four categories indicate that there is a diverse and heterogeneous landscape, but that this landscape is populated by ambiguity and potential tensions, since the principles are understood and applied differently across the different categories.

Second, by looking into practices of CE-inspired food initiatives, we are better able to put these practices in context, resulting in a more systemic and holistic approach to analysing potentials to transform the current linear food systems. Third, the typology helps us to disentangle the often confusing design principles as well as debates around circular economy. For example, it is still unclear whether all principles need to be followed to claim that a practice, a business model or a product is circular, or if circular economy should be understood as a "continuous improvement" type of process, which starts from closing loops of nutrients, and continue by trying to progressively include the other principles. Equally, it remains unclear for some whether, and if so how, circular economy differs from the concept of sustainability.

Finally, in our view the advancement of the typology also provides the basis to discuss the governance and political dimensions of circularity when applied to food systems design by, for example, shedding light on whether circular economy entrenches elite practices associated with food provisioning or whether the principles can be used to democratize it.

TABLE 14.1 Typology of cases using circular economy principles to design food systems

Type of innovation perspective	Level of implementation	
	Isolation	Collaboration
Technological development / innovative business models	***Islands of Pirates***: operating in relative isolation; they use technological/business model development as dominant approach towards implementing CE principles. *Examples:* • Friesland Campina circular dairy farming (farming, food production and processing) • Protix, Ynsect (food production and processing) • Ecovative (packaging) • Vertical farming (e.g. Philips–city farming)	***Spiders in the Web***: use technological/business model development but with emphasis and reliance on networked relations for implementation of design principles related to closing material loops. *Examples:* Agro-parks Bio-energy industrial clusters
Social innovation	***Towns of Renaissance***: operating in relative isolation; they are motivated by social innovation and social relations to implement CE principles. *Examples:* Permaculture initiatives (farming, food production) (Urban) food waste projects (food distribution and consumption) (e.g. GrowUp)	***Communities of Hope***: initiatives showing a strong reliance on collaboration to advance their CE designs. *Examples:* Organic agriculture networks Community-supported agriculture initiatives Resilient agriculture initiatives (e.g. FoodTank)

Source: authors' own elaboration

As noted above, the four categories that make up the typology share the idea that CE principles can be transferred into (business) practices, but that they also differ greatly in several ways. We have defined the first typology of cases as *"Islands of Pirates."* This category identifies initiatives that use technological/business model development as their dominant approach towards implementing CE principles and operate in relative isolation. These initiatives share an element of risk and uncertainty since they operate with ill-defined or unclear regulatory frameworks, dealing with new technologies, or threat of a low rate of acceptance of their innovation. Furthermore, these initiatives operate in isolation (in contradiction to the second CE principle: sharing and optimizing use of resources) primarily because they are motivated by competitive advantage. *Islands of Pirates* can thus be used to categorize initiatives developed within existing food companies which have limited cooperation with other businesses or societal actors. They also tend to develop new technologies and business models through selected, and very strategic, partnerships. Within the *Islands of Pirates* category, we also include entrepreneurs who are setting up new businesses in the food sector, using circular economy principles mainly as a guiding tool.

There are several examples of initiatives that fall into this category. For example, entrepreneurs have created new ventures using insects to close loops of food nutrients (e.g. using food waste streams) and to produce feed for fisheries and livestock industry (Protix, 2017; Ynsect, 2016). In the packaging sector, several entrepreneurs have been experimenting with bio-based regenerative processes to produce biodegradable packaging, again to valorize and re-use circularly food waste streams (see, for example, the Ecovative case (Ecovative, n.d.)).

Other "islands" tend to focus more on corporate-based projects. For example, a large dairy company like Friesland Campina in the Netherlands has teamed up with a Dutch-based circular economy think tank Circle Economy to develop a pilot project for circular dairy farming systems. In this project, alternative technologies and agricultural practices have been investigated, namely "optimized grazing," where land productivity is increased through combining biological and technological approaches, and "extensive grazing" which relies on biological processes and organic farming methods to close the soil-plant-animal-nutrient cycle locally (Circle Economy, n.d.). Initiatives promoting vertical farming are another example of project-based initiatives oriented to design food systems by using technologies to create closed loops of materials and energy, such as the Philips–city farming solutions project (Philips, 2017).

Although they are very different in terms of scope, type of CE principle used and stage of the food system they operate at, these projects all share features that position them into the *Islands of Pirates* category: (i) they foster technical, product and process innovation, promoting a different approach to use and re-use of materials and energy associated with food production and distribution; (ii) they introduce environmental goals through the introduction of new business models; (iii) they challenge corporate actors operating in a linear way to re-think their strategies in a more circular way; and (iv) they stimulate creativity and new forms of engagement between and among actors of the food system.

The second category in our typology is "*Spiders in the Web.*" This category is used to identify initiatives that have a more explicit network orientation and collaborative nature as compared to initiatives classified as *Island of Pirates*. Like the *Island of Pirates* cases, a key focus is on technological/business model development. However, these initiatives place emphasis on the implementation of design principles related to closing material loops as inspired by industrial symbioses and applied to bio-based nutrients and energy. Examples of such initiatives include food companies participating in so-called agro-industrial parks or clusters (Nuhoff-Isakhanyan et al., 2017). These parks are formed and managed in order to create an integrated system in which ties between companies are created on the basis of shared materials (i.e. waste industrial streams) and energy (Zwier et al., 2015). Several examples of agro-parks have been developed in northwestern Europe in both urban and rural contexts. These agro-industrial clusters are emerging all over the world, particularly in emerging economies such as China, Brazil and India, and more recently across Africa. Mimicking the concept of symbiosis, food companies operating in these parks promote an upcycling approach and innovative materials management practices, as well as increasingly producing and using energy from renewable resources. Agro-parks are an emerging example of how biological and technological cycles can be designed to reshape urban food systems and re-connect food, fibre and energy productions with local economies. Having described the two main categories of CE food initiatives marked by business models, our attention now turns to a description of categories for classifying initiatives more focused on social innovation.

First, we observed the implementation of a number of projects revolving around the idea of fostering restorative agricultural practices, for example, in aquaponics, permaculture or organic agriculture. These are developed mainly at the project or farm level. Similarly, several projects have been developed to close loops of nutrients, for example, when it comes to food waste in urban contexts or related to urban farming. An example is provided by the UK-based GrowUP start-up (GrowUp Urban Farms, 2014), which combines principles of closing loops with community engagement to foster social innovation when it comes to food and water waste, access to nutritious food products and application of technology solutions to food production in urban contexts. The Waste & Resources Action Programme (WRAP) provides another example of how circular economy principles have been directly applied to find solutions to food waste issues in urban contexts (WRAP, 2017). These are only a few examples of the group of initiatives which we call "*Towns of Renaissance*" to indicate that they operate at a small scale and provoke changes and innovation for a relatively limited group of participants. Still, they flag the presence of alternative ways to design food systems and to critique the conventional linear systems.

When these initiatives are marked by more collaboration (as opposed to working alone), we see movements or associations widely spreading the principles of regenerative agriculture, sustainable consumption and non-conventional food provisioning. We have labelled these initiatives "*Communities of Hope*." For example, FoodTank is a non-profit organization which actively connects projects and initiatives around regenerative agriculture and food production systems (Foodtank, 2016). Some Alternative Food Networks can also be categorized as operating in *Communities of Hope*. In line with CE principles, these actors are, for example, promoting regenerative agriculture and sharing resources, and in so doing are indeed reshaping and rounding food systems. Examples include community-supported agriculture (Urgenci, n.d.), solidarity purchasing groups, and consumer-farmer cooperatives engaged in fostering socio-ecological transitions in mainstream food systems (i.e. adoption of fair trade practices, organic agriculture, agro-ecological technologies, etc.). We note that Alternative Food Networks are also supporting the diffusion of the principle "celebrating diversity," particularly when it comes to socio-ecological diversities, as well as promoting practices to reduce waste, and by offering ways to design food production systems in which resources are carefully used and restored, reducing the dependence on non-renewable resources (The Food Waste Network, 2013).

Tensions, ambiguity and unsolved challenges in circular food systems

Thus far we have presented the key principles of circular economy. We then proposed a typology with four classificatory categories built on an examination of exiting cases where CE principles are being applied to aspects of food system design. The typology is presented to help us make sense of the emerging and diverse landscape of CE as it relates to food. While we are inspired by the progress being made, we are also cautious and cognizant of the need to take a step back and reflect on the implications of these initiatives, and the development of CE more broadly. In what follows, we identify a number of key points of attention that we believe need to be addressed if we want to fully realize the vision of CE.

The first source of ambiguity, and potentially tension, that we observe relates to the principles and the way they are interrelated and used to define a circular economy food system. In practice, it is hard to define a set of criteria to understand what indeed qualifies a system as being circular or not. Intuitively, the first principle of closing loops of resources seems almost redundant when compared to all other principles, since it is hard to envision a circular system without addressing the re-use and upcycle of materials. Further, the relationship between the principles remains unclear. Namely, can we consider a food system which is based on closing loops and regenerative practices but not on sharing or celebrating diversity circular? For example, in the vertical farming initiatives, and in several of the corporate-based projects, the element of sharing among different actors as well as using diversity as a design principle is fairly lacking if not completely neglected. Most of these projects are organized in-house, and often regulated through rigid intellectual property rights protocols, such that understanding the fine-grained details is difficult. From another perspective, it remains unclear how one principle is adding value to another.

Another point of ambiguity lies in the costs of re-designing food systems and the benefits or gains related to the re-design process. Many of the above-mentioned projects are not yet cost-effective or are operating at such a limited scale that it is practically impossible to predict whether they can challenge the more dominant linear systems. Moreover, the costs of transitioning and re-designing using the CE principles seem to limit their application outside the corporate space, thus exposing CE to corporate exploitation issues, or to projects revolving around the activities of foundations, non-profit organizations and volunteers, which may be restricted to limited number of actors.

The principles also lack reference to how conflicts on exclusive resources should be mitigated, and how different participants in the various loops and networks can regulate and negotiate their contributions and the gains attached to them. Although diversity is mentioned, it is not clear how it diversity is protected from risk of exploitation. This is particularly relevant since engagement between different types of actors with unequal relations of powers – as we might see, for example, in corporate-led initiatives – may result in so-called green-washing through CE, delegitimizing the transformational potentials of this framework.

Tensions and ambiguity can also be observed in relation to how CE principles can lead to the design of just and fair food systems. So far, our analysis suggests that the application of the principles tends to ignore the problematic issue of unbalanced and unfair access to resources between groups in society. For us, it is as significant as it is problematic that virtual value chains and online shopping are emerging as a best practice in a move towards dematerialized delivery systems. We question if, in line with principle three – *dematerialization and using new technology* – we dematerialize delivery, do we risk reinforcing increasingly disconnected food systems and move away from growing calls to shorten and localize value chains? Or can we see this as adding strength to movements that avoid selling to supermarkets?

The questions raised in this section highlight the pressing need for further reflection on the actual capacity of CE principles to inspire solutions that can tackle structural issues facing our food systems.

It is unclear how we can reconcile the principle of celebrating local diversity while also connecting places of consumption and production that are geographically distant or culturally distinct. A pending question remains whether to, and if so how to, re-conceptualize/re-shape global trade as a circular metabolism. Another conundrum revolves around the re-definition of rights over natural resources and living organisms. With respect to CE principles, "closing loops" and "celebrating diversity" invite us to re-define ownership over resources. Still, the issue of how to use technology in relation to living organisms and the property rights related to these processes are not included in the debate on circularity. For instance, it remains contested whether technologies based on genetically modified organisms could be seen as promoting and celebrating diversity (Laikre et al., 2010).

Concluding remarks

In this chapter, we have suggested that principles of circular economy can inspire new ways of designing food production systems that address the key limitations of linear models, and thereby provide a pathway towards a more sustainable food future. We have proposed a typology to help classify emerging initiatives and to support analysis of these initiatives. The typology is based on two distinct characteristics that marked the cases of CE uptake across the food system: the perspective on innovation and the level at which the innovation was being implemented.

Our research shows how real-world applications of these principles remain quite niche and represented by scattered and isolated initiatives. It appears that applications of CE principles to food are confined predominantly to agro-parks, urban metabolism pilots and projects related to corporate social responsibility strategies. From this perspective, it remains difficult to assess how CE principles can foster collaborative patterns of consumption and production, or how social justice and democratization can be enhanced. At the same time, we have identified a number of concerns and unanswered questions that require further reflection as the concept of CE is taken up and employed by a growing number of actors.

We can thus conclude that while CE invites us to re-design food production systems around principles of metabolisms of nutrients, it is still ambiguous when it comes to indicating how the actors involved in the metabolisms should shape their relationships. Although symbiosis is often indicated as a collaborative approach to business relationships, it also entails an increased dependency amongst actors, thus introducing issues of power imbalance and conflicting interests. We look forward to working with interested actors to answer the fundamental questions that still need to be addressed in debates about CE and food systems, including the ethical, cultural and political dimensions. In so doing, we are confident that CE can be a key component to moving towards a more just and sustainable food future.

RECIPE: FRITTATA DI MACCHERONI (LEFTOVER PASTA FRITTATA)

This recipe is a Neapolitan specialty, bringing in the important element of culture, as Stefano comes from Naples. The dish is also meant to make use of leftovers, thereby limiting food waste. You can add a diversity of ingredients and flavours to make it suit your mood. Try to find ingredients that reflect the principles of circular economy.

Ingredients

For each 100–150g (4–5 oz) of leftover pasta, add:

2 medium eggs
2 heaping tablespoons of grated cheese; we recommend parmesan or pecorino
Salt and pepper, to taste
Fresh parsley, finely minced (optional), to taste
Anything else that needs eating and would go nicely with the dish
Extra-virgin olive oil for frying

Method

1 Mix all the ingredients, except the oil, together in a bowl.
2 Heat a frying pan/skillet large enough to fit the pasta and egg mixture.
3 Add enough oil to cover the bottom, and make sure you swirl the oil around so that it coats the sides of the pan.
4 Pour the pasta and egg mixture into the skillet, cooking the frittata until golden brown on both sides.
5 Be sure to cook it gently, so that it does not brown before the insides are cooked!
6 Turn the frittata over onto a plate. Let it cook and enjoy!

Questions

1   What are the biggest barriers to implementing food systems that are circularly designed in your community?
2   Think of a local food product. How would you design a circular system in your community? Think of all the stages from pre-production to after you eat it! Don't forget to include the principles.
3   Circular economy principles are in the making. Can you think of a new principle to be added to the existing ones? Can you explain why it is needed?

References

Bernstein, S. & Cashore, B. (2007) Can non-state global governance be legitimate? An analytical framework. *Regulation and Governance*. 1 (4), 347–371.

Beus, C. E. & Dunlap, R. E. (1990) Conventional versus alternative agriculture: The paradigmatic roots of the debate. *Rural Sociology*. 55 (4), 590–616.

Booth, S. & Coveney, J. (2015) *Food Democracy: From Consumer to Food Citizen*. Singapore, Springer.

Braungart, M. & McDonough, W. (2002) *Cradle to Cradle; Remaking the Way We Make Things*. New York, North Point Press.

Braungart, M., McDonough, W. & Bollinger, A. (2007) Cradle-to-cradle design: Creating healthy emissions – a strategy for eco-effective product and system design. *Journal of Cleaner Production*. 15 (13–14), 1337–1348.

Ellen MacArthur Foundation. (2013) *Towards the Circular Economy: An Economic and Business Rationale for an Accelerated Transition*. Ellen MacArthur Foundation. Available from: https://www.ellenmacarthurfoundation.org/assets/downloads/publications/Ellen-MacArthur-Foundation-Towards-the-Circular-Economy-vol.1.pdf.

Ellen MacArthur Foundation & McKinsey Center for Business and Environment. (2015) *Growth within: A circular economy vision for a competitive Europe*. SUN in collaboration with the Ellen MacArthur Foundation & McKinsey Center for Business and Environment. Available from: https://www.ellenmacarthurfoundation.org/assets/downloads/publications/EllenMacArthurFoundation_Growth-Within_July15.pdf.

FAO, IFAD & WFP. (2015) *The state of food insecurity in the world: Meeting the 2015 international hunger targets: Taking stock of uneven progress*. Food and Agriculture Organization of the United Nations.

Ghisellini, P., Cialani, C. & Ulgiati, S. (2016) A review on circular economy: The expected transition to a balanced interplay of environmental and economic systems. *Journal of Cleaner Production*. 114, 11–32.

Kalmykova, Y., Harder, R., Borgestedt, H. & Svanäng, I. (2012) Pathways and management of phosphorus in urban areas. *Journal of Industrial Ecology*. 16 (6), 928–939.

Laikre, L., Schwartz, M. K., Waples, R. S., Ryman, N. & GeM Working Group. (2010) Compromising genetic diversity in the wild: Unmonitored large-scale release of plants and animals. *Trends in Ecology & Evolution*. 25 (9), 520–529.

Lang, T. (2003) Food industrialization and food power: Implications for food governance. *Development Policy Review*. 21 (5–6), 555–568.

McIntyre, B. D., Herren, H. R., Wakhungu, J. & Watson, R. T. (eds.) (2009) *Synthesis Report: A Synthesis of the Global and Sub-Global IAASTD Reports*. International Assessment of Agricultural Knowledge, Science and Technology for Development (IAASTD). Washington, DC, Island Press.

Nuhoff-Isakhanyan, G., Wubben, E. F., Omta, O. S. & Pascucci, S. (2017) Network structure in sustainable agro-industrial parks. *Journal of Cleaner Production.* 141, 1209–1220.

Oliver, T. H., Heard, M. S., Isaac, N. J., Roy, D. B., Procter, D., Eigenbrod, F., Freckleton, R., Hector, A., Orme, C. D. L., Petchey, O. L. & Proença, V. (2015) Biodiversity and resilience of ecosystem functions. *Trends in Ecology & Evolution.* 30 (11), 673–668.

Rasche, A., Waddock, S. & McIntosh, M. (2013) The United Nations global compact: Retrospect and prospect. *Business & Society.* 52 (1), 6–30.

Smol, M., Kulczycka, J., Henclik, A., Gorazda, K. & Wzorek, Z. (2015) The possible use of sewage sludge ash (SSA) in the construction industry as a way towards a circular economy. *Journal of Cleaner Production.* 95, 45–54.

Stuckler, D. & Nestle, M. (2012) Big food, food systems, and global health. *PLoS Med.* 9 (6), e1001242.

Tukker, A. (2013) Product services for a resource-efficient and circular economy – a review. *Journal of Cleaner Production.* 97 (15), 76–91.

van Weelden, E., Mugge, R. & Bakker, C. (2015) Paving the way towards circular consumption: Exploring consumer acceptance of refurbished mobile phones in the Dutch market. *Journal of Cleaner Production.* 113, 743–754.

Verfaillie, H. A. & Bidwell, R. (2000) *Measuring Eco-Efficiency: A Guide to Reporting Company Performance.* Geneva, World Business Council on Sustainable Development. Available at: www.wbcsd.org/web/publications/measuring_eco_efficiency.pdf

Vermeulen, S. J., Campbell, B. M. & Ingram, J. S. I. (2012) Climate change and food systems. *Annual Review of Environment and Resources.* 37 (1), 195–222.

Zwier, J., Blok, V., Lemmens, P. & Geerts, R. J. (2015) The ideal of a zero-waste humanity: Philosophical reflections on the demand for a bio-based economy. *Journal of Agricultural and Environmental Ethics.* 28 (2), 353–374.

Website/online resources

Circle Economy. (n.d.) *The circular dairy economy.* Available from: www.circle-economy.com/case/the-circular-dairy-economy/ [Accessed: 18th February 2017].

Ecovative. (n.d.) *Ecovative: We grow materials.* Available from: www.ecovativedesign.com/ [Accessed: 26th February 2017].

The Food Waste Network. (2013) *Our food waste stories blog.* Available from: www.foodwastenetwork.org.uk/ [Accessed: 22nd February 2017].

Foodtank. (2016) *Foodtank: The think tank for food.* Available from: https://foodtank.com/ [Accessed: 21st February 2017].

GrowUp Urban Farms. (2014) *Sustainable food for a local market.* Available from: http://growup.org.uk [Accessed: 22nd February 2017].

Philips. (2017) *Philips commercializing city farming solutions based on LED 'light recipes' that improve crop yield and quality.* Available from: www.lighting.philips.com/main/products/horticulture/press-releases/Philips-commercializing-city-farming-solutions-based-on-LED-light-recipes.html [Accessed: 18th February 2017].

Protix. (2017) *Protix.* Available from: www.protix.eu/ [Accessed: 15th December 2016].

Urgenci. (n.d) *Urgenci: The international network for community supported agriculture.* Available from: http://urgenci.net/ [Accessed: 21st February 2017].

WRAP. (2017) *WRAP.* Available from: www.wrap.org.uk/ [Accessed: 18th February 2017].

Ynsect. (2016) *Ynsect.* Available from: www.ynsect.com/ [Accessed: 15th February 2017].

PART V

Conclusions

15

CAUTION

Road work ahead

Jessica Duncan and Megan Bailey

Introduction

We concluded the first chapter by stating that the solutions proposed in this book can be read as an atlas of possibilities. An atlas is not an almanac: it does not try to predict the future. However, anyone who has ever poured over a map while planning an adventure knows that an atlas provides a starting point for identifying new roads, or in this case, pathways to more sustainable and just futures. But it is also possible that the atlas is incomplete, or not resolute enough, or that entirely new pathways for getting around are needed. And, while we remain uncertain about many things, we are convinced that road work is ahead.

The authors that contributed to this book started from the same place: a place of recognizing that food systems are marked by complex, multidirectional, messy problems requiring multiple solutions. But the consensus in some ways stops there. At times, these authors are even proposing divergent pathways. Indeed, there are contradictions across the solutions presented in this book. Perhaps this is not surprising given that contradictions have come to define many of the big problems we are currently facing. But rather than bury these contradictions, or pretend they do not exist, we accept them. Towards this end, we were inspired by A. David Wunsch's (2010, p. 4) review of Johnson and Wetmore's (2009) book *Technology and Society: Building our Sociotechnical Future*, where he proclaims that one of the book's strengths is in its aggregation of authors and essays that "frequently contradict one another and provoke discussion".

It is through these contradictions that we can uncover insights into the different ways individuals and groups in society view the world. These insights shed light on what people choose to value, and this in turns allows us to recognize that there is no single "right" solution; there is no final fix. As such, we are reminded of the importance of advancing new ways of thinking and new ways of doing that allow for this plurality of values. We need to build pathways that are aligned with these values.

What problems have we tried to address?

Taken together, the chapters in this book propose or problematize solutions to a number of key challenges facing food systems. They also answer a number of key questions about our prospects for a food-secure future (see Table 15.1).

In our conversations about our work, and our hopes for the future, we have often wondered why solutions are slow to surface, and why so many of the mainstream solutions fail to be innovative – or to put it bluntly: keep on proposing solutions that have already failed. Through our discussions, we came to identify three trends that serve to restrict the promotion of innovative new practices: notably, a lack of diversity, a tendency to research in silos, and a continued prevalence of binary – "either-or" – discussions.

TABLE 15.1 Matching key questions to solutions found in this book

Key questions about and challenges to the future of sustainable food systems	*Proposed solution*
• How can we challenge the hegemony of neoliberalism?	• In a word: resist! (Chapter 8: Gahman)
• How can we resist the conventional food system?	• Market practices that cannot be conventionalized (Chapter 11: Ajates Gonzalez)
• What is the role of women in sustainable food futures?	• Include women in local development projects that are also adapted to the local context (Chapter 7: Rainville et al.)
• How do we advance gender equality?	• Engage in an explicitly feminist politics that challenges language and practice (Chapter 8: Gahman)
• How can we think differently about values?	• Think of alternative economies and related currency, like soil currency (Chapter 13: Coleman)
• How can we better value what really matters to us?	• Support community-led programs to reclaim traditional and local food practices (Chapter 2: Hoover et al.)
• How can we overcome failed policies?	• Listen to people and recognize the values of their systems of knowledge and culture (Chapter 2: Hoover et al.)
• Who should bear the burden of regulation?	• Shift the burden of proof away from small-scale food producers to retailers (Chapter 10: Bush) • Train people in land rights (Chapter 6: Shilomboleni)

Key questions about and challenges to the future of sustainable food systems	Proposed solution
• How can we build trust in the food system?	• Foster community-supported agriculture (Chapter 3: Si) • Apply a place-based approach to analyzing food systems (Chapter 4: Klassen and Wittman)
• How can we improve access to markets?	• Better understand and support the work of intermediaries (Chapter 9: Schoonhoven-Speijer et al.) • Create place-based markets that connect producers to consumers (Chapter 3: Si; Chapter 4: Klassen and Wittman; Chapter 11: Ajates Gonzalez)
• Can technology support the development of alternatives to high-ecological-impact foods, such as meat?	• Consider the implications of cultured meat (Chapter 12: van der Weele) • Take up the design principles of the circular economy (Chapter 14: Pascucci and Duncan)
• How can we leverage technological innovations for the greatest benefit?	• Make sure that diversity is a key principle in the design of new technologies (Chapter 14: Pascucci and Duncan)
• How can we envision more collective futures?	• Push for more clarity on and relevant legal tools for supporting farmland commons (Chapter 5: Baxter) • In communities with a collective history and continued desire for community food sharing, support collective infrastructure like community freezers (Chapter 2: Hoover at al.)

Lack of diversity

When we talk about a lack of diversity, we mean diversity of people and ideas. One reason for this is that the dominant social-economic logic of economic growth and trade liberalization continues to set the terms of what is a "realistic" global solution. Another reason for the lack of diversity around solutions is that while food insecurity is likely to have major impacts on the global South, the mainstream solutions to counter this (and the related funding) are largely framed by the global North. Globalization and value chain coordination link developing and developed countries through food production and consumption, but solutions scholarship around food insecurity is still largely dominated by one set of voices. The result is that those likely to be most affected are most often excluded from the solutions conversations.

By contrast, a platform for diverse perspectives, including those who prescribe solutions and those who are to be governed by such solutions, may help elucidate multiple solution pathways and multiple possible futures (Leach, Scoones & Stirling, 2010). Such pathways are key to operationalizing timely strategies for a just and sustainable food future. To address this problem, we must actively challenge what we have a tendency to accept as "common sense" and push ourselves to reimagine how we operate in the world, or better yet, in one world among many worlds. We need to reject the tendency to call ideas that promote alternatives "unrealistic". Indeed, we wonder: at what point did it become realistic to have almost one billion people undernourished, over one billion people overweight, and to surpass key planetary boundaries (Steffen et al., 2015)?

Silos

The silo metaphor is often used to critique academic practices, but it seems particularly fitting when talking about food. Silos store and protect grain, and are thus fundamental to food security, but disciplinary silos separate ideas, concepts, and methods, so that many academics end up working in isolation from one another. From our own experience, we are surprised that people working on land-based food systems rarely interact with those working on marine-based food provisioning, even though capture fisheries and aquaculture provide 4.3 billion people with more than 15% of their average per-capita intake of animal protein (HLPE, 2014). We note that urban food provisioning remains of interest predominantly to city dwellers, but that this is changing with the advancement of concepts like the city-region food system (Blay-Palmer, Dubbeling & Renting, 2015). Indigenous food systems are consistently overlooked and left out of the conversation, even though their reliance on particular types of food and food systems may require specific governance considerations (Cisneros-Montemayor et al., 2016). Consumption is almost always discussed as separate to production, while the important processes in between (i.e., processing, distribution, marketing) are erased from most debates.

To develop future food solutions from within these silos is to ignore the complex dynamics of how people access food. As a result, solutions rarely surface that adequately and appropriately embrace complexity. Siloed scholarship leads to continuation of the status quo – a groundhog-day type reincarnation of crisis after crisis and a lack of visioning that things indeed could and should be better. In an effort to agitate the predominate food systems discourse, and to help provide new perspectives and visions for the future, we called on scholars and practitioners from around the world to contribute to this book.

The rationale was also to begin to develop an active and collaborative community of thinkers and doers. Scholars, notably young scholars, are increasingly being pushed to publish quantity over quality, and are generally not incentivized to consider radical or innovative directions in their work. With this book, we have aimed to provide a space where innovative ideas are the norm: where thinking and collaborating outside of the box (and outside of silos) is possible.

Binaries

A transition towards inclusivity, both in terms of knowledge and participation, involves moving beyond binary thinking. This concept, derived from linguistic studies, refers to pairs of related concepts that are opposite in meaning but are defined relationally: to understand big, you need to understand small. Common binaries that pop up in discussions around food include consumer/producer; organic/GMO; local/global; small-scale farming/industrial farming; rural/urban. It is important to recognize the tendency to interpret these binaries by reflecting on what might be the ultimate binary: good/bad. For many readers, good food would be organic, local, small-scale food production. The opposite would be framed as bad. Yet for others, industrial farming of genetically modified foods to feed a growing global population is what defines a good food system.

While binaries are indeed initially helpful for making sense of complexity, this is also part of their limitation. Binary thinking pushes scientific and societal debates into oppositional camps, effectively limiting the scope of debate to extremes, rather than presenting them along a continuum. This system of thinking can also lead to reductionism that does not serve us well when grappling with the complexity of food systems. A further critique of binary oppositions is that they create and reinforce barriers that can lead to prejudice and discrimination. Take, for example, the local-global binary. We understand the local in relation to the global, and vice versa. But, as Gibson-Graham (2002) highlight, there is a tendency to accept the view that the forces of globalization are inevitably more powerful than progressive, grassroots, local interventions. They call on us to question the positioning of the local as inferior to the global, and as a second-best (or worse) political terrain, as a way of destabilizing this binary but also to advance alternative futures (Gibson-Graham, 2002, p. 30).

The tendency to understand the world from a binary perspective is pervasive in Western thought and across the English language. By way of comparison, consider the Japanese concept of *satoyama*, literally, *sato* meaning arable and livable land, and *yama* meaning hill or mountain. While the term has only recently emerged, *satoyama*, as socio-ecological landscapes, have been developed through centuries of combined small-scale agricultural and forestry use. In reflecting on how to overcome the linguistic binaries that tend to structure our thinking, what makes a concept like *satoyama* interesting is that the name itself defies binary thinking. The construction of the word implies the inseparability of these spaces in terms of the landscape and related livelihoods, and in overcoming the binary, new pathways become available.

Overcoming the binary tendency is not easy. Even in this chapter, we invoked the binary of the West/East or West/Rest. We recognize that we are limited by our language, but we take inspiration from Ingold, who rejects (but not without effort) a West/Rest division, along with the association of terms such as "modern":

> Every time I find myself using them, I bite my lip in frustration, and wish that I could avoid it. The objections to the concepts are well known: that in most anthropological accounts, they serve as a largely implicit foil against which to contrast a 'native point of view'; that much of the philosophical ammunition for the critique of so-called Western or modern thought comes straight out of the Western tradition itself . . . that once we get to know people well – even

the inhabitants of nominally western countries – not one of them turns out to be a full-blooded westerner ... and that the Western tradition of thought, closely examined, is as various, multivocal, historically changeable and contest-riven as any other.

(Ingold, 2000, p. 63)

Ingold reminds us of the need to constantly reflect on the inherent assumptions and hidden biases of our language and practice. This is a key strategy for advancing sustainable food futures.

Why multidisciplinary solutions?

We are convinced that sustainable food futures are not to be found within the narrow confines of restricted diversity, silos, and binary thought patterns. Some solution pathways will certainly be found at the margins, but others will be found in the in-between spaces, or the middle. Solutions might pop up in places where the contemporary and tradition come together, only to be reassembled into something that works for particular people in a particular context, at a particular time.

The question of why we need multidisciplinary solutions may appear redundant after our discussion on the need to move out of disciplinary silos. However, the question we are asking here relates to the distinction that we see between disciplinary, interdisciplinary, and multidisciplinary scholarship. For us, the distinction is important for the development of solutions. From our perspective, interdisciplinary research starts from the same question and answers the question making use of the methods and theories from different disciplines. It is usually guided by the goal of developing one unified perspective at the end of the research journey (Beggs, 1999). A multidisciplinary approach, by comparison, maintains its disciplinary distinctness, and this is often seen as sub-standard to interdisciplinarity (Beggs, 1999; Collins, 2002). But we disagree, and appreciate that with multidisciplinarity, we can start with a shared problem, in this case, "what solutions can be advanced to support just and sustainable food futures?" From there, each author draws on their disciplinary expertise and positioning to develop relevant questions and corresponding research and solution formulations. From our perspective, this allows for a more complex and more academically rigorous scientific process. It also allows non-academics to ask the questions that are most relevant for them. As a result, there is potential for greater insight into the diversity of ways problems are defined and solutions are advanced.

On the importance of listening and learning

When envisioning solutions for a just and sustainable food future, there is no doubt that we require strong evidence to support solutions. But in saying this, we want to emphasize two related points. First, the best evidence is not always found in labs or through Western science (there we go again with the binaries). Often the most practical, applicable, and appropriate solutions are developed and applied every day by people facing challenges, and yet these solutions are often overlooked. Further, for any solution to work, it needs to be understood, accepted, and taken up by people.

We need to expand our understanding of what constitutes evidence, expertise, and knowledge. This is a difficult task, as it requires a new way of thinking. It requires that we learn to listen and learn what it means when an Andean potato farmer talks about the wisdom of potatoes, or when an Indian pastoralist expresses insights about erratic weather based on the quality of her cows' milk, or when the Inuvialuit communicate their knowledge of their land as an experience. This means learning more about each other: knowledge, in any form, only makes sense within its own cultural context (Mazzocchi, 2006). Listening to others, especially those outside our echo chambers, seems more important now than ever before.

This relates to the second point: the biggest problems we face cannot be solved by technical solutions alone. Even with all the evidence in the world, we must recognize that decisions about the future of food are fundamentally social and political. These are literally issues of life and death. And if you do not agree, then consider that all interventions have societal implications. This does not mean that we reject science, although we recognize that there is no scientific consensus about sustainable food futures. It does mean that if we accept that all solution interventions are also social interventions, then we must find ways of ensuring that people, especially those most affected by these changes, can participate in decision-making.

Drawing inspiration from the solutions presented in this book, we envision a future where not only the importance of consulting people most affected by particular interventions is recognized, but also that the designing of solutions starts with those most affected, be they the Inuit in the Arctic (see Chapter 2), or farmers fighting for their right to land in Mozambique (see Chapter 6). It also means recognition of, and respect for, the differences between stakeholders. Processes that include stakeholders tend to suggest that all participants have the same rights to participation. But not everyone has the same stakes in every problem. We need more nuanced multi-actor approaches that recognize that not all actors share the same stakes and that further recognize power asymmetries. Towards this end, innovative and transparent participatory mechanisms are emerging in communities around the world, all the way up to the United Nations. For example, the United Nation's Committee on World Food Security reformed in 2009. In this new form, civil society organizations autonomously organize to participate in the work of the Committee, including intergovernmental negotiations (Duncan & Barling, 2012; Duncan, 2015), and the Committee has as a key part of its vision to "ensure that the voices of all relevant stakeholders – particularly those most affected by food insecurity – are heard" (CFS, 2009, para. 7).

Key practices for sustainable food futures

In the introductory chapter, we outlined the four themes that were used to organize this book: Recognizing place; Enhancing participation; Challenging markets; and Designing sustainable food futures. Each of the chapters proposes solutions that directly address their related theme, but there is also a lot of cross-over between the themes and across the solutions. Recognizing this, we asked the authors that contributed to this book which practices were most relevant for their solution. It is by no means a scientific survey, but the results shed light on the important transversal practices that surround and enable solutions. Reflecting on them now is important as they may not have been explicitly highlighted in the chapters.

The majority of authors noted that **place-based** practices were central to their solutions. This serves as an important reminder of the limitations of categories, as in the end, we put only four chapters in this theme. It is also an important reminder that place, and by extension, context, plays a fundamental role in the success or failure of solutions.

Participation, another one of the four structuring themes, also emerged as a transversal practice. On this point, we would add that when speaking about participation, it is fundamental to distinguish between consultation, participation, and inclusion. Consultation refers to processes undertaken to solicit people's opinion on specific matters. In these cases, the problem is already defined, and so, too, the solutions. The participation we envision extends well beyond consultation. We are thus interested in inclusive participation. Following Quick and Feldman (2011, p. 272), we see inclusion as continuously creating:

> a community involved in defining and addressing public issues; participation emphasizes public input on the content of programs and policies. Features of inclusive processes are coproducing the process and content of decision making, engaging multiple ways of knowing, and sustaining temporal openness.

This is no easy task. It takes extra time, extra resources, makes trade-offs explicit, and opens up processes to conflict. However, we also note that such conflicts are not only unavoidable, they are fundamentally important insofar as they reflect the real-world contrasts in values and visions (Duncan, 2016).

Related to this, many of the authors agreed that **flexibility** was a very important condition to ensuring the success of their solution. We interpret flexibility as being able and willing to adapt to changing circumstances, changing values, and changing contexts. It requires mental flexibility, which can be challenging and confronting. This flexibility requires learning, which was the next practice that authors identified as important: **Learning** about other people's experiences, learning about, and from, other disciplines. Learning to listen, to be flexible, to participate. Entrenched within that is a commitment to equity, a key practice authors identified as central to their solutions.

Equity refers to fairness and justice with regards to the way people are treated. For us, this means being aware of the way oppressive institutions (e.g., racism, sexism, homophobia, transphobia, ableism, xenophobia, classism) are interconnected and impact peoples' lived experiences. We have to challenge our privilege, while also fighting for our own rights, in solidarity with others, and alongside others.

Equity is key to informing how solutions are organized and advanced. We cannot continue to advance solutions that privilege the few over the many, or that privilege some at the expense of others.

Finally, and perhaps not surprisingly, the authors noted that **sustainability** was important to the success of their solution. In this context, sustainability includes not only environmental sustainability, but also social, cultural, and economic sustainability. We want to press the issues of the social here, because at the end of the day, it does not matter how sustainable something is, or is not, if people are not willing to implement it. This said, we hope that the future people want is a sustainable one, and that the solutions and practices discussed in this book will support this.

Conclusion

Our original theme for this book was "Future Solutions for a Food-Secure World." It became obvious to us early on that, in addition to needing multiple solutions, we need space for multiple futures. That is, what exactly sustainable food systems will look like in the future is unknowable, and in fact, there are infinite possibilities, many of which may already be realized. For us, the road work ahead is needed, not to get us to a better absolute future, but rather to create the knowledge and practitioner infrastructure so as to assemble imaginative, reflexive, and representative futures. Just because things are, does not mean they ought to be, and it is this thesis that we want readers to take on board after they digest what this book has to offer. The atlas that past and present generations have thus far used for social-ecological navigation needs to be updated with contemporary and future routes that put us on pathways that allow us to imagine, define, and build (or disassemble) possible food-secure futures that are just and sustainable and multiple.

RECIPE: UGLY FRUIT FONDUE

We chose this recipe because it is versatile, communal, and you can use whatever fruit you have on hand. We have a hard time thinking of a single fruit that would not taste good dipped in chocolate, even ugly fruit. We called this "ugly" fruit fondue because we take issue, as some of our readers may, with the requisite "pretty" factor that many fruits and vegetables need to have to be considered for sale. So grab whatever fruit you can find at the market, or whatever fruit you already have in your home, and no matter what it looks like on the outside, dip it in chocolate and enjoy! Speaking of chocolate, this recipe also lends itself well to different budgets and dietary considerations and choices. Vegans can modify the fondue ingredients with dairy-free alternatives. We propose this as a dessert to be shared, but if you want to eat it all alone, go for it!.

Ingredients

2/3 C (160 ml) heavy cream
200 g chopped dark chocolate
Assortment of ugly fruit
Optional addition of 2 tbsp of liquor of your choice (brandy, Amaretto, Grand Marnier, etc.)

Instructions

1   Warm the cream over medium-high heat until it starts to rise up along the sides (small froth). Remove from heat and add chocolate, stirring with a whisk or a fork until melted. Add liquor if using, and stir.
2   Cut up the fruit into bite-size pieces and arrange them on a plate. Pass around sticks or forks, and then serve the fondue in a fondue pot or any other kind of pot that you have available. Dig in! It won't last long, and you can feel good about reducing food waste.

Questions

1   Which of the solutions presented in this book did you find most inspiring and why?
2   Identify the key binaries that inform discussions on sustainable food systems. How are these binaries used in everyday conversations? Is one part of the binary seen as more valuable, or better, than the other? What are the implications of thinking and acting along binary lines?
3   We introduced six key practices that authors identified as being important to the success of their solution: place-based, participation, flexibility, learning, equity, and sustainability. In your opinion, what other practices are important and should be included in this list, and why?

References

Beggs, D. (1999) 'Liberating ecological reason through interdisciplinarity. *Metaphilosophy*. 30 (3), 186–208. Available from: doi: 10.1111/1467-9973.00121 [Accessed: 10th March 2017].

Blay-Palmer, A., Dubbeling, M. & Renting, H. (2015) *City-region food systems: A literature review*. RUAF Foundation. Available from: www.ruaf.org/sites/default/files/City%20Region%20Food%20Systems%20literature%20review.pdf [Accessed: 10th March 2017].

CFS. (2009) *Reform of the Committee on World Food Security, final version*. Food and Agriculture Organization of the United Nations. CFS:2009/2 Rev.2. Available from: www.fao.org/fileadmin/templates/cfs/Docs0910/ReformDoc/CFS_2009_2_Rev_2_E_K7197.pdf [Accessed: 10th March 2017].

Cisneros-Montemayor, A. M., Pauly, D., Weatherdon, L. V. & Ota, Y. (2016) A global estimate of seafood consumption by coastal Indigenous Peoples. In: Clark, T. D. (ed.) *PLOS ONE*. 11 (12), e0166681. Available from: doi: 10.1371/journal.pone.0166681 [Accessed: 10th March 2017].

Collins, J. P. (2002) May you live in interesting times: Using multidisciplinary and interdisciplinary programs to cope with change in the life sciences. *BioScience*. 52 (1), 75–83.

Duncan, J. (2015) *Global Food Security Governance: Civil society engagement in the reformed Committee on World Food Security*. London, Routledge.

Duncan, J. (2016) Governing in a post-political era: Civil society participation for improved food security governance. In: Barling, D. (ed.) *Advances in Food Security and Sustainability, Volume 1*. Burlington, Academic Press, pp. 137–161.

Duncan, J. & Barling, D. (2012). Renewal through participation in global food security governance: Implementing the international food security and nutrition civil society mechanism to the Committee on World Food Security. *International Journal of Sociology of Agriculture and Food*. 19, 143–161.

Gibson-Graham, J. K. (2002) Beyond global vs local: Economic politics outside the binary frame. In: Herod, A. & Wright, M. (eds.) *Geographies of Power: Placing Scale*. Oxford, Blackwell, pp. 25–60.

HLPE. (2014) *Sustainable fisheries and aquaculture for food security and nutrition*. Committee on World Food Security. A report by The High Level Panel of Experts on Food Security and Nutrition. Available from: www.fao.org/3/a-i3844e.pdf [Accessed: 10th March 2017].

Ingold, T. (2000) *The Perception of the Environment: Essays in Livelihood, Dwelling and Skill*. London, Routledge.

Johnson, D. G. & Wetmore, J. M. (2009) *Technology and Society: Building Our Sociotechnical Future (Inside Technology)*. London and Cambridge, The MIT Press.

Leach, M., Scoones, I. & Stirling, A. (2010) Governing epidemics in an age of complexity: Narratives, politics and pathways to sustainability. *Global Environmental Change*. 20 (3), 369–377. Available from: doi: 10.1016/j.gloenvcha.2009.11.008 [Accessed: 10th March 2017].

Mazzocchi, F. (2006) Western science and traditional knowledge: Despite their variations, different forms of knowledge can learn from each other. *EMBO Reports*. 7 (5), 463–466. Available from: doi: 10.1038/sj.embor.7400693 [Accessed: 10th March 2017].

Quick, K. S. & Feldman, M. S. (2011) Distinguishing participation and inclusion. *Journal of Planning Education and Research*. 31 (3), 272–290. Available from: doi: 10.1177/0739456X11410979 [Accessed: 10th March 2017].

Steffen, W., Richardson, K., Rockstrom, J., Cornell, S. E., Fetzer, I., Bennett, E. M., Biggs, R., Carpenter, S. R., de Vries, W., de Wit, C. A., Folke, C., Gerten, D., Heinke, J., Mace, G. M., Persson, L. M., Ramanathan, V., Reyers, B. & Sorlin, S. (2015) Planetary boundaries: Guiding human development on a changing planet. *Science*. 347 (6223), 1259855–1259855. Available from: doi: 10.1126/science.1259855 [Accessed: 10th March 2017].

Wunsch, A. D. (2010) Technology and society: Building our sociotechnical future (Johnson, D. G. & Wetmore, J. M., 2009) [Book Review]. *IEEE Technology and Society Magazine*. 29 (1), 4–8. Available from: doi: 10.1109/MTS.2010.936435 [Accessed: 10th March 2017].

INDEX

adaptability 123, 180; Inuit 26
Africa *see* African Union; Mali;
    Mozambique; Uganda
African Union 78
agriculture 2, 49, 52, 77–9, 89, 91, 95,
    119, 129, 167, 175, 18, 186, 190,
    195; China 35, 37–9, 41; *see also*
    community-supported agriculture
    (CSA); organic
agroecology 41, 108, 146
Alternative Food Network (AFN) 7, 36,
    145, 146, 155, 195
Amazon 89, 92, 93; *see also* Bolivia
ambivalence 8, 165, 169
aquaculture 5, 6, 206; Bolivia 89–100;
    certification 133–4
arctic 17–28, 209; *see also* Canada
art 176; artist 107, 166, 167, 175, 177;
    bio-artist 166, 167
assets 121, 124, 125, 126–8, 129, 181, 182;
    soil assets 176, 177, 178–80, 183
autonomy 5, 103, 109, 111, 113, 154

binary 54, 67, 119, 120, 121, 127, 129,
    206–8
blueberry 49–55
Bolivia 89–100
British Columbia 62, 49–55
burden of proof 134

Canada 17, 19, 20, 21, 49–55, 63, 92, 104
capabilities 121, 125, 126, 127–8, 134, 136,
    137, 139, 189

capacity 67, 124, 127, 128, 134, 138, 140,
    149, 180; building 94, 95, 137, 139;
    production 52, 138
capitalism 103, 106, 107, 108, 109, 111,
    112, 204
cash flow 123, 125
Center for the Promotion of Peasant
    Agriculture (CEPAC) 92–8
cereal 20, 121–2, 123, 124, 125
certification 41, 46, 133–40, 146, 155, 191
China 34–42, 164, 195
climate change 5, 27, 52, 54, 89, 122,
    181, 187
collective action 64, 66, 67, 68
collective marketing 119–20, 190
Committee on World Food Security 78, 209
commons, community-resource 83;
    farmland 61–8
community 18, 22, 23, 26–8, 36, 48, 67,
    83–6, 94, 104, 107, 110, 177, 190, 195;
    community-led initiatives 19; farms
    152; freezer 21, 24; greenhouses 22, 25;
    ownership 152; researchers 206; resilience
    18; wellbeing 183; *see also* land rights
community-supported agriculture (CSA)
    26, 36–42, 64, 69, 155, 193, 195
consultation 2, 79, 83, 210
contracts 61, 64, 66, 67, 103, 119–20, 129,
    134, 136, 137, 154
conventionalization 146–7, 151
cooperative 79, 111, 119–20, 128, 129,
    138, 146, 148, 150, 152, 195; MSC
    (multi-stakeholder cooperatives) 149–55

co-optation 145–7, 154; *see also* conventionalization
currency: Bitcoin 178; Bristol Pound 177–8; soil 175–83

decolonization 103, 111, 113
democracy 67, 113; democratization 152–3, 197; *see also* participation
dichotomy 54, 169, 192
diversification 49, 51–2, 66, 89, 92, 139, 150–1, 167, 189
diversity 2, 6, 7, 52, 64, 67, 98, 150, 154, 182, 187; academia 204, 205–6, 208; biodiversity 61, 145, 146, 147, 163; celebrating diversity 188, 190–1, 195, 196, 197; conventional food systems 147
double label 153–4
double shift 136

economy 19, 36, 49; bio-economy 167; circular economy 186–98; moral economy 103, 107, 109, 111; political economy 68, 77; solidarity economy 150, 152, 155
ecosystem services 175, 177, 181, 182
education 19, 27, 28, 37, 41, 81, 93, 107–8, 109–11, 113, 139, 150, 163; trade schools 127–9; *see also* training
equity 47, 48, 82, 85, 111, 113, 180, 210–11
ethics 108
exchange 155, 175; financial 121, 123; food 48, 119, 120; information 65; knowledge 27, 128; market 54; rate 177, 179–80, 182
export 49, 51–3, 79, 81, 104, 120, 134, 138

factory farming 163, 167, 168, 170
farming 25, 35–7, 39, 41, 42, 66, 108, 110, 111, 119–20, 145, 146, 151, 167, 192, 193, 194, 207; fish farming 83, 89, 92, 97–8, 133; urban 170, 195; *see also* community-supported agriculture; factory farming; organic
feminist 151
fishing 27, 28, 93, 97; overfishing 8, 91
Food and Agriculture Organization (FAO) 78, 153, 163, 175
food availability 17, 22, 25, 120–1, 125, 127, 129
food movements 36, 46, 48, 55, 68, 79, 81–4, 113, 146, 150, 155, 195; *see also* organic
food security 17–20, 22, 28, 35, 48, 55, 61, 78, 81, 90, 97, 103, 120–1, 129, 145, 133, 171, 206
food sovereignty 18, 28, 79, 82, 83, 108, 110, 113, 151

garden 39, 41, 110, 175, 181; community garden 26, 109
gender 85, 90–6, 99, 150, 152, 155; gender equity 111–13; *see also* women
globalization 6, 48, 205, 207
governance 5, 64, 155, 192, 206; certification 133; decentralizing 103; land governance 66, 77, 78, 82–3, 85; normalization 135–6; self-governance 66, 67; *see also* value chain
government 79, 90; authorities 78–85, 149; local 27, 94, 149, 150; marketing 46; reform 77; responsibility 20, 80, 82, 91; *see also* state
greenhouses 22, 25–6

hunting 19, 21, 23, 26–8, 93

import 19, 104, 120, 134; nutrients 53
indifference 169
Indigenous Peoples 19, 49–50, 54, 206; Bolivia 90–1, 94, 97; Inuit 17–28; Mexico 104–6, 108, 110–11, 113 (*see also* Zapatista); Sami 25
innovation 167, 191–4; co-innovation 137, 139; grassroots 146; social 195; technological 7
intensive farming 151, 171
intersectionalities 152, 154
investment 23, 51, 65–6, 81–3, 122, 126, 133, 137, 186; foreign direct 62, 104; individual 94; labor 64; responsible 78, 151

knowledge 35, 38, 85, 98, 125, 147, 206; democratization 152–4; local 109; multiple 110, 155, 209; sharing 26–8; transfer 25, 41

labor 51, 52, 64, 95, 108, 111, 145, 152; collective 108; costs 8, 51; emotional 112; fair 47; family 133; farm 37, 180; intellectual 107; laborers 79, 82; *see also* investment
land rights 81–7; community 77, 78, 81, 83; customary-based land rights 77–8, 80, 81, 83; formalized 82; insecure 62; training 82–3
landscape 1, 27, 48–54, 192; cultural 169; diverse 196; food 190; indigenous 48; scale 66; socio-ecological 207
land transfer 78, 80, 81
land-use rights 77, 79, 81, 85
Life Cycle Analysis (LCA) 47, 167
Life Cycle Assessment (LCA) 187

livelihood 47, 52, 77, 89, 91, 92, 95, 97, 133, 152207; diversifying 99, 139; rural 37, 85, 98
livestock 53, 89, 93, 125, 163, 194
local 93–4, 153, 155, 177; delocalized 4, 35, 63; ecologies 109; economy 36, 46, 49, 89, 177, 195; food systems 18, 21, 25, 120, 149; governance 64, 79, 149; locally relevant 19, 24, 67, 109, 111; markets 40, 127, 182; re-localization 153; re-valuing 46–55; *see also* community; government; place

Mali 121–9
market 35, 42, 46, 51, 54, 62–3; access 52, 119–21, 128–9, 133–4, 137; alternative 151, 177, 181; challenging 6–7; development 94, 99, 152; fluctuations 52, 92, 126; free 104–8; global 77, 122, 128, 135; land 65–6, 78, 85; relations 39, 68, 134, 139; saturation 52, 53, 104; value 49, 63; *see also* exchange; local; price
marketing 151, 153, 206; collective 119–20, 129; state-run 46, 48, 79
meat 20, 24, 25–7, 47, 64; cultured meat 165–72; meat consumption; *in vitro* meat 165–6; *see also* hunting; pulses
Mediterranean 164
Mexico 51, 103–14
microbiome 171
Mozambique 77–85; *see also* National Union of Mozambican Peasants (UNAC)
multidisciplinary 9, 208
mutual aid 68, 108, 113

National Union of Mozambican Peasants (UNAC) 78–85
natural 41, 168; assets 125–6; breeding 50; capital 8179, 181; cycles 188; history 49; resources 18, 65, 68, 90, 94, 147, 177, 186, 188, 197; *see also* unnatural
neoliberalism 103–7
Netherlands, the 164, 166–8, 194; Dutch 164–72, 194
New Harvest 166–7
North American Free Trade Agreement (NAFTA) 51, 104–6
Nutrition North 20–1; *see also* Canada

oilseed 121–9
organic 2, 36, 39, 41, 108, 110, 149–53, 175, 181, 183, 188, 194, 195, 207; movement 145–6
Organization for Economic Co-operation and Development (OECD) 134, 191

participation 37–9, 42, 62, 67, 96, 155, 209, 210; barriers 19, 23; enhancing 4–5, 95, 112; *see also* women
participatory approach 5, 92
peasant 37, 39–42, 77–85, 90, 103, 154; marginalization 4; mobilization 79; *see also* Center for the Promotion of Peasant Agriculture (CEPAC); National Union of Mozambican Peasants (UNAC); Via Campesina, La
People for the Ethical Treatment of Animals (PETA) 166
pisteur 123–6
place 9; recognizing place 3–4
place-based 36, 42, 48–9, 51–3, 54–5, 210; education 109, 111
policy 19, 21, 63, 77, 85, 91, 129, 163; food policy 147; free trade 104; policy making 129; social policy 6; *see also* governance; government
poverty 89–93, 97, 98, 99, 104
price 21, 104, 119, 120, 123, 145–6, 153, 182; crops 89; fixed-price 120; market price 133, 135; predictability 128, 181; setting 39; share price 65; short-term price 134
principles: circular economy 188–91, 193–4, 196–7; cooperatives 151; organic agriculture 39; Principles for Responsible Agricultural Investment 78
produce flow 122–4, 126
property: intellectual 196; private 68, 108; public 78; regime 64; rights 61, 78, 94, 197; *see also* commons, community-resource
protein 25, 91, 97, 133, 164, 169, 171, 206
pulses 164, 170–1

rebel 104, 110
rebellion 104, 109
reindeer 22; herding 25
resilience 94, 98, 153, 189; community 48, 177; compassionate 113; ecological 49, 52; economic 62; house-hold 181; place-based 49
resistance 67, 106, 112, 190; collective 113; Lord Resistance Army 122; strategies 147, 153
retail 145, 146, 149–50, 153; certification 134–40; northern retailers 20
rice 37, 40, 79, 89, 92, 93
risk 36, 52, 55, 92, 124, 133, 136, 179, 193; co-option 147, 154; economic 49, 120; exploitation 196; food safety 34; food security 145; health 163; management 123, 138; minimize 124, 151; sharing 39; spreading 66, 124, 127

satoyama 207
seeds 38, 152; maize 84; saving 108, 153;
 sharing 153; *see also* oilseed
self-determination 111, 113
shepherd 150, 153
skills 4, 26, 110, 121, 125–8, 154;
 agriculture 35, 108, 110; lack of 19; life
 19, 21; marketing 151; training 27–8, 81;
 see also education
small-holders 133–5; *see also* small-scale
small-scale 195; agriculture 42, 89, 207;
 enterprises 94; family farms 92; farmers
 120, 127, 129; producers 121
social relations 35, 36, 54, 106, 107, 113
soil 51, 92, 108, 110, 175–6, 194; currency
 176–83; fertility 38, 53, 145; frozen 17;
 management 62; quality 61, 64
solidarity 108, 210; economy 152, 155;
 purchasing 195; savings 65
Somerset Rules 149
Spain 146, 150–5
specialization 51–5, 127, 150, 186
standards 191; access 134; aquaculture 133;
 compliance 134; eco 134, 135; export
 134; farm-level 139; production 41;
 quality 128; social 136; voluntary 133,
 136; *see also* certification; labor; organic
state 61, 63, 68, 77, 85, 110, 178; alternative
 65; cooperative 79; farms 79; neoliberal
 68; ownership 65; power 106; property
 78–9; repression 106; weak 138; *see also*
 government; policy
strategic ignorance 169
subsidies 20, 23, 94, 146; *see also*
 Nutrition North
supermarkets 46, 151, 152, 197
supply chain 34, 35, 39, 42, 190, 192; global
 48, 51; shortening 54; *see also* value chain
systemic change 155

technological fix 165, 169
tenure 90; customary 85; farmland 61–6;
 formalize 77, 78; insecurity 66–8;
 market-based 78; traditional 78; *see also*
 farming; land rights

traders 119–29
training 27, 128; business 94, 137; hands-on
 19, 26; law 81–5; peer-to-peer 95; *see also*
 education; skills
transparency 54, 85, 127, 128, 153; lack
 of 20
trust 68, 124, 125, 153; characteristic 150;
 consumer 34–42; distrust 37; land 65–8

Uganda 121–9
United Kingdom (UK) 145–55, 195
United States of America (USA) 47, 62,
 104, 166, 167, 181
unnatural 168; *see also* natural
urbanization 1, 122; China 35; Mexico 104

value 25, 49, 65, 108, 135, 146, 203; cultural
 18, 26; devalue 104, 111; economic 177;
 export 50; high-value 120; knowledge
 153; limited 41; market 63; nutritional
 19; in soil 176–9, 183; traditional 83;
 undervalued 54, 94; virtual 190, 197
value chain 93, 99, 136, 197, 205; global
 value chains 134, 139; governance of
 135–6
values 2, 210; environmental 36; land 83;
 redistribute 36; shifting 7; societal 6, 8,
 38, 39, 42
Via Campesina, La 79, 83, 150

waste 54, 62147, 186–7; asset 178–80; farm
 53; food 190, 192, 194, 195; human 38;
 organic 175, 181; zero 37
women 92–9; empowerment 95; impact
 62; responsibilities 95; stereotypes 95;
 women-led 92; *see also* gender
Women's Revolutionary Law 106,
 111–13
World Health Organization (WHO) 163

Yuck 168

Zapatista 104–13
Zapatista Army of National Liberation
 (EZLN) 104, 106–14